FOUNTAINS
in the
VALLEY

FOUNTAINS
in the
VALLEY

201
Devotionals

Joanne Peden

AMBASSADOR INTERNATIONAL
GREENVILLE, SOUTH CAROLINA & BELFAST, NORTHERN IRELAND
www.ambassador-international.com

Fountains in the Valley

Paperback: ISBN:978-1-64960-190-2
eBook: eISBN:978-1-64960-196-4

Printed in UK

Ambassador International

Emerald House
411 University Ridge, Suite B14
Greenville, SC 29601
www.ambassador-international.com

Ambassador Books and Media
The Mount
2 Woodstock Link
Belfast, BT6 8DD, Northern Ireland, UK
www.ambassadormedia.co.uk

I dedicate this book to my late grandmother

- Irene Blaine Hunter -

She was completely selfless and a cheerful giver who constantly poured herself into the lives of others.

Foreword

'*Fountains in the Valley*' is my third book. All three book '*A Myrtle Tree for Life's Briars*', '*Jewels of Jabbok*' and this one have been birthed from a valley of great suffering. The Lord has laid this devotional book upon my heart and given me the words to write. I hope that you will find within these pages words of hope from our precious Saviour and no matter what you are going through that you will not give up.

You see, I am no stranger to struggle. I live in the valley of suffering even now as I type these words. For the past almost 14 years I have been sick with severe M.E. In the early years I went through spells where I alternated between totally bedridden and able to function but in the past few years great deterioration came and I found myself confined to bed and in need of care at all times. M.E. is a disease of the brain (Neurological) and the immune system. Because the brain controls every system of the body – the body goes into shut down mode. It leaves the sufferer with no energy at all, immense weakness, pain, constant exhaustion, flu-like symptoms all the time, constant fainting (even in bed) dizziness and the list goes on. There is still no cure but they are still working hard in the labs of medical research to come up with a medication.

You may wonder why I have named this book '*Fountains in the Valley*'. The first devotion explains that in more detail, but the name came from the Scripture verse:

Isaiah 41:18 *"I will open rivers in the high places, and fountains in the midst of the valleys: I will make the wilderness a pool of water and the dry land spring of water."*

I have experienced the Lord bringing fountains of blessing during my greatest struggle. Even amid our greatest hardship, His presence brings refreshing. He makes a way to water our thirsty souls when we feel parched and think we are not going to make it. He is our Lord, our fountain in the land of suffering – the God who can bring water from a rock! Life can feel like a barren place at times but with the Lord our fountain bringing streams of refreshing in our hard places we can find the strength to go on. I pray that you will find great blessing and encouragement within the pages of this book and that it will be like water to your weary soul.

Through great brokenness, the Lord has sustained me and even during what looks impossible I will never lose hope that my Lord will make me His daughter whole again. As I wait I will continue to encourage. I run an encouragement page on Facebook. People follow that page from all over the world and through it, the Lord has given me the blessing of leading precious souls to Himself in Salvation.

May this book fire you up in your walk with God and may you sense His presence through it in a way you never dreamt possible. If you are reading this and don't know my Saviour then it's my prayer that you will find him within these pages.

Love Joanne Peden xxx

(November 2020)

1

Fountains in the Valley

Isaiah 41:18 *"I will make rivers in high places and fountains in the midst of valleys. I will make the wilderness a pool of water and the dry land springs of water."*

A fountain is described as: "A stream of water that is forced up into the air through a small hole, or a structure in a lake or pool from which this flows."

A valley is a low dip between hills, a hollow place. In the context of this verse, the valley referred to is an extremely dry wilderness. Imagine walking through your lowest valley, dry with thirst, weary with continually not being able to find water to refresh yourself. Then suddenly, a fountain of pure water springs up, you run into it, your weary, heat-stricken body is cooled, you drink of it and quench your thirst. You have been in a low place for so long, plodding wearily. Your life has been a barren valley, just barely coping and no hoping when suddenly, this fountain of refreshing strength, hope and blessing springs up when you least expect it. Your weary spirit is revived and refreshed. The Lord fills you with hope and fresh strength for the fight. You are still in the valley, but your vigour and courage have been restored and you have drunk freely from the Spiritual fountain of your Saviour and your dryness of spirit is gone.

If this is you and you are plodding through the driest most barren valley you've ever been in - then the Lord is promising to cause fountains of refreshing to spring up in your wilderness to keep you going in Him until you emerge from that valley. In the meantime, ask the Lord to let fountains of refreshing spring up in your driest place to bring an end to your weariness and hope drought.

I liked these words from Pastor Ken Davidson's book, *'Finding God's path in a dark season.'*

"There are different valleys that everyone encounters in their lives. We may not go through them all but one valley that we will all experience is the valley of tears. The valley may be the loss of a loved one, a dream that came to a sudden end, removal of a car or house, or the doctor saying, 'I can do no more for you.' Always remember when a dark season closes in, the sun still shines behind those dark clouds. Likewise, the Son, Jesus Christ our Lord still reigns no matter what stands in front of us! Did Jesus not say: *"I will never leave thee, nor forsake thee?"* Hebrews 13:5."

Our fountain amid our lowest valleys is our precious Lord and Saviour, Jesus. He is our fountain of life that continually refreshes us in our weary valleys. I know that through all my years of illness in the places that have been filled with such drought - Jesus my fountain of life has always sprung up from within my heart to sustain me with scripture, with a comforting song, with a word of encouragement or thoughtful gift.

Psalm 36:9 *"For with thee is the fountain of life, in thy light shall we see light."*

Jesus is our fountain of living water! With Him as our Saviour and sustainer, we will ALWAYS find refreshing in the driest and bleakest of places.

2

Breath of God

I watched an episode of the Walton's where an injured seagull appeared on Walton's Mountain. The bird had a broken wing. The children got him in a box, and they tended to him, but he would not eat. Grandpa said, "That's the funny thing with injured birds they either decide to get well or die. This one just hasn't decided yet." Eventually, the bird did begin to eat, his wing was healed, and he flew to freedom once more.

Sometimes things in life happen to us that totally break our spirits. A tragedy can happen, circumstances can feel like they are falling apart. Maybe someone has spoken extremely cruel words over you and your heart is breaking in pieces.

Whatever has happened to break your spirit, know that the Lord is with you, tending to you, looking after you, trying to breathe new life into your spirit so you can fly again, so your heart can mend again.

Dear brother, dear sister you will mend again. It might not look like it now. It might look like the most impossible thing ever but like the seagull, you will soar again.

Even if you are in the pit of despair right now and can no longer see light at the end of the tunnel, the Lord can see what you cannot see. He can see farther down the road. Maybe you can only see a dead-end sign now, but God sees the 'New Life' sign that is just hidden from your view. God's new breath of life upon you can change things!

Job 33:4 *"The Spirit of God hath made me and the breath of the Almighty gives me life."*

Ezekiel 37:4-14 *"Behold I will cause breath to enter you that you may come to life....and put breath in you that you come alive; and that you will know that I AM the LORD."*

Genesis 2:7 *"And the Lord God formed man of the dust of the ground and breathed into his nostrils the breath of life, and man became a living soul."*

If you have become lifeless as a result of pain ask the Lord to breathe life into you again. Only the breath of the Almighty can cause dead, depressed numb spirits to come alive with hope again and to blossom and bud. I love the words to this old hymn:

Breathe on me breath of God,
Fill me with life anew.
That I may love what Thou dost love,
And do what thou wouldst do.

Breathe on me breath of God:
Till I am Wholly thine.
Until this earthly part of me,
Glows with thy fire divine.

If you have been in a bad state for a long time you need the Breath of the Living God to cause your lifeless, hopeless mind to come alive.

My prayer for you all today is that the Lord would breathe on you, lift you out of the pit of despair and make a way where there seems to be no way!

3

Spontaneous Blessings

I was reading a Christian fiction book called *'Spring Weddings.'* I learned something that I did not know before. A lady happened to be weeding the church garden just before dawn when suddenly she heard voices. There were a bride and groom, a wedding registrar, a man playing the guitar and about half a dozen people watching the proceedings. The lady hid in the bushes and said out loud, "I'm covered in dirt and trapped in the middle of a guerrilla wedding!"

I had no idea what such a wedding was, so I googled it! It is where a couple with very little money appear at an unpaid for destination. They marry before anyone will notice and usually do not have any guests, just themselves and the wedding officiant.

So, the lady hidden in the bushes got to witness the spontaneous blessing of watching a romantic daybreak wedding.

I've seen a few spontaneous blessings recently like being sent flowers (pink roses - my favourite), having a package full of goodies left on the doorstep including lovely perfume and then just recently a package of edible treats.

Life is hard being bedbound and extremely ill with the severest form of M.E. but it hasn't blinded me to see the spontaneous blessings of God in the midst of it.

Maybe you could make it your aim this week to spontaneously bless someone who is suffering! The miracle of being able to bless others is in our hands. Making time for others makes a massive difference in other's lives.

What about you today? Are you in a dark place and finding it hard to see the blessings that are right in front of you because of the darkness? Look around! These might not be spontaneous blessings but I thank God for them every day: A roof over my head, warm pyjamas, food and water, a family's love, the love of friends and people who pray for me are to name a small number. But sometimes the 'out of the blue', I love you and I care blessings can truly bring so much light and love into the life of someone for whom life is not easy. I now call them my 'guerrilla blessings' because they are spontaneous and unexpected!

James 1:17 *"Every good and perfect gift is from above, coming down from the Father of the heavenly lights who does not change like the lifting shadows."*

2 Corinthians 9:8 *"And God is able to bless you abundantly so that in all things, at all times having all you need, you will abound in every good work."*

Lamentations 3:22-23 *"It is because of the Lord's mercies* (or blessings) *that we are not consumed, because his compassions fail not. They are new every morning; Great is thy faithfulness."*

Despite our circumstances, despite our tears and all our fears, God's many blessings still abound in the midst. His blessings keep us from being consumed by all our pain, they cause us to abound and still be fruitful for Him no matter how useless we feel. He sends us His good and perfect gifts from above to remind us that His hand is still strong upon our lives even when we cannot sense Him and that He delights in us and loves us dearly! He blesses us so we can be a blessing - let us follow in the Lord's footsteps today and bless others. Let us be thankful for the blessings that remain amidst the storm.

4

Choose Life

After reading a series of Christian fiction books called 'Winter Brides' they all struck me so much. There were lessons from God in each of them but the last one struck me most. It began with a bride on her wedding day adorned in a dress which had been passed down from her grandmother to her mother to herself. However her family had a history of failed marriages and as she stood in the heirloom dress, she fled and ran because she believed if she married her beloved she would break his heart. She felt that it was some kind of curse that was on her family to be unable to stay married.

If you are in Christ, then you are a new creation. It does not matter what unhealthy patterns have been in your family history - they can end with you! As God's child, you can choose to honour Him and follow His word. I heard of a family where the grandfather was angry, controlling, verbally abusive and manipulative. The traits passed down to the son, but they ended with the grandson for he had chosen God's way over the fleshy pattern in that family that had repeated itself for years.

> Deuteronomy 30:19-20 *"I have set before you life and death, blessing and cursing; therefore choose life that both thou and the seed may live. That thou mayest love the LORD thy God and that thou mayest obey his voice and that thou mayest cleave unto him, for he is the length of the days."*

> Galatians 5:1 *"Stand fast therefore in the liberty wherewith Christ hath made us free, and be not entangled again with the to the role of bondage."*

A speaker in my church once said, "The thing we learn most from history is that we don't learn from history."

History has a habit of repeating itself. However, as a blood washed believer in Jesus Christ, you are being instructed to continually choose life. That means choosing to feed the spirit through prayer and worship. It means endeavouring to become more like Jesus with every passing day. To choose death means that you have a worldly attitude, you neglect God's word, you neglect prayer. You are not growing in Christ, you are in stagnant waters and in that place of feeding the flesh, you will become in bondage to your fleshy ways and lose your walk with God.

We are told to stand fast in the liberty wherewith Christ has set us free. Having tasted true freedom and what it is to have a real living relationship with the LORD why backtrack and start to go back to old behavioural patterns that you have already been set free from?

Our calling is not to a life that feeds the flesh that leads to our destruction but to love the Lord with all our hearts, obey His voice and cleave unto Him with our all. To cleave means to stick to something like glue.

Walk daily by your Saviour's side. Be quick to repent from bad attitudes and make it your goal to be a history maker for God and touch as many lives with His Gospel while you still have time.

5

Serving God's Purpose

Recently I had to order a couple of new pairs of pyjamas. My fleecy pyjamas from last year were well worn and no longer kept the heat in as they had been through the wash so many times. I am deeply grateful for my new warm pyjamas that hold the heat as I always feel stone-cold in summer and winter (a symptom of my illness). My old pyjamas were no longer fit for purpose! Their only purpose was to go to a clothing bank.

> Jeremiah 32:19 *"Great are your purposes and mighty are your deeds. Your eyes are open to the ways of all mankind; you reward each person according to their conduct and as their deeds deserve."*
>
> Job 42:2 *"I know that you can do all things, no purpose of yours can be thwarted."*
>
> 1 Peter 2:9 *"But you are a chosen people, a royal priesthood, a holy nation, God's special possession, that you may declare the praises of him who called you out of darkness into his wonderful light."*

The Lord has placed us on this earth for His divine purposes. He breathed life into our lungs for a reason. As His children, we are His treasured possessions who are chosen by Him. He called us out of darkness into His wonderful light when He saved us and His greatest purpose for our lives is to shine His gospel light into the lives of the unsaved.

I was listening to a sermon about a preacher who was drowning in the icy waters that horrendous historic night in 1912 when the Titanic sank. He fought to stay afloat and every time he drifted near someone he called out; "Are you Saved?" and then cried out Act's 16:32, *"Believe on the Lord Jesus Christ and thou shalt be saved."* That preacher was going to die that night but he had such a compassionate heart to see souls snatched from hell's fire that he fought with all his might to serve God's purpose till he finally succumbed to hypothermia and sank. His body was never recovered. But many who were rescued testified to getting saved that night because of that preacher's great passion for souls.

My old pyjamas were no longer serving the purpose that they were made for therefore making them unusable.

What about you? What about me? Are we serving God's purposes for our lives the most important things to us or have we become apathetic to the great need of all the lost around us? No matter what your limits are you can still fulfil the very last command that Jesus gave before He ascended to Heaven - to go into all the world and make disciples.

The Lord is the potter and we are the clay in His hand. Are we willing to follow Him wholeheartedly? Are we willing to be His vessel who is wholeheartedly willing to be broken and spilled out for Him so that every purpose that He has set us on earth will be accomplished? Can we say, *"Here I am wholly available. As for me, I will serve the Lord."*

6
Becoming All Glorious Within

Psalm 45:13 *"The King's daughter is all glorious within, her clothing is of wrought gold."*

Colossians 3:12-14 *"Put on therefore as the elect of God, holy and beloved, bowels of mercies, kindness, humbleness of mind, meekness, long suffering. Forbearing one another and forgiving one another. And above all these things put on charity which is the bond of perfection."*

Do you ever notice as you scroll through social media or watch the television how beautifully adorned Royalty are? No expense is spared. Their beautiful gowns cost a fortune and they are adorned with the most expensive accessories.

The Lord cares more about what we look like on the inside. The King of all Glory wants His sons and daughters to be all glorious within.

The verses in Colossians are the very wardrobe that He wants His children to adorn themselves in!

Believer's Bible commentary (page 2010-2011) "Because we are objects of God's love it gives us a desire to please Him in every way. Tender mercies speak of a heart of compassion. Kindness speaks of the unselfish spirit of doing for others. It is an attitude of affection or goodwill.

Humility means lowliness, the willingness to be humbled and to esteem others better than oneself. Meekness does not speak of weakness but rather the strength to deny oneself and walk in grace to all men. If humility is the absence of pride then meekness is the absence of passion.

Longsuffering speaks of patience under provocation or offence. It combines joy and a kind attitude towards others along with perseverance in suffering.

Bearing with one another describes the patience we should have with the failings and odd ways of our brothers and sisters. But we must bear with one another and forgive one another as Christ forgave us.

Love (charity) is spoken of here as the outer garment which binds all other virtues together to make up perfection. All that we do must be done in a spirit of love for others. Our actions should not be grudging but should be born out of wholehearted affection."

If we pray through all these things then ask the Lord for grace to put them into practice, He truly will make us all glorious within. Outer beauty fades but the inner beauty of Christ reflected through a beautiful, genuine heart will never fade.

I came across this quote by Maddie Hodgetti. "The other day I looked in the mirror and didn't feel so pretty. So I said, God I need a reminder what do you see when you look at me? So He said, you are my beautiful creation. So I said, yeah but what do others see when they look at me? So He said: They see me! And suddenly I felt beautiful."

Let us abide in the Lord's presence. Let us soak up His character. Let us become all glorious within that the world might see Jesus.

7

Saviour Still Amidst Brokenness

Ezekiel 34:16 *"I will seek that which was lost, and bring again that which was driven away, and will bind up that which was broken and will strengthen that which was sick."*

Has there ever been a time in your life that you have got physically lost? Maybe as a child, you got separated from your parents in a crowd and felt such a sense of panic and fear. I cannot say I was ever lost in that sense.

Do you remember a time when something you loved broke and was unfixable? I remember that happening with my favourite china doll. Or maybe you broke a bone and had to go to the hospital to have it bound up in bandages so that the bones could heal again?

Have you ever been physically sick and felt so weak that you longed for strength to return?

Or maybe in an emotional and spiritual place within you, life has got you feeling confused and utterly lost right now. So many things have been thrown at you and you feel disconnected from life. Maybe you feel broken and your nights have been spent in tears for so long that you do not see yourself as fixable. Maybe you are long term sick either physically or mentally and healing feels so far away. You are feeling lost, broken, and sick and in desperate need of the Saviour's touch.

Through this verse I sense Him saying: "My Child, I understand how lost you feel. In all seasons I understand your pain and confusion. Take my hand precious one and let me lead you back to solid ground. I know that you are broken; I know that you are sick. I have promised to seek out my lost child, to bind up your broken places and strengthen you in your sickness. You are deeply loved. You are in a season of pain now but remember it is only a season and in my time, I will fulfil all my promises to you. Keep drawing near to me for in me you will find a refuge from the storm and peace amidst the confusion. I am here for you and will always be here. I never forsake my children, people might forsake you, but I will not. Come unto me my weary one and I will give you rest."

I love the words of this song, *'Beauty for Brokenness'*.

Some of the words go as follows: "Beauty for brokenness, hope for despair, shelter for fragile lives, cures for all ills... Rights for the weak. Voices to plead the cause of those who cannot speak... Friend of the weak, give us compassion we pray. Lighten our darkness, breathe on this flame."

Jesus is the one who brings beauty for brokenness and hope for despair! He is the shelter for our fragile lives in which to dwell! He is the friend of the weak who is full of compassion! He will lighten our darkness and breathe new life on our flickering flame. You are not too lost for Him to find, not too broken for Him to fix or too sick for Him to strengthen.

8

Deep Affliction

Isaiah 63:9 *"In all their affliction he was afflicted, and the angel of his presence saved them: in his love and pity he redeemed them; and he bare them and carried them all the days of old."*

Affliction means, a cause of pain or harm, suffering, trouble, misery. Affliction is not limited to physical suffering. It can come as the direct result of someone who caused you pain or harm on purpose.

Some people think of bullies as being people in the schoolyard years ago. But the fact is there are adult bullies who are always on the lookout to destroy or harm a genuine servant of God. They are motivated by jealous, insecure spirits but their words can truly destroy. They can stop someone in their service for God because satan can use their words as lies to block them from continuing. In this type of affliction, the child of God becomes distressed, they feel destroyed. Even if they forgive the bully immediately the damage has already been done.

When your spirit is crushed by any type of affliction and crying your heart out and on the brink of giving up! You are not alone. In your entire affliction, the Lord Himself is afflicted too. He knows what it was like to be bullied, lied about, and accused falsely. He took the lashings of a cruel beating before His death on a cruel cross. In ways, I wonder if the cruel lashings of hate-filled tongues tortured Him more than what He endured physically. When you are in pain because of suffering or harm caused by other people, the Lord feels that pain too. He is touched by the feelings of your infirmities.

He sends the angel of His presence to you in those times. Maybe you cannot feel Him for you are crying so sore, you cannot feel Him because your heart is pierced, and the cruel lashings of unfair words spin round your mind. Even when you cannot feel Him, He's there and in His love and pity, He'll carry you through.

Your afflicted state will not last forever. The Lord will be your help. I wrote this poem:

My child, I feel your pain. I was in pain too.
I know about the cruel lashings of words and also
physical suffering and how they wound your spirit
and make you feel blue.
But I care, it afflicts me to see my child sad but I promise
to hold you close and carry you through.
My child, I died for you. I will bear you up.
Don't listen to satan's voice, listen to mine for it is
honest and true and with all my heart I'm saying:
I LOVE you!

Never think in your valley of suffering that the Lord is distant and remote for He's right there with you. He is stronger than any type of affliction that comes up against you. Pour it all out to Him and let Him hold you close.

9

Let The Lord Have His Way

Do you ever remember a time when you wanted things to go perfectly but it ended up being a total disaster?

For one of my A-levels, I took Home Economics. We had to learn about the science of food and nutrition for different categories of people etc. There was very little practical cookery in the A-level setting. However, a very small portion of our result, something like 5% was based on our ability to plan and cook a three-course meal and carry it out within a certain time frame.

I was so nervous at being watched and scrutinised so closely by a teacher. When the day came nerves got the better of me. My practice run at home had gone perfectly without a glitch but when it came to the actual day to perform so many things went wrong. I was so focused on the teacher grading me that I could not focus on what I was supposed to be doing! I was running behind time, the lid came flying off the blender making a huge mess, my sauce would not thicken as it had at home. I kept dropping things! Yes - the meal did turn out perfectly - the starter, the main course and dessert. But most of the grade was based upon how you carried out the task and my nerves just beat me! (I did do well in the actual written exam though so thankfully I did not fail). Things just did not go to plan that day!

Ever feel like in life that things are not going your way? The plans and dreams you had just did not materialise and you feel disappointed deep in your heart!

Proverbs 19:21 *"Many are the plans in a person's heart, but it is the Lord's purpose that prevails."*

Sometimes our way just isn't God's way even though we may not understand why. Life may not have gone the way we wanted it too, but the Lord's purpose will still win!

Our lives may look messy at times and out of control, but God has them in complete control. Even in the mess, He knows what He's doing. He can bring good out of seeming disaster.

He wants us to continually seek His face and His way in everything for He knows what is best for us. He has a purpose for each of our lives. He wants His will to be done through you and for you to accomplish all He set you on earth for His glory.

Sometimes He blocks things that we have planned for ourselves because He knows they will lead to harm.

No matter what state we are in life we need to be continually submissive to Him and let Him have His way. He is the one who sees the bigger picture. He sees what we cannot see. He sees how our lives fit into His grand scheme of things even when we cannot. Believe me, I know! The dreams I had for my life did not come to pass because of suffering. Yet God is the master expert at causing His purposes for our lives to prevail no matter how many times satan has tried to strike us down. I may not understand the why's and how's of things, but I trust God for He is good and sovereign and what He says He will do. His plans for your life will not be messed up by anything.

10

Self-Sacrifice

I was reading a book called, *'Among the Poppies'* by J'nell Ciesielski. It was set during WW1. A Girl called Gwen went out to the battlefield in France as an ambulance driver and medic. The sights she sees are horrific. I know it was a fiction book, but women did go out to the battlefield as ambulances drivers, medics, and nurses etc. They were determined to make their lives count. They were determined to help others and make a difference. They put themselves in danger to help the wounded and dying and because of their risk, many of them were captured and held hostage by the Germans.

They were willing to do all in their power for those in need no matter what the cost. It showed bravery, selflessness, kindness, and care to the extreme and hearts of pure devotion motivated by the desire to help.

I thought about how it shows how we should be as Christians with the needy and the unsaved. To be brave, selfless, caring, and willing to do whatever it takes to help these people even if it costs us dearly.

Romans 12:1 *"I beseech you therefore brethren by the mercies of God, that ye present your bodies a living sacrifice, holy acceptable unto God which is your reasonable service."*

We have been called to lay ourselves down in sacrifice and to make God's word our primary priority and to give it all our devotion. Jesus laid down His life for us in the ultimate sacrifice of all sacrifices and He wants us to follow in His footsteps.

A song that we used to sing at Scripture Union keeps coming into my head.

> We are willing to pay the price;
> we are willing to lay down our lives,
> as an offering of obedience as a living sacrifice.

Are we willing to do all in our power as servants of Christ on this earth to be self-sacrificing vessels to a needy world? Are we willing to follow in Christ's footsteps and give our all to care for the needy and the unsaved? Excuses like, 'I don't have time' are not valid for when we have surrendered our all to Christ, our hearts should beat for the same things that His heart beats for. He wants us to be His hands and feet on earth. He wants us to go to the lonely and afflicted, the sick and depressed and bring them the comfort and hope of our Saviour. He wants us to devote our lives to winning the lost for Him for His heart is in agony over those who do not yet know Him and will not be safe in Heaven when they die.

Do all you can do make a difference. This life is over in a blink and the only treasures that we take with us are the treasures of souls won for our Master.

11

Memories

I didn't sleep well one night, and I was thinking about all the best times of my life. For some of them, unfortunately, I've no photos and I regret that!

One of my favourite pre sickness memories occurred just eleven months before I was struck down with illness. It was one of my closest friend's wedding, my dear friend Joanne that I lived with at Bible College. I bought a disposable camera for the day but sadly it was a dud and only two photos turned out. One of the bride on her father's arm and one of the newlyweds on the church step. I had been excited for weeks about the wedding! I bought a pink skirt, pink jacket, white top, and a pink hat! I have rarely had any occasions to get dressed up, so I felt like Cinderella going to the ball!

It was a God filled day from start to finish. I have never been at a wedding before or since that I sensed the presence of God so strong. His blessing was all over it. It was such a precious day.

Do you ever have days that you look back on during painful times? You search through your memory bank and savour everything about those times before life changed and pain came.

Memories are good but sometimes they are a way of escapism. Escaping the present by reliving happier times. I'm aware that at times I do this, and the Lord spoke to me about it recently.

Philippians 4:11 *"Not that I speak in respect of want for I have learned in whatsoever state I am, therewith to be content."*

I need to not just dwell on the happy times in the past as a form of escape, but I need to learn to be content in the here and now. In this place with all its suffering and pain, I need to get to a point where I can say like Paul in whatever state I am in, I have learned to be content.

Content means in a state of peaceful happiness, fulfilled, cheerful, glad delighted, serene, at ease.

When your daily circumstances are dire it is hard to learn how to be content, yet they were dire for Paul and he still wrote these things from a prison cell.

Here are some things that I jotted down to find contentment in a barren place.

1. Take your eyes off circumstances and place them on the goodness of God.

2. Abide in His presence for that is where He strengthens you in the inner man and fills you with peace.

3. Look for the tiny blessings every day and be thankful for them.

4. Have a spirit that is full of praise to God. He honours those who honour Him and when He sees His children praising Him anyway despite their pain, He sends blessings.

5. You can be fulfilled and at ease no matter what your state. Seek God's will and way in everything and He will direct your paths and use your weaknesses to bring Him glory.

12

Making God Our Hope When All Seems Hopeless.

Psalm 38:15 *"For in thee, O Lord do I hope; thou wilt hear me, O Lord my God."*

:21-22 *"Forsake me not, O Lord, O my God be not far from me. Make haste to help me, O Lord of my salvation."*

In seasons of great hopelessness, David made the Lord his hope. His emotions may have been spinning out of control. He may have felt in the depths of despair, but he still exclaimed, 'I still hope in you for I know you will hear me.' He then goes on to plead with the Lord to not forsake him and make haste to help him. He was in an extremely dark pit, but he still called out to God from within it.

Does your life look like a hopeless pit today? Do you feel as if you are sinking? Then the Lord is asking you to be like David and make Him your hope even when you do not feel like it.

Maybe you feel like you cannot hope anymore. You feel numb and like a shadow of your former self. The Lord will help you. He will not leave you. I wrote this little poem; I pray it blesses you.

How do you keep hoping when your hopes all gone?
How do you continue when you feel like it's been night forever
and you'll never see the dawn?
By the Grace of God and His sustaining strength,
He'll give you His might to go on.
He won't leave you desolate,
He'll do all in His power to see you through till you see light
again and the curtains of life are once more drawn.

I sense this is what the Lord's saying to weary hearts today.

"My Child I see your hopelessness and pain. I long for you to call out to me to be your help and hope. I see the innermost parts of your mind. I know how great the struggle is. I am touched with the feelings of your infirmities and I weep for you. I long to hold you close but in your panic, you are running from my arms and looking to people to be a healing balm. Only I, your Lord, can provide the healing balm of my love and hope to bind up the deep wounds within you. Return to my arms child. Abide in me. I will restore hope unto you. I will hear your cry. Even now I am making haste to help you, even now I have not forsaken you. I am your fountain of living hope and I will supply you with all you need to face every battle that you face."

You are not alone! Your Saviour is right there with you. Believe things will not always be this way. You will not dwell in the thick darkness forever.

13

Perfectionism

God made us first and foremost as human beings NOT human doings. As important as it is to labour for God and do as much to extend His Kingdom while there is still time, it is also important to note that our worth does not come from our doings. If we put all our sense of worth into the things, we can achieve we can easily become discouraged and depleted. We can be extremely hard on ourselves and constantly feel we should be doing more. This constant need to put our worth in what we can do blinds us to the fact that our worth comes from being God's child.

He is proud of us for who we are in Him before we even speak or do one thing. It is like a parent with a baby. That baby cannot 'do' anything, but they love that child for who they are not what they can do for them and our Heavenly Father's love is just the same.

I know that this is something that I struggle with and I am still trying to learn. In my healthy days, I found my worth in what I could accomplish for God and my years of sickness have been no different for I've strived even harder to accomplish things for God from my bed and make my life count.

I never did anything with false motives of wanting vain glory from man. My motives have always been to bring glory to my beloved Lord. But I am extremely sore on myself. If I don't achieve as much writing in a week as I want too I instantly feel like a failure and worthlessness and uselessness set in.

I'm learning afresh though I'm finding it hard to learn that all my worth comes from Christ living in me. He delighted and rejoiced over me when I was a tiny baby in my mother's womb!

He delighted in me because I was made in His image and He loved me with an unquenchable love before I was born!

Here are some scriptures about our worth to God:

Psalm 139 *"I am fearfully and wonderfully made. Wonderful are your works."*

Matthew 10:31 "Fear not therefore, you have more value than the sparrows."

Isaiah 43:4 *"You are precious in my eyes and honoured and I love you."*

Zephaniah 3:17 *"The Lord your God is in your midst, a mighty one who will save. He will rejoice over you with gladness, he will quiet you with his love, he will exalt over you with loud singing."*

Let this sink in. You are precious, a jewel to the Lord, His treasured possession. Beautiful in His sight. His blood washed you from sin and when He looks at you, He doesn't see all the faults and failings - He only sees the blood of His crucified Son and calls you son or daughter! He is proud of you simply because you are His! Your existence brings Him joy.

We need to surrender the perfectionist spirit to God, that spirit that causes self-blame, self-condemnation, guilt, and feelings of failure for the Lord does not want us to be trapped in our spirits like that. We'll find when we completely surrender it all, God will come and remove all the perfectionist rubble and build in its place a mirror where we can see Christ living in us and accepting us for who we are. Then our walk with God will be deeper than we ever imagined because we will finally know that ALL our worth comes from the Lord. Do not keep inflicting a yoke of bondage by self-condemnation upon yourself when Christ has already set you free!

14

The Kindness Of Our Lord

Psalm 63:7-8 *"Because thou hast been my help therefore in the shadow of the wings will I rejoice. My soul followeth hard after thee; thy right hand upholdeth me."*

As I was having my quiet time the scriptures that I have written at the top jumped out at me. I thought how amazing my God is!

He has been the God of many a sleepless night spent crying since the beginning of my illness. He has been my help amidst sufferings. He has hidden me in the shadow of His wings many a time when I thought that the suffering would break me.

I remember one summer I had been rushed to hospital in a stroke-like state. They discharged me as they could not help me since it was the M.E. that had left my body in that state. I could not lift my head of the pillow and could not even lift a glass to sip from it. I could not read, write, or go on social media. All I could do was lie still.

I remember one Sunday I was listening in to the service at Whitewell Metropolitan Tabernacle, Belfast, Northern Ireland (a church that I listen to online that I am deeply fond of). I could barely speak but yet when the worship came on I was trying with all my might to sing. Mum was on the phone to a friend at the time and she heard noises coming from my room and was worried that I needed water or something was wrong. She stood in the doorway and listened. She told her friend that she was doing all in her power to sing. She later told me that her friend had said, "What has she got to sing about when her body is in a stroke-like state?" The answer to that question was because despite how dire things were, I felt at peace, felt truly hidden under the shadow of my Lord's wings and was determined to utter my love for Him during the worship. Through the worst of times, I have been conscious of His right hand upholding me! With young babies, parents must be careful to always support the child's head, holding them otherwise the head will just flop for it is so delicate. I think Father God cradles us like a child in His arms with His strong hand supporting our heads and holding us up lest we crumble.

The words, "My soul follower hard after thee" couldn't be truer! As a teenager, I had a collie dog called Tessa. She was affectionate, followed me everywhere and constantly wanted to be near me. The Lord wants us to follow Him in both the best of times and the worst of times. He wants us to seek Him with our all no matter what our circumstances are. In reflection, I wrote this poem.

You have ever been my help, my beloved Lord.
You have cradled me like a child in your arms.
Through the storms, you've ever kept me hidden in the
shadow of your wings and haven't let me come to harm.
Your right hand has ever held me up
in the best and worst of seasons.
So I praise you, Lord, for your love so deep.
You are my purpose for living. You are the reason.
So my soul will follow hard after you all the days of my life.
When the skies are sunny
and in times of black turmoil and strife.
Continue to hold me close to you and ever sense you near.
Thank you for all you've done for me.
To me, you've been so dear.

15

Put away all Bitterness

I received a lot of books, Amazon vouchers for books and money for books over Christmas! I am a real bookaholic and love reading so much! I am enjoying them all so much. They are all Christian fiction and they have such powerful biblical messages.

In one of them, *'Where we belong'*, by Lynn Austin, a lady struggled so much with her childlessness. She was a Christian who had used her great wealth to start up many orphanages. At one point two boys came to one of the orphanages. She strongly felt that the Lord wanted her to adopt them but she felt so much bitterness in her spirit at God for not blessing her with her own children that she fought against His will and didn't adopt the boys. Her bitterness got in the way of God's perfect plan for her.

In another book by Lynn Austin, *'Wonderland Creek'*, bitterness almost destroyed a lady called Maggie. She had come as a missionary to a small town and fallen in love with one of the men there. Both her husband and child died, and she became so bitter and angry at God that she tried to kill the man who she blamed for her husband's death. She had wanted her husband to go to college, but his friend Mack told him to stay and keep working in the coal mines as that is who he was and what he loved doing. Because the man died in a mining accident, Maggie was so angry that she was biding her time to try and kill Mack. She shot him but thankfully he lived.

Bitter thoughts lead to bitter actions. Allowing yourself to become bitter because of hardships only destroys you by blocking your walk with God. He cannot abide in the same heart as rebellion against His will and a heart that is bitter and angry.

He wants our hearts to be in perfect harmony with His! Becoming bitter with God and people is like pressing the self-destruct button that stops you accomplishing God's will on earth.

> Ephesians 4:31-32 *"Let all bitterness, wrath and anger and clamour and evil speaking be put away from you with all malice. And be ye kind one to another, tender-hearted, forgiving one another even as God for Christ's sake hath forgiven you."*

As the words of the Disney song go, "Let It Go!" Whatever grudge you are holding against someone in your heart, whatever bitterness you've stored up against God because He hadn't done things your way, whatever anger and unforgiveness that you are clinging tightly too PLEASE, for the sake of your walk with God, Let It Go! Get on your knees before God and repent. Tell Him you are sorry you have hurt Him and ask Him to make your heart pure and tender-hearted always willing to do what He asks no matter what the cost!

Part of a song I once sang as a solo in church went like this:

> Oh, for a heart to serve my God.
> A heart that is ever broken to His will.
> O for a heart to serve my God my King,
> a heart that is ever delighting in Him.
>
> O that I may be made pure.
> That I would strive to love Him more.
> That every work of my hands, would accomplish all His plans so that He may be glorified.

The only way that God can be glorified through us is when we have pure hearts that are ever broken to His will and heart's that aim always to bring Him delight. Bitterness and anger do not fit that category so cast it away before it destroys you and stops you from being a powerful vessel for God to pour His glory through.

16

Teamwork For The Kingdom

I remember years ago as a teenager, I went on a youth team-building weekend with a local organisation. Everything was about working together, leaning on one another, not doing things independently but putting all our ideas together. We stayed outside in tents at night which I loved. We did all sorts of things like designing wedding dresses out of toilet paper, to going out blindfolded and crossing a small stream and doing a walk being wholly dependent on one another.

Another thing we had to do was build a boat that would hold one person out on the sea without sinking. We were given hard plastic, plastic rods, and rope. Whatever group built the boat that did not sink won! I found it a daunting task. I am not very skilled with my hands when it comes to making things but the other's got their ideas together and I just did all they told me to do. Since I was the lightest, the team chose me to go out in the boat! I was terrified! I am a strong swimmer, but the sea was so rough on that March day. I was convinced that I was going to sink! But I did not! Our boat floated and our team won!

It was teamwork that achieved everything that weekend and it is the same for us as Christians. We all need to pull together as a team to accomplish the task of winning souls to Christ while there is still time before we pass away or before the Lord Jesus returns to earth.

1 Corinthians 12:4 *"Now there are a diversity of gifts but the same Spirit."*

:14 *"For the body is not one member, but many."*

:18 *"But God hath set the members everyone in the body as it has pleased him."*

We all need to lean upon one another for the Lord has set us all as members in His body and one part is not more important than another part. Each of us using the gifts that we have for the extension of God's Kingdom is what the Lord wants.

I once heard of a soloist in a certain church who only went up to the platform to show off how amazing her voice was. She was not getting up to sing so that others might come to know the Lord. She got up to sing in a spirit of rivalry, jealousy, and competition to show the other singers in the church that she was the best. Then when it came for the other's turn to sing, she tore them down and spread nasty comments about them.

Every soloist or group in a church is of equal value. The aim should be to encourage God's children and pray that the words that you are singing might soften the hearts of the unsaved that Jesus might be seen through them.

It is the same in all ministries. We are all called to be a team and unite our gifts for the Lord's sake. As the famous saying goes, "There's no I in TEAM." We are all to encourage one another to use our gifts so that the enemy cannot sow seeds of discouragement to hinder the work of God's Kingdom. The enemy loves it when he gets God's children to be in a spirit of disunity for then God gets no glory, and nothing happens for the sake of the Kingdom.

Just like I once united with a group of teenagers that I did not know before that weekend to build a boat, determine to unite with all your brothers and sisters to build God's Kingdom together! No one is more important, and no one is lesser! We all have our necessary part to contribute too.

17

More Than Conquerors

Romans 8:37 *"Nay in all these things we are more than conquerors through him that loved us."*

This verse has been on my mind so much. We are all victors and champions in this battle of life for the Lord has said we are.

Feelings can scream the opposite so much of the time, but no matter how defeated you feel right now, God still sees you as more than a conqueror. The one who loves you deeply is going to get you through this.

I talked to a girl over Christmas who was struggling. The battle had gotten too much for her. The girl is a born again Christian but satan was tempting her strongly with suicidal thoughts. The week before a lady had attacked her with the cruellest words and lies and it made her feel like she did not deserve to live. For her, those words were the straw that broke the camel's back. Every ounce of the fight went out of her and she yearned for death. A few nights later she told me that randomly she received a message from a Christian lady who had no idea what was going on in her head. The lady said, "I don't ever do this, and this might sound silly, but I feel that God is saying to you that your time on earth is not yet up. He has great purposes and plans to fulfil through you for His Kingdom before it is time for going home to Heaven. He's saying your life matters so please don't give up."

The girl who received it was so astonished, that she told me peace filled her heart. The next day she told me for the first night in so long she did not cry herself to sleep and felt God's presence surround her. God had used that other believer's words to erase the enemy's suicidal thoughts from her and let her know how loved she was and how much she mattered. I was in awe of God over it too! That lady - His precious darling child had been under attack from satan and he used the perfect timing of that other faithful believer to remind her that her life was not over. That she was more than a conqueror and that her work on earth was not yet done.

How amazing are God's ways! We can give up on ourselves, but God never gives up on us.

So where are you today? Extremely low? Anxious? Worried? Feeling like a failure to God? Feeling that you do not matter and that your life does not matter? The Lord wants to say otherwise to you:

"My dearest child, I know you've grown weary. Remember that I the Lord who formed you from your mother's womb can see your innermost thoughts, feelings, and emotions. I weep with you and for you when I see that inside you feel like you are losing the fight. But that will never happen! You will not lose the fight; I the God of Angel armies won't let that happen. I will always swoop in in the nick of time speaking through my Word or another believer to revive your fainting heart and remind you that you are still more than a conqueror in my eyes.

Even when feelings scream the opposite, you are not going under my dearest Child. Your life matters and satan only attacks you so viciously because you are accomplishing so much for my Kingdom. But I will not let him win. He is already a defeated foe and you are mine! No one can snatch you from my hand. I am holding you tight. You are dearly loved. I see you as treasure and delight over you with singing. So, my conquering child keep going for 'Greater am I your Lord within you than he that is in the world.'"

18

Moving Forward

Deuteronomy 31:8 *"And the Lord he it is that doth go before thee; he will be with thee, he will not fail thee, neither forsake thee; fear not neither be dismayed."*

As we advance forwards, we know that we are advancing into battle with the Lord on our side. He has gone before us every step of the way. He has promised to be with us and not fail or forsake us. He is asking us not to fear for He will help us through every obstacle.

Did you ever get your car stuck in mud or the snow? You are doing all you can to make it move forward but it refuses to budge. Maybe right now you feel stuck and like you are not moving anywhere? The Lord will give you His divine push into causing you to advance into the battle of life quickened by His spirit to be all you are meant to be.

Let nothing hold you back in your spiritual walk. Do not be looking over your shoulder constantly trapped in the past. The Lord does not want you to dwell on the past He wants you to match forward.

Remember the words to the old hymn *'Onward Christian Soldiers'*.

Onward Christian Soldiers, marching as to war,
with the cross of Jesus, going on before.
Christ the royal master leads against the foes;
Forward into battle, see his banners go.

Advance into battle, determining to be 100% devoted to Jesus. Make being a soldier of the cross and your highest goal to be a soul-winner your heart's desire. I wrote this poem.

Moving Forwards

Lord I'm not looking back to things long gone by.
I desire to match forward and bring your Gospel
to lost souls before they die.
Don't let fear or distractions hold me back
from being a mighty soldier for thee.
For I long with all my heart to keep plodding on through
thick and thin to win the victory.

Somethings in life come from our foes to hold us back.
Never let us give in to fear and discouragement,
but rather obey you in all you want
us to do and never slack.
So, empower us from on high to be going forward
all the way and not trapped
in a defeated trapped place.
Oh, be our battle shield and sword for the fight.
Anoint us with your glory
and keep us going by your grace.

Maybe in your mind, you are like Lot's wife in the Bible. She was so busy looking back to the life of sin that she had enjoyed that she never got to move forward into all God had for her, as he turned her into a pillar of salt for her disobedience.

Make obedience and living a Holy life and letting the Lord have His way in you be your top priority and God will do the rest in getting you His soldier ready to advance into satan's domain.

19

Throw Them Away

Hebrews 12:1-2 *"Let us lay aside every weight and the sin which doth so easily beset us and let us run with patience the race that is set before us. Looking unto Jesus the author and finisher of our faith."*

I used to love running before I took sick. When I was running, I felt as free as a bird. But imagine an athlete trying to run a race with a rucksack of heavy rocks on their back and heavy rocks tied to their arms and legs? Do you think they would get very far? The answer is no! In life, we too are running a spiritual race. We are battling to keep moving forward and keep looking to Jesus no matter what life throws at us.

If you have heavy chains of oppression that are tied to you, cast them off. Cast your burdens on the Lord and let Him sustain you. If there are weights of persistent sins tied to you then repent of them and let the Lord throw them into His sea of forgetfulness.

Satan loves it when God's children keep carrying heavy weights and keep their eyes off the Saviour for then he can weigh them down under burdens of guilt and condemnation and stop them from being all that God intended them to be. They will be hindered in prayer, bible study, witnessing and satan loves that. He loves it when God's children carry these weights and sins for then they carry no threat to him. They are not furthering the Gospel in any way and he loves that.

So, be determined to cast aside all weights and sins that hinder you running the Christian race so that your life can be a real powerhouse for God and a real threat to the enemy.

Run with patience the race set before you. Do you ever notice in marathons the runners need people to cheer them on? The encouragement keeps them going when they feel like stopping. All of us who have given Jesus our lives are runners in this race, that is why we need the Church and need one another. We need to encourage and encourage others for we can all become weary especially if satan has been throwing fiery darts at us. We are not to compete with one another as we all share the same common goal - bringing the Lord as much glory with our lives as possible and bringing lost souls to our Saviour. So, we are to cheer one another on. Encourage people to build on the gifts that you see in them for the Lord's glory. Whatever your gift is use it that others will see Jesus clearly through it.

Look unto Jesus the author and finisher of our faith. We are in a battle and the only way to make it through this spiritual battle is to keep our eyes firmly fixed on our Saviour and the prize of our eternal home in Heaven. I love this song:

> To keep your lovely face, ever before my eyes.
> This is my prayer, make it my strong desire.
> That in my secret heart, no other love competes.
> No rival throne survives, and I serve only you.

Keep your eyes on Jesus' lovely face and He will help you to keep running the race and be all you can be for Him. Lose the weights of hindrances and sins today and make running the race that brings your Saviour great glory your biggest life goal.

20

New Year's Day

Isaiah 43:19 "Behold I will do a new thing; now it shall spring forth; shall ye not know it? I will even make a way in the wilderness and rivers in the desert."

We do not know what a year will hold or bring but we do know the one who holds our lives tightly in His hands. The verse that I have written at the top is a promise that the Lord gave me years ago. I've yet to see the fulfilment but maybe this will be the year when the suffering ends and I will step into the new thing that the Lord has for me.

The Lord's new things spring up like rivers in the desert in miraculous ways when we least expect them. What have you been believing God for, for so long? Do not lose the hope of the Lord doing that new thing in your life just because the past few years have been barren drought years.

I thought that my prayers for my late Granny's salvation were not going to be answered as she wasn't softening her heart in any way. Yet two days before she died, once more I asked her if she would accept Jesus as Saviour and to my surprise, she said yes and together we prayed the sinner's prayer! That was God making a way where there seemed to be no way.

Hold onto the hope that God can make a way where there seems to be no way. Some of you are in a difficult place right now. The calendar changing from year to year did not miraculously change your circumstances, but this is what I sense the Lord saying to me and you.

"My child don't fear for the new year. I know how many hairs are on your head, I can see everything that this year holds for you. I am asking you to trust me. To hold my hand tightly and let me lead you through every high and low place for the praise and glory of my name. Never stop believing that I can do a new thing in your life. Never stop believing that I can cause rivers of living water to flow out of your wilderness. But for now, let your focus be on 'The New Thing.' Be concentrated on newness in your walk with me. Focus on walking with me more closely, focus on drawing even nearer and let me handle and work out the things that are beyond your control. I am making all things new in your life precious one - trust me even though right now you cannot see beyond the bleakness. I am ever with you and I love you deeply."

I wrote this poem in my first book, *'A Myrtle Tree For Life's Briars.'*

Newness of life,
Being birthed from my strife.
After years of being under the Master surgeon's knife.
It's the feeling of excitement
that precedes a maiden becoming a wife.

Newness of life springing up within me.
I'm going from winter to spring with a heart filled with glee.
It's God's appointed season
like a prisoner released I'll be free.
After walking in darkness for so long
with my eyes daybreak I shall see.

Newness of life covering me like Heaven's blanket.
The haze is lifting, fears are dispelled.
I've no reason to fret.
I stand in awe of God, to His mercy and love I'm in debt.
Mine eyes are ever toward the Lord
for He shall pluck my feet out of the net.
(Psalm 25:15)

21

New Year's Eve Reflection

What kind of year have you had? I like to spend some time reflecting on the old year before entering the New Year. Maybe like me, your year has not been easy. Maybe it has been a brilliant year where you have got engaged, married, or had a child. Maybe it has just been a non-eventful year of work and church and nothing out of the ordinary has occurred.

But whatever kind of year you have had, you are still standing. For those of you who have had a horrific year - you are making it through, still loving Jesus just as much which is a real testimony to His grace and mercy in your life! If it has been a year of blessing, then praise God with a thankful heart for pouring His loving-kindness on you.

We can all end the year in a spirit of thankfulness no matter what has gone before us for the God that we serve is loving and good and He deserves the glory for all He has done for us and all He has brought us through.

Here are just a few Bible verses that highlight praising our Lord.

Daniel 2:20 *"Blessed be the name of God for ever and ever: for wisdom and might are his."*

Jeremiah 20:13 *"Sing unto the Lord, praise ye the Lord: for he hath delivered the soul of the poor from the hand of evil doers."*

Psalm 75:1 *"Unto thee O God, do we give thanks."*

He has encouraged us through every season. He has protected us from every fiery dart of the enemy. His might has held us up through every circumstance. His wisdom has shown us the way forward in times of confusion.We can sing unto Him for all He has provided - a home, warmth, shelter, food, water, people to love us. We can praise Him for who He is compassionate, loving, caring, good, faithful, ever-present just to name but a few.

As I reflect on this year though it has been hard due to continued illness. I can still praise and thank God for the few things I have mentioned and far more. I can look back and say that the circumstances were not good, but my precious Lord was good!

I have written this poem as a reflection of thankfulness and praise.

My dearest precious Lord as this year ends.
I lift my voice in thankfulness.
You've held me close and protected
me from satanic foes.
Everything I've needed you've given
in abundance and for this,
I bring you praise.
Oh Lord, you are beautiful and ever so faithful,
this is the tender song today I raise.

You are most high, Lord my Master.
Lord my Shepherd and my peace.
You are Father, you are the provider.
You are my help. In famine, you are my feast.
So I look back and marvel in gratefulness.
Thank you for keeping me safe all the way.
You've ever been my rainbow of hope
when skies have been grey.

22

Wise Men From The East

Matthew 2:1 *"There came wise men from the east."*

:9 *"Lo, the star which they saw in the east went before them, till it came and stood over where the young child was."*

:10-11 *"When they saw the star they rejoiced with great joy. And when they came to the house they saw the young child with Mary his mother, and fell down and worshipped him and when they had opened their treasures they presented unto him gifts; gold, and frankincense and myrrh."*

We do not know much about these wise men from the east. The Believer's Bible Commentary explains (page 1207).

"They might have been pagan priests whose ritual centred around the elements of nature. Because of their knowledge and predictive powers that they were chosen as counsellors to Kings. It was the star in the East that somehow made them aware of the birth of a King whom they came to worship.

Possibly they were familiar with O.T. prophecies concerning the Messiah's arrival. But it seems more probable that the knowledge was communicated to them supernaturally. That the star they followed stopped right over the house where Jesus was is so unusual that it can only be accounted for a miracle.

The treasures that they brought spoke volumes. Gold is a symbol of deity and glory; it speaks of the shining perfection of His divine person. Frankincense is an ointment or perfume; it suggests the fragrance of the life of sinless perfection. Myrrh is a bitter herb; it predicts the sufferings He would endure in bearing the sins of the world."

I always found it so amazing that a star would miraculously appear in the sky and lead these wise men to worship the King of kings and Lord of lord's! Neither did they come empty-handed. What beautiful symbolic gifts they brought with them.

At Christmas, we have all opened gifts. Gifts that people thoughtfully selected for us. I know when I'm giving a gift, I do my best to put great thought into it and consider what the person might like or value. But the gifts that the wise men brought were more than thoughtful, they were prophetic. They were signs of what was to come.

When I think of the wise men offering gifts, the verse from the Carol, *'In the bleak midwinter'* comes to mind.

What can I give Him, poor as I am.
If I were a shepherd, I would bring a lamb.
If I were a wise man, I would do my part.
Yet what can I give him - give my heart.

Bringing gifts to Jesus is not a Christmas thing. It is an all-year-round thing. We can bring the gift of our wholehearted love for Him, the gift of walking closely by His side, the gift of our service in sharing our Saviour's heart and bringing the gospel to the lost, the gift of a loving, caring heart that reflects Him to a world in great need. Let your daily life be the best gift in His sight so that one day you will hear the words, "Well done good and faithful servant. Enter into your reward."

23

The Holly And The Ivy

I remember years ago I received a little pop-up carol book and cassette tape as a Sunday school prize. One of the songs on the cassette was the '*Holly and the Ivy*'. I love these words:

> The holly bears a blossom as white as lily flowers
> and Mary bore sweet Jesus Christ to be our sweet
> Saviour... The holly bears a berry as red as any blood
> and Mary bore sweet Jesus Christ to do poor sinners
> good. The holly bears a bark as bitter as any gall, and
> Mary bore sweet Jesus Christ to redeem us all.

The prickly leaves of the Holly represent the crown of thorns that Jesus wore when He was crucified. The berries represent the drops of blood that were shed by Jesus because of the thorns.

Mary's child - God incarnate was born to die. His mission was to come and die a most horrendous death to take our place so that it is now possible to be right with God through repentance of sin and surrendering one's life to Him. We could not earn our way into Heaven by ourselves, we needed someone pure and Holy to die in our place so that after placing our trust in Him we will for sure go to heaven when we die.

Matthew 27:28-30 *"And they striped him, and put on him a scarlet robe. And when they had platted a crown of thorns, they put it upon his head and a reed in his right hand and they bowed the knee before him and mocked him saying, Hail King of the Jews. And they spit upon him and took the reed and smite him on the head."*

Oh our precious King of Glory what He suffered, and this was only just the beginning of it all. Oh, what a contrast to that starry night in Bethlehem, when He was cradled safely in His mother's arm and shepherds rushed to bow down to the King of kings and Lord of lord's.

Holly and Ivy are Christmas decorations but what they represent is the destiny of this tiny babe. Those thorns that were platted and pierced into His brow were not like the tiny thorns we have here, they were extremely long. The pain of that crown of thorns being platted into our dear Saviour's brow would have been excruciatingly painful. They stripped Him naked and put a flimsy scarlet robe on Him to mock Him, pretend to worship Him and spit on Him. The King of all Glory who came to this earth to bring hope and forgiveness to all who would accept Him and an eternal home in Heaven based on His redemption alone was being treated like a criminal. The real worship that He had experienced as a babe was now mock. A band of people cruelly mistreating Him.

He bore it all because He loves us deeply. If you know Him as Saviour today examine your heart. He went to extreme lengths to make you His child. Are you willing to go to extreme lengths for Him? Is your worship real like the praise that the shepherds brought to the babe born in Bethlehem or do you merely go through the motions? Going through the motions of worshipping with your mouth and singing empty words when your heart is a far off grieves our Saviour.

> Matthew 15:8-9 *"This people draweth nigh unto me with their mouth and honoureth me with their lips but their heart is far from me. But in vain do they worship me."*

Let your worship of the Saviour be from your heart. He does not want lip service; He wants people who will worship Him with their all, in purity of heart. He bore sheer agony for us the very least we can do is draw near with our whole heart and worship Him in Spirit and truth. The King of Glory deserves all our adoration and devotion.

24

Joy To The World

This is my favourite Carol. The lyrics I like most in it are: "Let every heart prepare Him room."

Isaiah 7:14 *"Therefore the Lord himself shall give you a sign; Behold a virgin shall conceive and bear a son and shall call His name Immanuel."*

That prophecy came through long before this:

Luke 1:26-27 *"The angel Gabriel was sent from God unto a city of Galilee, named Nazareth to a virgin espoused to a man whose name was Joseph, of the house of David and the virgins name was Mary."*

Look at Mary's response after the angel had told her that she would conceive a son and call Him Jesus and that to His Kingdom there would be no end. First, she asked how it could be since she was sexually pure. But the angel told her the Holy Ghost would come upon her and place the miracle inside her.

Her response was: Luke 1:38 *"Behold the Handmaiden of the Lord; be it unto me according to the word."*

Her response was one of humble submission. She prepared room in her heart to be God's instrument through which He would send the promised Messiah. We are talking about a young girl here. In Bible days girls usually got married around fifteen. The cost of expecting a baby outside of marriage was to be stoned to death yet she still said, *"Be it unto me according to thy word."* Or in other words, I am wholly yours Lord, do what you want in me and through me whatever the cost.

Mary teaches us to always be ready to submit to what the Lord asks of you even if there is a high cost to it. She gave all of herself and held nothing back. She had a spirit of, I am thine Lord, completely abandoned to you, here take all of me. Mary had a beautiful spirit.

What kind of year are you having? Is it a year full of so much busyness and clutter that you have hardly any space in your life for the Saviour you claim to love? Have you daily prepared Him room in your heart by coming to His precious word so you could hear His voice and daily pray to Him to draw even nearer to His heart? Have you made time for prayer meetings? Have you obeyed the Lord's call to reach out with the gospel? Does Jesus inhabit your whole life because you are so devoted to Him and your heart beats in tune with His Word? Or does a room in your life look so cluttered and filled with junk that Jesus is squeezed into a tiny corner with hardly any breathing room? You have filled your heart with everything but Him, not even taking time to have a time of devotion.

Determine to change that this very day. Be a Mary! Open your whole heart to Him. Prepare your Saviour room to enter. Start walking with Him daily again. Start making Him a priority once again, obeying His word again and doing all that He lays on your heart. For at the end of the day all that matters is Jesus. We can be constantly busy but not fulfilling His most Holy calling of carrying the light by spreading His Gospel so that other's will prepare Him room and accept Him as Lord and Saviour.

Open wide your life and heart today. Make Mary's prayer yours today! *"Be it unto me according to thy word."*

25

O Holy Night

'O Holy Night' is my second favourite Carol! The words are so precious. I could listen to it repeatedly. Consider some of the words.

O Holy Night the stars are brightly shining. It is the night of our dear Saviour's birth... A thrill of hope the weary world rejoices for yonder breaks a new and glorious morn... His law is love and His Gospel is peace. Chains shall He break for the slave is our brother, And in His name, all oppression shall cease. Fall on your knees. Oh hear the angel voices. Oh night divine. Oh night when Christ was born.

> Luke 2:7 *"And she brought forth her first born son and wrapped him in swaddling clothes and laid him in a manger, because there was no room for him at the inn."*
>
> :8 *"And there were in the same country Shepherds abiding in the field keeping watch over their flocks by night. And lo the angel of the Lord said unto them, Fear not; for behold I bring you great tidings of great joy which shall be to all people. For unto you is born this day in the city of David, a Saviour which is Christ the Lord."*

It truly was a Holy Night! The Saviour of the world born from a virgin's womb came to planet earth. Redemption's plan started in a filthy stable but the babe, the Lord Jesus Christ would not do what He came to earth to do until He was thirty-three years old. Then on an old rugged cross, in utter agony, He died for all people so they could have forgiveness of sins and a home in Heaven if they will accept His gift of Salvation.

But consider that Holy Night. The long-awaited Messiah had arrived on earth. Consider the amazement of the shepherds when the sky filled with angels heralding the arrival of the Saviour. Had I been a shepherd I would have passed out in shock to see the sky filled with angels. It was the night of the miraculous! The words, "A thrill of hope a weary world rejoices, for yonder breaks a new and glorious morn." These words say it all.

This truly was that hope-filled glorious morn. You see God's people had been waiting thousands of years for this day. This was something that they had prayed for nonstop and while the world slept, God the Father brought to pass His promise that had been prophesied years ago. This touches me to never give up on what you are praying for, for when God's appointed time comes to 'perform' that thing in your life your weary soul will truly rejoice in amazement.

The other line, "Chains shall He break for the slave is our brother and in His name, all oppression shall cease." This teaches me that no chain of oppression that we struggle with is too great for Jesus. He sees the pain that your heart is in and He will come and comfort you and give you peace and release. Though we will not see an end to all oppression on earth until the Lord Jesus returns and ends satan's reign on earth by casting him into the lake of fire. Then there will be no more suffering, sickness, or death.

"Fall on your knees, oh hear the angel voices." The greatest gift you can bring the Lord Jesus after you've made Him your Saviour is to continually bring Him the gift of worship and let your life bring Him praise. No matter how hopeless our circumstances may seem we can always celebrate Jesus by bringing Him a sacrifice of praise. Our beloved Saviour born that Holy night is now seated at the right hand of the Father ever praying for us! He is our hope!

26

Changing Our Thinking To God's Way Of Thinking

Philippians 4:8 *"Finally brethren, whatsoever things are true, whatsoever things are honest, whatsoever things are just, whatsoever things are pure, whatsoever things are lovely, whatsoever things are of good report; if there be any virtue and if there is any praise, think on these things."*

The Lord wants our minds to be pleasant places. He does not want His children's minds to be full of trash, negativity, and gossip. He wants us to follow His instructions from this verse to be on track to having a pure mind like Him. Whatever you are feeding into your thought life will indeed spill over into your words and actions.

Proverbs 23:7 *"As a man thinketh in his heart so he is."*

If your mind and heart are full of trash how can you expect the Lord to dwell there also! Light cannot dwell amid darkness!

Believer's Bible commentary (page 1979)

"The Bible everywhere teaches that we can control what we think. It is useless to adopt a defeatist attitude saying that we simply cannot help it when our thoughts are filled with unwelcome things. The fact of the matter is that we can help it... A person cannot entertain evil thoughts and thoughts about the Lord Jesus at the same time. If then an evil thought should come to him, he should immediately get rid of it by meditating on the person and work of Christ.

The more enlightened Psychiatrists of the day have come to agree with the Apostle Paul on this matter. They stress the danger of negative thinking.

You do not have to look very closely to find the Lord Jesus in verse eight. Everything true, noble, just, pure lovely or of good report, virtuous and praiseworthy is found in Him. True means not false or unreliable but genuine and real. Noble means - honourable or morally attractive. Just means righteous both toward God and man. Pure would refer to the high moral character of a person's life. Lovely has the idea of that which is admirable or agreeable to behold. Of good report has also been translated of good repute. Virtue of course speaks of moral excellence and praiseworthy is something that deserves to be commended."

If you put bread into a toaster, you will get the bread out again. If you put milk into a milk jug, milk will come pouring out. If you put junk into your mind junk is going to come back out.

Examine your thoughts today. The Lord knows and sees all. There is not a fleeting thought that He misses, and He longs for you to honour Him with your thinking. If it were possible to portray your secret thought life onto a TV screen where all the world could watch your thoughts, would you be embarrassed by what they are seeing/hearing? That TV screen is one that the Lord himself can view 24/7. So with that knowledge does your thought life please your Saviour or grieve His heart?

27

Make A Difference

I recently watched a Christmas film about a little boy who had no family living. He was found by new tenants, of an old house that had stood derelict for years, in the basement. Every foster home that William had ever been placed with he ran away from too scared to get attached to anyone else in case he would lose them too.

But William did finally open to the lady and her daughter who had found him and grew to love them. They adopted William, the previously unwanted child and gave him a home in their hearts.

There are so many people in this world who are extremely lonely. They have known abandonment, the death of loved ones, of rejection's sting in the form of bullying.

We as God's children are called to open our hearts wide to those who are lonely and in need. We are called to minister to them as we would to Jesus.

Matthew 25:35-36 *"For I was hungered, and ye gave me meat, I was thirsty and ye gave me a drink. I was a stranger and ye took me in. Naked and ye clothed me; I was sick and ye visited me; I was in prison and ye came to me."*

:40 *"Verily I say unto you; Inasmuch as ye have done it unto the least of these brethren, ye have done it unto me."*

Jesus is saying that every time that we reach out with arms of compassion to others on earth that we are doing it for Him. When we send clothes to the homeless or poor, we are sending them to Jesus. When we support an organisation that gives food and water to some of the neediest people on earth, it is as if we are feeding the Lord Himself.

Every time you show kindness and hospitality to strangers it is like we are reaching out to the Lord Himself. Every time we show kindness to those who are sick in the body it is as though we are touching the Lord Himself in infirmity. When we support the organisation for the Gospel to be taken into prisons we are showing Christ's mercy, forgiveness and compassion and again He says what you did for the least of people in the eyes of the world you are doing for me.

As His children, the Lord has placed within our hearts the ability to love, to care, to be tender-hearted and to make a massive impact on this world. Jesus wants us to be His hands and feet in this life reaching out to the lonely and abandoned 'Williams' of the world and seeing beyond ourselves and our own needs to the needs of others. Maybe for a long time you have been too self-focused to care - well the Lord is saying it's not too late for you to start.

James 1:27 *"Pure religion and undefiled before God and the Father is this, to visit the fatherless and widows in their affliction and to keep himself unspotted from the world."*

Do you truly care for others? Do you hate to see them suffer? Then make a massive difference with your life while you still have time and live to serve your Lord and majesty by pouring yourself out upon the needs of others.

28

Heartbreak

I once heard about a girl that was engaged to a man that she adored. Sadly due to circumstances beyond her control, the engagement ended. The girl still loved him and could not forget him, so she never looked at another man again. She just prayed and hoped that her first love would come back for her. After thirteen years she heard that her first love had married another, and it rekindled her heartbreak because she now knew for sure that he would never come back to her. He belonged to another.

Many situations in life can cause us great heartbreak.

Heartbreak means overwhelming distress, grief, sorrow, sadness, anguish, trauma, agony, desolation etc.

Scientists and doctors now agree that heartbreak can affect your physical health and lead to heart problems. Someone suffering from heartbreak will be under immense stress. Stress affects the heart. People have been struck down with severe illness as the direct result of the trauma of heartbreak.

Psalm 147:3 *"He healeth the broken in heart and bindeth up their wounds."*

Psalm 34:18 *"The Lord is nigh unto them that are of a broken heart."*

You have a Lord who understands your heartbreak. He knows whether it is over a failed relationship, a failed friendship, sickness in your own body, sickness in a loved one's body or over extremely bad news that you have just received. But His word says that He is close to them that are broken in heart and wants to bind up those wounds.

I feel like He's saying: "My child, I see your heartbreak. I see your grief and agony of spirit. I see the many tears that flow in secret that others know nothing about. I see the despondency and the hurt that is deep within your heart and I want you to know that I ache alongside you. I hate to see my darling one suffering so much. You have a High Priest who sympathises fully with your infirmities. I care! I want to stop the inner bleeding by binding up your wounds in the balm of my love. I long to heal your brokenness. Bring to me all that heartbreak right now. Child, release it to me, place it into the hands that were pierced and wounded for you. Give me all the broken pieces and let me be your Heavenly heart mender. I will not ever fail you. You can trust me with all that is on your heart for I AM your Lord and wonderful Counsellor. I am right here waiting for you to stop striving in the flesh and just let me take over. I love you my dearly beloved one."

I remember singing a song at a children's camp that went like this:

Heartaches, broken pieces.
Ruined lives are why You died on Calvary.
Your touch is what I long for.
You have given life to me.

Let His tender touch sweep over your spirit even this day so you might know comfort and then full release from the heartbreak.

29

To Reflect Jesus

I was re-reading a series of Amish books by Beverly Lewis called, *'The Rose Trilogy'*. They were about the lives of two sisters. Hannah who had made a hasty decision and married without her parent's approval and left the church. (Though in the end she made things right with God and her husband received Christ.) The other sister - Rose was the reliable, caring, unselfish one. Their mother had been injured and confined to a wheelchair since an accident years ago. Rose ever faithfully tended to her mother's needs.

Rose reminded me of a person of beauty, humble, loving, selfless, devoted to God and others. Rose showed me all the qualities that my dear Saviour has.

There is so much emphasis placed on outer beauty these days. But there is little emphasis placed on the hidden inner person of the heart who reflects the Saviour in Spirit wholly.

Here are a few characteristics of Christ.

- Humble service. (John 13:1-5)
- Holiness (1 Peter 1:15-16)
- Righteousness (I John 3:7)
- Purity (1 John 3:3)
- Love (Ephesians 5:1-2)
- Forgiveness (Colossians 3:13)
- Endurance (Hebrews 12:2-4)
- Submission (1 Peter 2:21-24)
- Humility and Obedience (Philippians 2:5-8)

- Kindness (Luke 6:35)
- Generous Giving (2 Corinthians 8:1-9)

Looking into the mirror of God's word and seeing my Saviour's heart makes me want to reflect Him to the world. I want to be like and set apart for my Master.

I want my life to be one of humble service towards others, kindness, and generous giving love.

I want my life to be a beautiful reflection of His holiness that is not in any way tainted by trying to serve two masters and being corrupted with the world. I want to live the way He wants me to live in all holiness and purity.

I want to reflect His righteousness. Jesus did not tolerate sin or hypocrisy when He was on earth. He was quick to speak out the truth. We as God's children need to never lose our passion for standing upon God's word and speaking the truth.

I want to be full of forgiveness towards others, the way He is towards me. I want to endure whatever life throws at me. Just like the way Jesus endured the cross.

I want to be submissive, humble, and obedient always ready to do His will whatever it is.

I want to reflect my beloved to the world and do not want my life to put any others off coming to a saving knowledge of Jesus.

We all need to ask the Lord to make us more like Himself so that we can shine with the light of His glory in this dark world and lead many to Him.

I will finish with the words of this hymn: *'O to be like Thee'*.

Oh to be like thee, blessed Redeemer.
This is my constant longing and prayer.
Gladly I'll forfeit all of earth's treasures Jesus thy
perfect likeness to wear.

30

Soar High

It was my beloved late Grandfather who taught me how to swing. For a long time, I just could not get the hang of it, I was pumping my wee legs but getting nowhere! I remember saying, 'Grandpa, please just push me for I can't do this.' But he would not push me, he kept saying, 'I believe you can do it yourself.' With his confidence in me, I kept pumping those wee legs until finally, I was soaring through the air myself with screams of joy!

I must admit that I still love swings to this day! Although it has been years since I was on one, I love that feeling of freedom as you soar higher and higher through the air!

Isaiah 40:31 *"But they that wait upon the Lord shall renew their strength, they at all mount up on wings like eagles, they shall run and not be weary and they shall walk and not faint."*

Maybe right now you are like the wee girl version of me. You are pumping your legs hard so to speak but you are not moving anywhere. You're doing all in your power to soar high again and burst through the shackles that are holding you back but no matter how hard you try, you still find yourself in the same place.

Do you know where you are? The waiting room of life. Our period of waiting will not last forever, but the Lord has said that once it is over you will once more soar. You will be like a strong and mighty eagle soaring through the air with more strength in God than you had before your season of waiting. It is hard and frustrating now, but it will not always be this way!

Eagles are admired all over the world as living symbols of power, freedom, and transcendence. It is one of the biggest and most majestic birds!

Transcendence means, existence or experience beyond the normal or physical level. Greatness and magnificence.

Maybe right now you feel confined, like you are in a tight spot, like a bird in a cage. Circumstances have you extremely limited and you yearn to break free from the constraints of your cage.

Keep waiting upon God in your season of suffering and waiting. Keep praying, keep studying His word, keep worshipping, keep doing all in your power in your little ways to serve Him with a humble heart. For when this season is over you will soar high like an eagle. You will have a greater awareness of God's power because of what He did in your season of waiting. You will have a greater sense of freedom in God - you will no longer be the caged bird! You will soar to heights in your walk with Him that you never dreamt possible. You will have more freedom to serve Him in more ways than you can now! The shackles will lift. The limits that are placed on you now will be taken away! You will know the greatness and magnificence of your God in amazing ways.

So keep pumping those wee legs on the swing of life, even when you feel limited and like you are getting nowhere! You will not always be the caged bird! One day you will soar like an eagle.

31

Freshness In Our Walks

At the end of every year, I have each one of my journals for that entire year burned. My journals are extremely private. I pour out my feelings, pour out prayers to God. Write what I have learned from Scriptures that I have been studying that day and what I believe the Lord is saying to me through that season. But unlike some people who keep their journals to look back on, I prefer to get rid of them as I don't believe it's healthy to re-read them and go through all the pain of what I had been feeling at certain times again. They are all between the Lord and I and I would rather do as Paul said in Philippians 3:13-14 *"Forgetting those things which are behind and reaching forth unto those things which are before, I press toward the mark for the prize of the high calling of God in Christ Jesus."*

I want to keep the freshness in my walk with Him by moving forward and forgetting the painful times of the past year so that I might press on in God and fulfil His calling for me. I want nothing holding me back or shackles of old memories or feelings holding me back.

I remember reading a parable in Matthew 9:16-17

"No man putteth a piece of new cloth unto an old garment... Neither do men put new wine into old bottles else the bottles break, and the wine runneth out and the bottles perish but they put new wine into new bottles and both are preserved."

New Bible Commentary (page 916)

"The patch and new wine are images of a powerful, effervescent new relationship with God which bursts out of the dried-up confines of formal religion."

Effervescent means, active, positive, and full of energy.

I do not want to be full of clutter of the past, old feelings, bad memories etc to keep the Lord from filling me afresh with His Spirit and keeping my walk with Him fresh and close! I want to be active for Him and enthusiastic, not held back by anything.

Maybe you feel all shrivelled up inside spiritually. You become dead inside and dried up. But you long for the deep passionate walk with the Lord that you once had! Ask Him to remove all that's a hindrance, all that is dried up and ask him to pour the freshness of His Holy Spirit into your life so you can start anew with an uncluttered heart, ready to be and do all that God wants you to do. Most of all He wants you to walk closely with Him. Keep drawing nearer and nearer to Him for He longs for your cup to be flowing over so that you can spill Him into the lives of everyone you meet. The closer you walk with Him the more you will bubble over and sparkle with His love. You become like the company you keep and the best person you can become like is God! I will finish with this little verse I wrote:

Let my walk with you be fresh.
Take all the clutter away.
Never let me walk in my old dried up flesh.
But to walk by your Spirit every day.

32

I'll Praise My Maker
While I Have Breath

Psalm 146:2 *"While I will live, I will praise the Lord. I will sing praise to my God while I have my being."*

I bought a book for my late Grandfather years ago with lots of hymns and their history in it. Both Grandpa and I loved the hymns most of all out of Christian music. I used to sing them to him all the time. When he passed away my Granny gave me back the book as it represented a special bond that I had with Grandpa. I was reading through it recently and came across a hymn by Isaac Watts that I was not very familiar with. It is called *'I'll Praise My Maker While I Have Breath.'* Dated from 1719. The first verse goes:

> I'll Praise my maker while I have breath,
> And when my voice is lost in death,
> Praise shall employ my nobler powers,
> My days of praise shall ne'er be past.

Isaac Watts once wrote: "Death to a good man is but passing through... one little dusky road of his Father's house into another that is fair and large, lightsome and glorious and divinely entertaining." Isaac Watts certainly did praise his maker all the days of his life and even on his deathbed, he was still praising his Saviour.

Do you ever feel yourself getting so numb and depressed that you no longer feel like singing? You want to praise God, but your spirit has sagged so low within you that it is the last thing you feel like doing.

It is in those seasons of great distress that we need to force ourselves to worship. Force ourselves to praise our Saviour even when you are hurting like crazy. I find the Christmas season hard especially this year with it being my 13th Christmas Ill. The other night I was feeling so low. The last thing that I felt like doing was worshipping God. Not because I feel bitter against Him but because numbness of spirit had set in. But this Scripture came into my head:

Psalm 150:6 *"Let everything that hath breath praise the Lord."*

I sensed the Lord saying, "Worship me, you've still got breath in your lungs." At first, I struggled. It felt like I was going through the motions but then like a spring pouring forth from me, I knew great release. I sang my heart out to my Saviour despite how low I felt. I focused on His Salvation, on Heaven, on His faithfulness, on His goodness on all the blessings He has poured over my life and when I had finished I knew my Lord's presence so strong and my focus was no longer on circumstances. I once heard a song where one of the lines went, 'You can praise the hurt away.' That was true for me!

I read these quotes: "Worship will get you through the roughest times in your life because it shifts your focus from the problem to the problem solver."

"Even when the fight seems lost, I'll praise you. Even when it hurts like hell, I'll praise you. Even when it makes no sense to sing, Louder then I'll sing your praise."

I may be extremely sick but there is still breath in my lungs and even when it's hard, I'll fight against the hopeless feelings and bring a sacrifice of praise to the one that I love and adore most - my precious Jesus! So like Isaac Watts said, 'I'll praise my maker while I have breath', for that is still something of great value that I can do in service for my King.

33

Divine Strength When We Feel None

2 Chronicles 15:7 *"Be ye strong therefore and let not your hands be weak, for your work shall be rewarded."*

Isaiah 40:29 *"He giveth power to the faint; and to them that have no might he increaseth strength."*

I just sense the Lord saying through this: "My child, I see how faint-hearted you've become. You are weary and afraid. I am still your God during extreme weakness. I am still here. I want to impart my divine strength into your fragile heart. You have been trying to pour from an empty cup for too long. You have tried to keep going in your strength instead of letting me breathe my divine strength into you and now in your heart, you have fainted. It has all got too much for you. But right now I'm saying to you, my faint-hearted child who has no might left, that I am going to breathe fresh hope upon you and once more, increase your strength and endurance to cope with the things that life has thrown at you.

I will give you the power to continue in ministry for me and service for others, even though right now your spiritual hands are weak.

I will not let you stay this way; I love you too much! Be clothed in the garments of my divine strength which I am giving to you now and continue in the mighty work you are doing for you shall be greatly rewarded. Give me your weakness and let me give you my strength."

Did you ever see a flat bouncy castle? It is of no use for its purpose until a lot of air is pumped into it, then it inflates and becomes a happy place for children.

Maybe right now you feel like a deflated bouncy castle and you might not feel like you are fit for your purpose, but the Lord is saying otherwise today. His divine strength and breath will fill you up again, the colour will return to your cheeks, the dreary distant look in your eyes will be replaced with eyes that sparkle life again! Lean on your God, the strength of your salvation even now and let Him replace your powerlessness with His power. Let Him be the strength of your life today!

34

Still God In The Crisis Moments

Almost six years ago a scary phone call came through to our landline on a Friday night. My brother had been in a car accident. He had been on his way home from church where he was a leader at a youth club, and he fell asleep at the wheel and hit a wall. My parents went and stayed with him at the hospital. I was in an utter panic in the house myself. I did not know if he was going to live or die. The tears where flowing thick and fast and I had no idea how I was going to make it through the night. I was not well enough to be at the hospital too and I was in utter despair. But despite the despair and panic, God was with me in that time of crisis, soothing me despite the terror in the pit of my stomach.

We were later told by the ambulance men that it was a complete miracle that he was still alive. The car was smashed to pieces. The only answer to his still being alive was a complete miracle from God!

Maybe you are amid a crisis right now. Fear is consuming you and you are at breaking point. Please know that God will not let you break. He will soothe you and carry you through the agony.

There is a story in Scripture about God working a miracle in a crisis. 2 Kings 4:18-37

Earlier in this chapter, Elisha was staying with a family. The lady had no children and her husband was old. The prophet told her that she would conceive a son and that precious miracle of life happened.

When the child was grown, he was out in the fields with his father when he suddenly cried out with pain in his head.

:20 *"And when he had taken him and brought him to his mother, he sat on her knees till noon, and then died."*

During the crisis, she cried out to her husband to get the man of God back again. Elisha came immediately.

:34 *"And he went up and lay upon the child and put his mouth upon his mouth and his eyes upon his eyes and his hands upon his hands and he stretched himself upon the child and the flesh of the child waxed warm....and the child opened his eyes."*

Before their eyes, they witnessed their son coming back from the dead! God was with them in their crisis time. That is what we witnessed in the life of my brother! He fought for his life in hospital for weeks, but God in His mighty power worked a miracle and we still glorify His name for it!

Though I understand some crisis times do not end like this. My heart breaks when I hear of a child passing away from cancer or illness. My heart bleeds for victims of road traffic accidents who did not pull through. It is a crisis when a young mother passes away leaving behind heartbroken children. But God is still God during every crisis. He stands with arms wide open weeping, feeling the pain, longing to scoop every sufferer of a crisis into His strong arms to let Him soothe and breathe hope and strength into them and carry them through the pain.

If you have suffered from some kind of crisis this year, then run into the arms of the Lord. He truly cares and wants to stand with you, holding you tight while you cry. We do not always understand why the outcomes of certain situations worked out the way they did but nothing that comes our way can ever change the fact that God is good and faithful and loves us as no other could!

35

Eliphaz

Job 4,5, 15 & 22

I listened to a sermon about Eliphaz. He was one of the so-called friends who came to comfort Job in his suffering! But with friends like Eliphaz who needs enemies! Eliphaz accused Job of being sick because of some sin that he had not repented of. He also accused Job of being mean and selfish in his time of plenty. He said that Job had probably ignored the poor and those in need in his time of plenty and this was God's punishment to him. Did this man truly know his friend before he was hit with suffering for this is what God said about Job?

> Job 1:8 *"And the Lord said unto satan, hast thou considered my servant Job, that there is none like him upon the earth, a perfect and an upright man, one that feareth God and escheweth evil."*

The Lord considered His servant Job to be the most Holy and good follower of Him on earth. Eliphaz's accusations were total lies and how much they must have hurt Job during agony.

I had an Eliphaz once. Someone who knew the ultra-active me before my illness. Yet when suffering struck me, she seemed to forget the healthy, determined, lie down to nothing Joanne that I had been. She came to visit me at a time when I could not even lift my head off the pillow and started to throw Eliphaz statements at me. The one that hurt me most was when she said, if I had a baby, I would have no other choice but to push myself out of bed (implying that I could get out of bed if I wanted too.) If I could push my body and make it do what I wanted it too I most certainly would. No one wants to lie in bed all the time when they could be living. And to mention a baby was rubbing salt in the wound for she knew my heart's desire in life was to be a wife and a mother. I cried sore in deep distress and pain when my Eliphaz left. I forgave my Eliphaz but after that, she was no longer part of my life. A real friend would not come into the room of someone suffering deeply and say the whole list of things that she said. I felt Job's pain that night. Someone whom I had once called friend came into my bedroom and instead of offering words of comfort or holding my hand, she assaulted me with cruel statements. The pain of that memory is long past. It only surfaced when I heard the sermon on Job and felt convicted to write this.

If you have a family member or friend who is suffering please do not be an Eliphaz. Do not try and make up reasons as to why they are suffering and assault them with your theories about what you think they should be doing. Be a tender-hearted, compassionate friend who stands by them through thick and thin, who sends edifying words to encourage their spirits. Maybe they are not well enough to have visitors, but you can make your presence known to them that you care through text or social media, letter, or card.

I have witnessed one of the Godliest woman who loved God with all her heart and constantly poured out love on others, suffer and die a long and cruel death from cancer. She did not do a thing to bring on her suffering. She was not to blame. She had not even touched alcohol or smoked in her life. I believe that God would have said of her, 'Consider my servant who is perfect and upright and honours me.'

Do not blame people for their suffering with silly theories like Eliphaz did. Be there for them, love them, care for them, and most of all show kindness. Like it says in 1 Corinthians 13, the greatest of all the spiritual gifts is a heart of love.

Do not be an Eliphaz be an edifier. Believe me, sickness is a battle, without being heaped with guilt and criticisms.

36

Do What You Can

John 4:37 *"One soweth and another reapeth."*

Mark 14:8 *"She hath done what she could."*

Do you ever get discouraged when trying to win others to the Lord? I remembered a time I had felt discouraged and like I was making no headway at all with people I was earnestly praying for. I was living in a student house in my second year of Bible College and I felt strongly that I had to try and reach out to our next-door neighbours. So I went to Tesco, bought some chocolates and buns, and put a Gospel tract in with them and knocked on their door. They just snatched the bag from my hand and slammed the door in my face. So I left it a wee while and tried again. I went over with more goodies and a different Gospel tract hoping they would at least chat to me on the doorstep for a few minutes but again they snatched the bag from me and the door was slammed.

I tried one more time and the same thing happened. I tried but I felt like I had failed until I remembered the scriptures that I quoted at the beginning. I had done what I could. I had sowed the Gospel seed. It would be someone else's joy to reap that harvest someday and lead them to Jesus.

1 Corinthians 3:6 *"I have planted, Apollos watered but God gave the increase."*

:8 *"Now he that planteth and he that watereth are one. And every man shall receive his reward according to his own labour."*

It did not matter that Apollos had got to reap what Paul had sown. Both were vital links in the chain to leading others to Salvation.

If you are feeling discouraged, please remember this: keep ploughing and sowing the Gospel seed into others' lives even if you are not the one who gets the joy of kneeling with them and leading them to the Saviour. Do your best and do not stop! Keep going for you are having more impact on lives than you think even if you've been given the cold shoulder many times!

I came across this poem by Adelaide Anne Proctor called, *'Sowing and Reaping'*. I will share three verses of it.

Sow with a generous hand,
Pause not for toil or pain,
Weary not through the heat of the summer,
Weary not through the cold spring rain.
But wait till the autumn comes
for the sheaves of golden grain.

Sow for the hours are fleeting,
And the seed must fall today,
And care not what hands shall reap it,
Or if you shall have passed away,
Before the waving cornfields
shall gladden the sunny day.

Sow, and look onward and upward,
Where the starry light appears,
When in spite of coward's doubting,
Or your own hearts trembling fears.
You shall reap in joy the harvest,
You have sown today in tears.

37

The Persistent Widow

Penny Crayon was a character from a cartoon that I used to watch as a child. Every picture she drew came to life! I thought, imagine if that were reality - we could draw a picture of the things we have prayed for and they will miraculously appear. Sadly, we don't live in a cartoon world, but God does honour persistent prayer.

In Luke 18:1-8 we find the parable of the persistent widow.

"Men ought always to pray and not to faint. There was in a city a judge which feared not God neither regarded man. And there was a widow in the city and she came unto him saying, Avenge me of mine adversary. And he would not for a while: but afterward he said within himself, though I fear not God nor regard man, yet because this widow troubleth me, I will avenge her lest by her continually coming she weary me. And the Lord said, hear what the unjust judge saith. And shall God not avenge them speedily. Nevertheless when the Son of man cometh, shall he find faith on earth?"

The Believer's Bible Commentary says this (pages 1437-1438).

"The parable of the praying widow teaches that men ought always to pray and not lose heart. This is true in a general sense of all men and all types of prayer. But the special sense it is used here is prayer for God's deliverance in times of testing. It is prayer without losing heart during the long weary interval between Christ's first and second comings. The parable pictures an unrighteous judge who was ordinarily unmoved by fear of God or regard for his fellow men. There was also a widow who was being oppressed by an unnamed adversary. The widow came to the judge persistently asking for justice that she might be delivered from his inhumane treatment. The judge was unmoved by the fact she was being treated unjustly and didn't move to action. However with the regularity with which she came before him, promoted him to act. Her persistence brought a decision in her favour. The Lord explained to the disciples that if an unjust judge would act on behalf of a poor widow, because of her persistence, how much more will the Just God intervene on behalf of His elect."

The Lord wants us to have the same persistent faith that the widow had. She was not giving up until her cry had been answered.

Persistence means continuing in a course of action despite difficulty or opposition, perseverance, endurance, dedication, being steadfast.

Sometimes we can get weary lifting the same need for other's or ourselves before the Lord, but He wants us to keep going for He honours that kind of determined faith that refuses to give up. That unsaved loved one that you are weary of bringing to God - keep bringing them to the throne regardless and the same for any other situation you face. His answer might not be what we want or we might not see the request granted in our lifetime but He wants us to *'pray without ceasing'* (1 Thessalonians 5:17) even when we feel we've hit a brick wall, for he is a fair God and prayer changes things.

38

When You Can't Understand

I heard a song on the radio that had the words, 'God knows what He's doing'.

Maybe you have spent endless days and nights crying, for everything is so confusing and even though you love the Lord deeply you just cannot see His hand working amidst your circumstances. Maybe you relate to this poem that I wrote.

When you're scared and your heart's full of pain.
When you can't see the way
and are collapsing under the strain.
When you plead with God to send you hope
but nothing stops your bleeding heart's drain.
When you get to the point where things
are so bleak that you can't see God reign.

Then today He is saying:
My child I am still right here.
You might not understand but I know what I'm
doing and to me, you are precious and dear.
My strong hand of love won't let your weak
one go and I'll bring you through the fear.
Don't lose hope my darling one,
despite your pain ,
come near to me and let me dry every tear.

David must have been struggling deeply in Psalm 119 for he says:

:25 *"My soul cleaveth unto the dust: quicken thou me according to the word."*

:28 *"My soul melteth for heaviness, strengthen thou me according unto the word."*

:41 *"Let the mercies come also unto me O Lord, even the salvation."*

David was in a bad way. He said his heart was melting because of heaviness and he pleads with God to let His mercies and deliverance come unto him. At this point, he had hit an all-time low. He probably could not understand what the Lord was doing amidst his despair.

But as the song I heard says, 'While our heart's break we have to believe that God knows what he's doing.'

He still knows what He's doing even when we can't understand and we're struggling to hold on. You may feel like you are going through hell but keep persevering as the Lord has set His heart on doing wonderful things through you!

As the old song goes: 'When you can't see His hand trust His heart.'

His heart is always one of pure love, compassion, and devotion to you. He adores you! Even if it now feels like you have boarded a bus blindfolded and do not know where you are going to end up trust God's eyes. He sees and He will make it clear to us in time.

For now keep fighting hard through all the horrible feelings that are coming against you, for the Lord's mercies and deliverance will come to you in His time!

Isaiah 60:22 *"When the time is right, I the Lord will make it happen."*

39

Revival

3 John 11 *"Beloved, follow not that which is evil but that which is good. He that doeth good is of God: but he that doeth evil hath not seen God."*

1 John 2:15 *"Love not the world, neither the things of the world, if any man love the world the love of the father is not in him."*

There are many directions that a child of God could be pulled in today, but God clearly says that we are not to follow that which is evil but that which is good.

There is a spirit of compromise with the world going around today. But the Lord does not want us to follow that which is worldly. You cannot claim to love God and serve satan at the same time. It is an age of lukewarmness, but the Lord is calling us to be fired up for Him wholeheartedly, holding nothing back and not holding any worldly compromise in our hearts. The Lord is looking for a people of complete devotion and passion for Him. A people who long to see souls saved and long to see revival come to our land. God cannot send revival unless His children are pure clean vessels who walk daily with Him, long for nothing else but Him and who pursue Him with their all.

The last revival that broke out in our land in 1859 came about because of a few faithful people meeting every week in the little village of Kells. Pleading with God to come in all His power and save and restore backsliders to Himself. And the Lord heard their earnest cries of these pure clean vessels and poured out His Spirit on this land. Thousands of people were falling to their knees in the streets, repenting of their sins and crying out for God to save them. Thousands of backsliders returned to the Lord. The pubs closed as there was no one to frequent them. This was a land ablaze with the Spirit of God.

> 2 Chronicles 7:14 *"If my people, which are called by my name shall humble themselves and pray and seek my face, and turn from their wicked ways; then will I hear from heaven and will forgive their sin and heal their land."*

We are called not just to humble ourselves and pray for our nation to be changed, but also, we are called to turn from our wicked ways. To turn from anything that smells of sin, worldliness, and compromise so we can be pure vessels, ready for the Lord to move in revival power.

I wrote this poem years ago when I was at Bible College, but I feel it contains that which the Lord wants me to share on turning away from evil and truly seeking revival with all our hearts. I read this out in church at a youth service in 2002. It may not be popular, but I've vowed always to honour my Lord and truth above anything else.

Revival

Land of mine
Now is the time,
To awake from your sleep.
There's a harvest to reap.

Minds fed on lust and porn.
Abortion kills babies unborn.
Some TV and films to watch seem harmless fun,
But can you truly watch them in the presence of God's own Son?

Eerie music and blood on the screen.
Swearing and filth upon which the land is so keen.
Sure what does it matter, it's a laugh you know?
Jesus the Saviour doesn't think so.

The box in the corner has taken the place,
Of worship and prayer thanks for His grace.
Feeding our minds on total trash,
The movie just a waste of cash.

Out the next day early and bright,
Ready to start a doctrinal fight.
Super holy we think we are.
Close to God? No, we're far!

Some scowl at the way the neighbours live,
And the recent scandal with Bob and Viv.
Gossiping in our holy huddles.
Throwing more mud in dirty puddles.

First at church on Sundays.
First at the pub for a drink on Mondays.
First to point out another's fault.
Last to live as light and salt.

Terrorism and wars breaking out in rage.
Famine and suffering, oh hear my pledge.
Humble yourselves, come to Jesus.
The Spirit's coming, oh feel the breezes.

Why live morally we're saved anyway?
I've got an answer for you today.
Jesus is returning and our nation's blind,
Won't you do something to change their mind?

Our world is searching for answers,
Amidst fury, fear, and cancers.
We need to buckle up and shine the torch,
Or precious souls in Hell's fire will scorch.

Do you care I ask you now?
If you do with me please bow.
Lord renew your vision in me,
And let worldliness from me now flee.

Let revival fall on our land.
Each soul be marked with Jesus brand.
Child of God, desperately pray,
As if your last hour was today.

40

Rejection

I read a book called *'The Big Blue Soldier'* by Grace Livingston Hill. In it, a soldier returned from WW2 to find that his fiancée had become engaged to another man. He also found himself to be financially destitute too. He came home but had no real home to go too. He wandered the streets and as circumstances too complicated to explain worked out he was invited to stay with an elderly lady. He was suffering from pneumonia and the elderly lady and a young neighbour nursed him back to health. It then emerged that something he had invested in had brought him a great fortune. His old fiancée then turned up at the door wanting him back because he had money now! She did not want him for who he was, only for the wealth he could give her, so he turned her away. By this stage, he had fallen in love with young Mary, the girl who had helped nurse him back to health. At the start of the book things were awful for the soldier - rejected and destitute, but by the end, he found love, acceptance, security, and greater joy than he had ever known.

> Isaiah 53:3 *"He is despised and rejected of men, a man of sorrows and acquainted with grief and we hid as it were our faces from him, he was despised and we esteemed him not."*

> Psalm 94:14 *"For the Lord will not cast off his people, neither will he forsake his inheritance."*

I do not know if you have ever felt rejection's sting, but it hurts badly. You start to blame yourself and feel like you are not worthy of being loved. People can be extremely fickle - The person you once called your closest friend can drop you like a hot potato and to them, you no longer exist.

If anyone knew what rejection's sting was like it was Jesus while He walked on earth. He came to His people and they just saw Him as the carpenter's son and not the promised Messiah. Religious leaders constantly scorned Him and looked for ways to trip Him up. People came to Him for what He could do for them - i.e. healing, but in His hour of greatest need everyone fled wanting no association with Him. These fickle people wanted Him for what He could do for them but did not love Him for who He was. He truly was a man of sorrows and was well acquainted with grief. So there is no one better to understand your rejection and pain like Jesus. Like the psalm said He will never cast off his people. People may cast us away like old newspapers but never Jesus!

If you are feeling the deep pain of rejection's sting today, take your pain to the Lord and let Him soothe you. At the end of the Grace Livingston Hill book, all things worked together for good and God will do the same in your life! Please know dear friend that you will not always feel this way. The Lord will send comfort, love, and acceptance in rejection's place. Until then remember the words of the old hymn.

> What a friend we have in Jesus.
> All our sin's and griefs to bear.
> What a privilege to carry,
> everything to God in prayer.
> Oh, what peace we often forfeit.
> Oh, what needless pain we bear.
> All because we do not carry.
> Everything to God in prayer.

Carry it all to the one who loves you most and will not ever cast you off or forsake you. He adores you and longs to share in your pain. He knows the pain that other people can cause, and He wants you to go straight to Him with it. He is our precious Saviour, the one who never rejects nor casts away His dear children.

41

The Everlasting Arms

Deuteronomy 33:27 *"The eternal God is the refuge and underneath are the everlasting arms."*

This verse came into my head as I was lying singing a hymn we sang at church. Verse 3 especially struck me:

> What have I to dread, what have I to fear,
> Leaning on the everlasting arms?
> I have blessed peace with my Lord so near,
> Leaning on the everlasting arms...
> Leaning - safe and secure from all alarms.
> Leaning on the everlasting arms.

Over the years of illness, I have found so much comfort from this Bible verse and the hymn about it.

When I feel battle weary, I close my eyes and picture the Lord holding me in His everlasting arms. Arms that are strong, compassionate, tender, gentle, supportive. I imagine myself as a child in my Heavenly Father's arms. He is holding me up and is not going to let me fall. I cannot crumble or stumble when I am safe and secure in my Father's arms. When things are overwhelming, I can lean back and ask my Lord to hold me tight in His arms.

I remember when my late Grandfather used to scoop me up and set me on his shoulders. I was never afraid of falling in that place. I felt happy, secure, and confident in his ability to hold me.

In life, it can feel at times like we cannot go on. Maybe circumstances have kept us trapped so long that we begin to dread and fear the future. We get into a place where we focus more on circumstances instead of upon our Lord. But despite the times when fear and panic is at its worst, the Lord is still holding us firm in His embrace. We might feel like everything is spinning out of control, but it is never spinning out of control because we are held in our Heavenly Father's arms.

He is our refuge. Refuge means the state of being safe or sheltered from pursuit, danger, or difficulty. We are constantly safe and sheltered from all fiery arrows that satan sends at us. We are wholly protected. Satan can try to destroy us, but he cannot win.

When I was held tightly on my Grandpa's shoulders, I was afraid of nothing. It is the same for us, His children, when we're making Him our refuge and leaning hard into His everlasting arms. Sickness, rejection, grief, loneliness, hardships of all kind cannot remove us from His sovereign protective care. I wrote this poem.

Thank you for being my refuge.
Thank you for holding me tight.
No matter what life throws at me
in your arms everything is alright.
When fear threatens to cripple my mind,
squeeze me tighter
and do not let me be engulfed by fright.
In your arms, I am a child again safe
in Grandpa's firm hold.
I can praise you here in this haven.
I can approach you, and be bold.
Help me to lean upon you harder in the storm,
and never let my love grow cold.
I'm so thankful to be one of your precious
flock ever safe in your fold.

42

Freddie

I was listening to a Christian radio station and a speaker told the following true story.

A mother who had been permanently disabled after all her cancer treatments and operations had an adult son called Freddie, with Down's Syndrome. She was not able to get welfare and she and Freddie were living on the breadline. Freddie got a job clearing tables at a coffee shop. He worked so hard and staff and customers adored him. The pittance that Freddie earned kept food on the table and kept him from being removed from his mother. It came to be that Freddie had to go for heart surgery. Down's Syndrome patients often have problems with their heart and Freddie needed a valve replaced. He was going to be absent from work for three months until he recovered. Every customer missed him and asked where he was. One trucker declared loudly, 'How are they going to pay for Freddie's medical treatment, it's not right to see them suffer so much.' After that, every single day napkins would be left on the table with, 'For Freddie' written on the outside and inside they were full of money.

When Freddie returned to work three months later with his disabled mother accompanying him, his boss directed them to a table that was covered in napkins. There were ten thousand American dollars in those napkins. Freddie and his mother cried as they were so touched by everyone's generosity! They were no longer on the breadline.

About generosity the Bible says:

Proverbs 11:25 *"The Liberal (generous) soul shall be made fat and he that watereth shall also be watered."*

2 Corinthians 9:7 *"Each man according as his purposeth in his heart, so let him give, not grudgingly or of necessity: for God loveth a cheerful giveth."*

Psalm 112:5 *"A good man sheweth favour, and lendeth."*

A generous spirit that gives and pours out of themselves freely is a Christlike Spirit. The Lord wants us to be like the people in the cafe and give freely to those in need. Jesus constantly, sacrificially, gave of Himself and He's calling us to do the same. We cannot financially meet every need in the world, but we can choose some causes to donate too and faithfully give. We are not supposed to give reluctantly but instead out of a heart that is abounding in love and compassion for others. There is a story in John about a lady who broke her alabaster jar to anoint Jesus. This expensive perfume would have been this woman's everything. Perhaps used as a dowry in a future marriage. In other words, it was her life's savings - yet she gave it all to Jesus. Her giving was an expression of her love for her Master.

Our giving is supposed to be an expression of our love for our Master too. This selfless pouring out of ourselves to lift someone else who is in dire need. We are called to be the Lord's hands and feet on this earth. It is not enough to pray, 'Oh Lord bless so and so they are going through a hard time.' Answer the prayer yourself and bless them yourself. Maybe leave a food hamper on their doorstep or a supermarket voucher.

There is no point in hoarding all our earthly possessions - they cannot be put into the coffin with us when we die. Give as much of your money, time and talents to your Saviour's service while you still have breath in your lungs, for at the end of the day it's more important to give your all to Jesus than to constantly hoard things and 'get' all the time. It is Jesus we will spend eternity with. Dare to have a Christ-like spirit and make a difference while you can.

43

Do Not Harden Your Heart

I did not sleep well one night, and something came into my head that I had forgotten about. Many years ago I was visiting someone in the hospital. I felt hungry afterwards and stopped at a little fast-food van along the road. I decided that I'd go and visit my grandparents, so I ordered 'sausage and bacon baps' for the three of us. The woman who was cooking was chatting away to me. She was talking about her life with all its tragedies. I told her that I was a Christian and that Jesus loved her. She asked me to step into her van to talk more. Her eyes were flaming with fire. How can you love a God that lets people suffer from cancer? How can you love a God that lets orphans starve and lets natural disasters happen? She said bitterly, 'if you ask me God is cruel and I hate him'.

I tried my best to explain that God never intended for there to be suffering in the world, but people choose their way over Him. I tried to explain how Jesus came as Saviour and gave His life as the greatest act of love that we might know Him and if we trust in Him, we have the certainty of Heaven.

But she just sighed and said I was young and naive and that someday something would happen to me and I would be bitter at God. I paid for my order, left her a Gospel tract and left praying for her the whole way to my Grandparents house, that the Lord would draw her to Himself and remove all bitterness and anger.

Newsflash to that lady! Something did happen to me! I am going into my thirteenth year of severe illness. My life was taken away from me completely! The girl once known for her boundless energy now is bedbound and depends on her mother for everything. But I can honestly say in these years of illness I have not once shaken my fist at God in anger and bitterness for the presence of suffering is NOT His fault!

This lady's bitterness made me think of Job's phase with bitterness amidst his suffering, he blamed God at one point.

Job 10:1 *"My soul is weary of life... I will speak in bitterness of my soul."*

:8 *"Thine hands have made me and fashioned me together round about; yet thou dost destroy me."*

:19 *"I should have been as though I had not been. I should have been carried from the womb to the grave."*

Those words, *'Thou dost destroy me'* show Job's anger and bitterness at God for what was happening to him.

Job's suffering came from satan. God only permitted it as a test of faith, but the root of his suffering was not God it was satan and the presence of evil in this world due to man's rebellion against God.

At the end of the book, Job repented of his bitterness. I do not have all the answers, no one does this side of Heaven but if you are suffering today and are a believer, do not blame God. He hates suffering.

Jesus even said in John 16:33 *"In this world ye will have trouble but fear not, I have overcome the world."*

We have an eternity of pure bliss to look forward to where there will be no more tears, sickness, and death. Jesus will win in the end! His word tells us so!

Amidst suffering, thank God for His goodness. Praise Him, He is still sovereign and good and in control and full of deep love for you. Do not harden your heart to Him because of temporary suffering on earth for He loves you deeply.

44

Impact

I read a book by Grace Livingston Hill called, *'In the Way.'* After a girl's mother died, she was informed that her mother had never been her real mother but her Aunt who had adopted her as a young baby when her real mother died. So she discovered that after all those years that she had two brothers. Her father had died years ago, so she learned that these brothers lived alone in an old farmhouse. She was eager to reconnect with them and packed everything up to go and live with them. She realised that neither of her brothers knew her Lord as Saviour. It became her daily passionate prayer for them that they would find her Lord. She also took on a Sunday school class at the local church and won many of her young girls to Jesus. Her name was Ruth and her life was one of mighty impact. Her only desire was to live a life that reflected the face of her Saviour and one that was in close communion and obedience to Him.

Reading about Ruth made me think of the book of Esther. She was just an ordinary girl of God who was called by God for the huge task of saving God's people from destruction. To do so, she had to risk her own life for she could have got killed for going before the king without being summoned.

Esther 4:14 *"Who knoweth whether thou art come to the Kingdom for such a time as this."*

And it was so that when the King saw Esther the queen standing in the court that she obtained favour in his sight, and be held out to Esther the golden sceptre that was in his hand. Esther was willing to perish for other's salvation and deliverance! God blessed her obedience by causing the King to show her favour.

Esther was a woman of impact. In her quiet way, in obedience to her God, she accomplished so much. Are our lives having an impact on the lives of others? Impact means a marked effect or influence. The name Esther means 'Star', and she truly shone like a bright star for God. She let herself be a vessel fit for the Master's use and only wanted what He wanted.

Could the same be said of you? Are you living to make a mighty impact for eternity or are you muddling through life just doing your own thing, wasting time? God is calling us to be men and women of impact. I wrote this poem some years ago after a personal Bible study, but it fits into this devotion today. It applies to men too just substitute Handmaiden for servant!

A Woman of Impact

A Woman of unswerving devotion,
Passionate, steadfast and loyal.
Not swayed by every passing notion.
Self-sacrificing and obedient.
Always eager to set the Lord's plans in motion.
Bold and ready to be counted.
May my life stir up in satan's kingdom great commotion.
Impact with a capital 'I' is what I want
to have on my nation.
May being a handmaiden for you,
be my most important occupation.
My cry is that you would use my life to bring the hope of
your Gospel to this population.
Being a stream from you my source
brings me great elation.
So now flow through me as I completely surrender.
May I be bursting with compassion
and have hands like yours, so tender.
May I reach out always
and be many a lost soul's befriender.
Sold out totally and ever ready to pour out my all to you
my precious Heavenly sender.

45

When Things Don't Turn Out The Way We Planned

I remember in an A-Level class we were given the task of making apple flavoured jam. None of us had ever made jam before so it was the first attempt for us all. We did not get it right though, much to our teacher's despair. It looked more like runny syrup than it did jam! We had not put enough of something necessary in it! But it did taste good even if it was runny!

Proverbs 19:21 (NIV) *"Many are the plans in a person's heart, but it is the Lord's purpose that prevails."*

We planned to set jam, but that plan did not happen. But on a more serious note, we as God's children make so many plans, so many wants and wishes.

Maybe according to your plan you're going to marry a man who doesn't love your Lord and you know that you are intending to go against scripture when it says, *'Do not be unequally yoked with unbelievers.'*

Maybe you are planning a job change or course of study that you have not consulted the Lord about. You are charging full speed ahead without asking His guidance. That can lead to disaster and finding yourself out of the perfect will of God.

Maybe you are in a relationship with a man or woman who say they are a Christian but who are living in compromise with the world. You continue to tolerate it as you are afraid that you will not find anyone else. But have you sought the Lord in prayer about this person or just jumped in headfirst, not thinking how it might affect your faith?

I do not know what your plans are, only you know that. But if these plans do not line up with God's word, they can have disastrous results.

Often God's children are too quick to run to people for their opinions on their plans, rather than running to the one who created mighty plans for their lives before they were born.

The latter half of this verse says it is the Lord's purpose that prevails in the end.

Prevail means to prove more powerful, or superior, to be a victor, to conquer.

1 Chronicles 22:19 *"Now set your mind and heart to seek the Lord your God."*

The Lord wants us to be daily walking with Him and daily seeking His face to make sure the plan that you've dreamed up in your heart is His vision for you, to make sure that your plan with His will and isn't just your way. For at the end of the day seeing the Lord's purpose prevail in our lives and living lives that honour Him is all that matters. I will end with a poem I wrote as I thought about this subject.

Lord if my plans aren't your will for me.
Then give me the strength to leave them be.
Let me seek thy face instead so my life may honour only thee.
Let my will and plans be in tune with Heaven
for only in your will am I truly free.
Give me the wisdom to know the difference
between what I covet and your way.
For I want your purpose to prevail,
even if it comes at a great cost, this I pray.
Keep me walking a path that brings you great glory
and honour and never let me stray.
I love you Lord and want what you want all the days of my
life. Mould me, for you are the potter and I am just clay.

46

Lack of Supplies

Psalm 34:10 *"The young lions do lack and suffer hunger; but they that seek the Lord shall not want any good thing."*

Philippians 4:19 *"But my God shall supply all your need according to his riches in glory by Christ Jesus."*

As a teenager, I did my 'Duke of Edinburgh' award scheme at school. One of the expeditions was to hike several miles in one day, camp overnight and hike the rest of the allotted miles the next day. We girls over-prepared! Our backpacks were overflowing with food. We did not mind the extra weight on our backs because we knew it would be worthwhile.

Evening came and we put up our tent, cooked our sausages, then I boiled up some water and made tea and we all enjoyed a packet of buns. The evening was so light and the mountains so beautiful! I even washed my hair in a fresh mountain stream. The four of us had a lovely night in the tent, chatting and laughing.

The next morning we were cooking breakfast from our ample supplies and then the boys appeared! The boys had set up camp in the opposite field. They came begging for food! They thought that by not packing food it would make hiking easier on them! But the next morning they were ravenous. They had no cooked supper the night before or the luxury of tea and buns and by morning they were ready to faint with hunger. One of the girls said we should not feed them; it is their fault for their stupidity. But I said we had plenty and that they would never make it through the rest of the hike without nourishment. So on went extra sausages, bacon, and eggs for the boys. They ate it like they had never seen food before in their lives.

The incident came into my head as I thought about the Scriptures that I quoted at the beginning: *"They that seek the Lord shall not want any good thing."* Also, *"My God shall supply all your need."*

God never leaves us in dire need. He will not let us lack anything that we urgently need. He is not some cosmic genie that grants our every wish and bends to our every whim. But He is a loving, faithful father who will provide each great necessity that has arisen in our lives. Think of earthly parents they would go without to see their children fed, clothed, and having shoes to wear. They see to their children's needs before they even ask.

You and I are the Lord's beloved children and He will not let us lack any good thing that we badly need. Oh, He sees your need before you even ask but He longs for you to bring it to Him, to pour out your weary bottled up spirit to Him, commune with Him as a friend to friend and trust that He will meet your need whether it is financial, emotional or physical. He has promised to supply all your needs. Not one true need will He omit. He does not cater to our greed, but He does meet genuine needs and does not miss one.

So if you are in a difficult place today of great need, know that if you have brought your lack to the Lord in prayer that He will hear and answer. He is faithful, loyal, true, and loving! Do not fret dear child of His, God's got this!

47

When God Amazes You

Jeremiah 32:17 "Ah Lord God! Behold thou hast made the heaven and the earth by thy great power and stretched out arm and there is nothing to hard for thee."

I was listening to an online service and a man called David Hathaway was speaking. He told how his father had fought in WW1 and that he was eight years old when the second world war broke out. His life has been used as a mighty instrument in the Lord's service. At eighty-six, he says I do not have time to get sick or die, there is still too much to do in God's work!

He smuggled Bibles into the Soviet Union when it was under communism and at one point was jailed for a year. He was meant to be in jail for ten years, but God in His grace made a way of escape.

What struck me from his speaking and made the shivers go down my spine was his retelling of miracles that he had seen in his life! I mean we all believe God is powerful, that he made the heavens and earth with His power and that nothing is too difficult for him. But still, when we hear of mighty miracles we look to God in amazement and go - wow!

David told the story of his healing from cancer. He had a massive inoperable tumour in his tummy. Nothing could be done about it; it was too dangerous to operate so he was told that he would not live. He went home and said to the Lord, 'Look if I'm still needed in your service then I need you to take the cancer away.' The next time he was at the hospital they had a tube down his throat and into his tummy. What did they see? No tumour and just scar tissue where the tumour had been. The doctor got angry and asked him what surgeon had removed the tumour? David simply replied God did it.

I was amazed when I heard that! What a mighty answer to a man's prayer. Also, he was in a foreign country holding tent crusades, seeing thousands saved and thousands healed when he heard a whisper from Heaven telling him to go to the hospital the next day. He obeyed and walked into one ward. He asked the first man what was wrong. The man replied that he had a broken back. So he prayed healing over the man, and he got up and walked fully made whole. He went to the second man who also had a broken back and after praying for him, he also got up and walked. He came to the third man he said he was blind. He prayed for him and reached him a Bible to read and he could see as clear as day.

The next day the officials of the land wanted to see him. They were angry and asked him what he had done at the hospital the day before. To which he replied that he just prayed for three men and then left. He was then informed that the healed blind man had gone around every ward in the hospital and told everyone what the Lord had done for him. Every patient in that hospital got saved and healed! They had an empty hospital on their hands with no sick to tend too.

I still marvel as I write these things down. We truly limit God when we pray. Maybe it is because we see so little miracles in our wee land. But it does not change the fact that we serve the same Lord of power who formed the world out of nothing, who made us out of the dust, who rose from the dead! He has said that nothing is too hard for Him and wants us to believe His word. Keep praying and keep waiting upon God for that which you are praying for, for He hears you and is still great in power today!

48

The Crossroad of Crisis

I heard the title of this devotion mentioned on the radio and it struck me. Sometimes in life, we reach crossroads of crisis. We cannot turn back because that is a dead-end and we cannot move forward for everything is so bleak and uncertain. There are roadblocks on the left and right, so you are in a very confusing place and do not know what to do.

I think Proverbs 3:5-6 helps us to know what to do at the crossroad of crisis. I know it is a familiar passage but it is jumping out at me today.

Proverbs 3:5-6 *"Trust in the Lord with all thine heart, and lean not into thine own understanding. In all the ways acknowledge him and he shall direct thy paths."*

Firstly, we are to trust the Lord with ALL our hearts. Not part of our hearts, but ALL. For when our hearts are filled up with half distress and half trust then we become weary, depressed, and even more afraid.

Trust means a firm belief in the reliability or ability of someone or something. Confidence, faith, assurance.

The Lord is worthy of all our trust, confidence, and faith for He is the only one who can see the full picture for our lives and can guide wholly. Trust Him with every piece of your heart. He needs all the pieces in His hands to put it all back together again.

Secondly, do not lean on your understanding. I have found that when I lean on my limited understanding of my illness and when I am going to recover, I get into great panic and distress. The doctor's words of, "You'll never be well Joanne", flash through my mind and I panic, cry, or become scared. Leaning on your understanding leads to fear. Fear brings chaos. It intensifies the crisis that we are already in.

> 2 Timothy 2:7 *"For God hath not given us a Spirit of fear; but of power and of love and of a sound mind."*

Looking to yourself for answers brings terror. I admit I do it at times, but I shouldn't! When you invite Jesus into your heart to be your Saviour, His Spirit automatically enters our hearts. His Spirit living inside us is one of power and love and a sound mind. So lean on the Lord's understanding. He sees the end from the beginning and let Him fill you with His love and power amidst the crisis.

Lastly, we are told to acknowledge Him in all our ways, and He will direct our paths. In all your ways acknowledge Him means to remember the Lord in all you do even during the confusion. Look to Him to guide you and give you the wisdom you so badly need. He sees where you are. He sees your crossroad of crisis and knows that you do not know what to do but he is calling you to acknowledge Him as the only guidance counsellor and obstacle breaker that we need.

Even in confusion, even in your hardest bleakest time, the Lord has not forgotten you. You are His beloved child and He will show you the way forward. In Joshua, He showed His people what to do in their crossroad of crisis. They were to march around the city walls until God told them to stop. Do you know what happened? Those walls came crashing down! What looked humanly impossible became possible with God before their eyes. So keep looking to Jesus, obey His whispers to your heart. Wait and trust in Him, not looking to yourself but constantly acknowledge Him every waking moment.

49

A Selfless Heart

I watched a true-life film called, *'The Heart of a Child.'* It was a very moving film that moved me to tears. It followed the lives of two married couples who were both expecting babies. One couple was told that their child would die within hours because the baby had something wrong with her brain. The other couple were told that there was something wrong with their child's heart and he would die without a transplant.

It worked out that the first couple gave their daughter's heart for a transplant and the second couple's baby who was going to die without a heart received the baby girl's heart and their child lived.

It moved me so much. The first couple were struggling too much knowing that they would only hold their daughter for a few hours after birth yet amidst their pain and grief they did the most beautiful selfless thing by donating her heart so another child so it could have life.

It made me think, we can go through the hardest trials in life, but God doesn't want us to be self-focused or selfish. He wants us to surrender our all to Him so He can use our pain for the help and blessing of others. He wants us to be outward-looking and selfless no matter what we are going through.

Philippians 2:3-5 *"In lowliness of mind let each esteem other better than themselves. Look not every man on his own things but every man also on the things of others. Let this mind be in you which was also in Christ Jesus."*

Jesus is calling us to have selfless hearts like His. Jesus did not have an easy life the thirty-three years that He was on earth. He was rejected by many, scorned by religious leaders. Yet He was constantly giving, showing compassion, comforting others, healing the sick. Oh, He knew that many who came to Him to have their needs met would disappear and no longer follow Him at His time of great need when He was arrested and on trial. Yet He still selflessly gave of Himself with compassionate, unconditional love. He is calling us to walk as He walked and even begin to think like Him. What way did He think? Well, despite all His hardships He was constantly focused on meeting the needs of others. As the hymn puts it:

> He had no tears for His own griefs
> but sweat drops of blood for mine.

He knew His life was going to end with one of the most horrific deaths ever but even in His hour of greatest agony, He was sweating drops of blood over everyone else that they might trust in Him and know Him as Saviour.

No matter what you are going through today please do not close your heart to wallowing in self-pity. Ask the Lord to help you focus on Him and pour yourself out in compassion and love for in doing so the Lord receives great glory. I wrote this poem:

> Let me have a selfless heart Lord, one, like thine.
> One that's like a fountain pouring out your love.
> Despite my hardships may I ever have a heart
> that's all about you and others, not I, me and mine.
> Use me to point as many to you even in my pain.
> Oh, this is my heart's cry my precious Heavenly dove.

50

Messy Cookies

I remember when I was a teenager seeing an appeal to bake and sell cookies to raise money for Childline. I immediately sent away for the kit which contained recipes, and a couple of cookie cutters in the shape of Childline's telephone symbol. I enlisted the help of two friends from school and so we began our marathon evening of baking! We bagged them all up and could sell them at a parent's evening at school. I cannot remember what the final amount raised was, but I know it was a grand sum.

Only one person was not happy though! My mother! We were messy bakers and had left her kitchen in a state. We had cleaned it, but Mum was still finding sticky cookie dough in random places and crevices of cupboard doors weeks later! Needless to say, us three fourteen-year-old bakers, where banned from using Mum's kitchen for a while!

It made me think. Life can feel like such a mess at times. Circumstances spin out of control and we can feel stuck in the mud. Did you ever see a tractor get stuck in the mud? The wheels are spinning, dirt is flying everywhere but that tractor is not moving anywhere.

David was in a messy, stuck in the mud type of situation.

In Psalm 40 1-2 he writes: *"I waited patiently for the Lord and he inclined unto me, and heard my cry. He brought me up also out of an horrible pit, out of the miry clay and set my feet upon a rock and establish my goings."*

We've no idea what horrible pit that David was in. He was in a messy place. Stuck in deep mud. His life was not going anywhere, the mess of circumstances had engulfed him, and he could not get himself free. Life was not so nice at all. But David in his godliness waited patiently for the Lord to come and lift him out of a horrible place, out of the mess. And God did answer! I do not know how much time had passed from David first pleaded with God until he answered and *'set his feet upon a rock.'*

He went from a horrible messy place. A place where he was drowning in mud to a firm, solid, place where the mess was cleaned up. And you know what! His nasty experience wasn't wasted for in verse three he declares:

> *"And he hath put a new song in my mouth, even praise unto our God: many shall see it and fear and shall trust in the Lord."*

God will replace the mess by giving us a new song in our hearts! Others will see what the Lord did in your life and will place their trust in Him!

He will use the mess, the stuck in the mud circumstances, the horrible pit that you are now dwelling in all for His glory! You cannot see it now because all you can see is a mess, but God can see the bigger picture. He can see beyond the mess to the beauty He is going to create. I know it is hard when all you have seen is a mess for so long, but God is creating something of great beauty out of you. So hold on like the Psalmist did and wait patiently for Him. In due season the Lord will come - you will not dwell in mess and chaos forever!

51

Amazing Grace

Ruth 2:10 *"Then she fell on her face and bowed herself to the ground, and said unto him, why have I found Grace in thine eyes that thou shouldest take knowledge of me, seeing I am a stranger."*

:12 *"The Lord recompense thy work and a full reward be given thee of the Lord God of Israel, under whose wings thou art come to trust."*

I was reading this passage and the part that struck me was, *'Why have I found grace in thine eyes?'* Boaz went on to explain that she had found grace in his eyes because he had heard of her selflessness in leaving her home country and devoting herself in love and care to her mother-in-law. He told her that the Lord would recompense all her work and a full reward be given her by the Lord.

I thought it was so beautiful. It made me think of my relationship with Jesus! His grace never fails to amaze me! I often think like Ruth declared, 'Why have I found grace in thine eyes.' I have found grace in my Lord's eyes through no merit of my own. He poured out His grace upon me the day I gave Him my life, repented of my sin, and let His precious blood shed on Calvary wash over me.

Ephesians 2:8-9: *"It is by grace ye are saved through faith and not of yourselves, it is the gift of God, not of works, lest any man should boast."*

Our acceptance of His saving grace is why we find grace in His eyes. His grace that knows all about us and yet still loves us! That thought amazes me. His strengthening grace to carry us through our hardest days. His comforting grace that holds us close on days when all we can do is cry!

Grace means unearned kindness. We cannot work our way to Heaven, but we can accept Jesus' sacrifice and become His child.

Out of a heart of thankfulness for the Lord's Salvation will naturally come a desire to honour our Lord and love as He loved. To reach out in kindness because we are following in our Saviour's footsteps. These 'things' we do cannot save us, but they do bring great delight to our Lord's heart. He sees every act of kindness and service to Him that you have done in secret and He will honour you when you come home to glory with Heavenly rewards. He is saying to you today what Boaz said to Ruth: *"The Lord recompense thy work and a full reward be given thee of the Lord God of Israel."*

He sees your labours for His Kingdom. He is proud of you and misses nothing done for His glory, not even the smallest act. Oh let your response to His gift of grace be a life that brings Him honour, a heart that meets others with the same grace that the Lord gives us. Live a life that bestows favour and beauty to others for in all this our Heavenly King is well pleased.

You are His special creation, placed on this earth at this time to reflect His grace to a sin-sick world. Heed His call today and dare to be a giver of His divine grace all the days of your life.

52

When Self-doubt Causes You To Freeze

Years ago before I took sick, I was asked to speak to the children for a Children's Day Sunday at a large Presbyterian church. I said yes but afterwards fear set in. What if I start and I freeze? Nevertheless, I went on with my preparations for it and borrowed two large puppets from the Bible College children's ministry department and I got my message ready. On Sunday as I drove into the church car park, I thought what am I doing? What if I get my notes mixed up or mess up working with these puppets? So when I was introduced to come and speak, and all the children came forward I became so aware of the huge congregation and I froze! A quick Lord help me and one reassuring smiling face from the congregation smiling at me and I knew the Lord was saying you can do this! I threw myself into it heart and soul and thoroughly enjoyed it! I took many more children's addresses in churches after that and each time God gave me the strength.

When God calls you to do something, He'll also equip you with His power.

In Judges 6:12 an angel appeared to a man called Gideon and said, *"The Lord is with thee, thou mighty man of valour."*

The Angel was telling Gideon that he was being called to save Israel from the hand of the Midianites. But Gideon froze and was filled with self-doubt and replied:

:15 *"Oh my Lord, wherewith shall I save Israel? Behold my family is poor in Manasseh and I am the least in my Father's house."*

In other words, he was saying, not me Lord, I cannot! I do not have the courage! I am a nobody! The Lord called him a mighty man of courage, yet he felt anything but courageous. He was terrified. He did not believe God could use him in that way. Nevertheless, Gideon did eventually obey God and he was used of God in the way that the Angel had told him off.

What has the Lord asked you to do for him, yet you have said oh, not me Lord, I could not do that. Obey the call of the Lord for he will give you strength and all the courage you need. Even when feelings of self-doubt creep in or you freeze up in fright, remember that you have the power of the living God inside you and you can do what He's called you to do. Step out in faith even if you are trembling at first, for God sees you as a person of courage and he will not let you down. I wrote this wee poem.

Go forth and obey for the Lord is with thee,
He's called you for a divine purpose so go and don't flee.
He will equip you with all the courage you need
to heed His call and set other's free.
Though you may tremble and be filled with fear,
leaning on your Saviour for strength is the key.

Jesus will be all the strength you need and far much more and you will have all the courage that you need.

53

The Storm

There was a severe storm recently. The wind was howling and lashing against my bedroom window. I was in a haven. I was sheltered from the storm. Protected by the walls and roof of our little bungalow.

There is mention of a storm in Mark 4:35-41

"And there arose a great storm of wind and the waves beat into the ship so that it was now full."

:37 *"And he (Jesus) was in the hinder part of the ship asleep on a pillow, and they awake him, and say unto him, Master careth thou not that we perish?"*

:39 *"And he arose and rebuked the wind and said unto the sea, Peace be still. And the wind ceased and there was great calm."*

I am not keen on storms and yet I am always sheltered from them. But how much worse would it be to be in a boat with the wind howling and tossing you from side to side and the huge crashing waves filling your boat with water. How would you feel then? I would have been filled with fear and panic. I would have felt like I was going to drown.

Amidst their fear the disciples only ran to Jesus to accuse Him of not caring if they perished. Jesus, the Son of God was in that boat with them, yet they still believed that they were going under. Yet Jesus arose despite their fear and lack of faith and spoke the glorious words *'Peace be still'*, and the storm ceased. The disciples didn't know Jesus in all His power and glory at that point for their reaction was to be afraid and to ask each other, *'What manner of man is this, that even the wind and sea obey him?'* They had gone from the feelings of terror to being fearful, in awe that the Lord they served had the power and authority to control the wind and the waves.

Is your life like a storm? You are overwhelmed, the winds and waves of circumstances are fiercely rocking your little boat and you feel like you are going to drown. You love the Lord, but you feel like there is no way that you are going to make it without going under. Your little boat of life is storm-tossed and you are weary with coping. Run to Jesus for He is with you in the boat of circumstances that you are in and He has the power to turn things around with three spoken words, *'Peace be Still'*.

Then the miraculous happens and the raging storm calms. The Lord's peace and presence flood your heart in an amazing way and you feel the strength of your God carrying you, so you know you are going to make it!

I love the words of this song called *'Master of the Wind'*.

My boat of life,
Sails on a troubled sea,
Where there's a wind in my sail,
But I have a friend who watches over me,
When the breeze turns into a gale.

I know the Master of the wind,
I know the maker of the rain,
He can calm the storm,
And make the sun shine again,
I know the Master of the wind.

Let Jesus calm your storm,
Make the sun shine again,
He is the Master of the wind.

54

The Death Of A Dream

I watched a Christmas film where the girl had dreamt her whole life of becoming a professional ballet dancer. She finally found herself living the dream when she was accepted for a New York ballet company. Her oldest sister Beth had always been her greatest encourager, the one who cheered her on and helped her see her vision come to pass. However, one night as she prepared to dance the dream role of the sugar plum fairy in the Nutcracker that she had coveted all her life, she got a phone call. Her sister Beth had died in a car accident. With that one phone call, she gave up her dream and went home to raise Beth's daughter Sadie. Her heart was so broken over Beth that she vowed never to dance again. For eight years she ran a fitness studio and abandoned her life's greatest passion. But it so came about that Sadie loved Ballet and was chosen for a part in New York. Her life's passion and dream that had been long shattered and lying in ruins returned to her and returned to her passion.

> 2 Corinthians 1:20-22 *"For all the promises of God in him are Yea, and in him Amen, unto the glory of God by us. Now he which stablisheth us with you in Christ and hath anointed us in God; who hath sealed us and given us the earnest of the Spirit in our hearts."*

If the Lord has given you a promise for your life know that He cannot lie. If He has laid something on your heart and said it will come to pass, then you can be sure it will. When He says that His promises are 'Yea and Amen' then He means that! Even if you get lost for a while in a black cloud of discouragement and lose hope of seeing that promise come to pass it doesn't in any way stop the Lord from working behind the scenes to unfold His precious plan for your life.

No matter how low you feel, you are still anointed of God. You still have His Spirit living in your heart. Even if you have lost hope right now - God's promises always come to pass. Sometimes things will take longer to unfold than we would like and over time we can lose sight of the promise but rest assured that God never loses sight of His promises.

Ecclesiastes 3:4 *"There is a time to mourn and a time to dance."*

That *'time to dance'* means the time when the Lord fulfils His promise to you and there is much celebration and joy.

The Lord will always make a way to have you accomplishing all you can for His Kingdom. While you wait take heart! When you stand waiting in a queue at the supermarket, your time does come. While you wait on that bus or train and feel fed up, you know it will eventually come. Even if the promise the Lord has given you is delayed it is not forgotten.

Keep battling on dear brother, dear sister and in your weariest day remember, your time of the promise fulfilled, your *'time to dance'* and celebrate what the Lord has done in you WILL come to pass so don't lose heart.

55

Chance Encounters

I read a book by Grace Livingston Hill called, *'The Girl of Wood'*. In it, a chance encounter brought a young man, in great distress, in contact with a young lady who was in the area for a short time picking her late mother's favourite flowers. It was a chance encounter, but the girl greatly encouraged the young man in his distress to turn to God. The chance encounter led the young man to find the Lord as his Saviour.

I believe all our chance encounters in life are for the glory and honour of our Lord. He wants us to use our chance encounters with everyone we meet to speak of Him.

1 Peter 3:15 *"Be ready always to give an answer to everyman that asketh you for a reason of the hope that is within you with meekness and fear."*

Believers Bible Commentary (page 2271)

"People often ask us questions which quite naturally open the door to speak to them about the Lord. We should be ready to tell them what great things the Lord has done for us. The witnessing should be done in either case with gentleness and reverence. There should be no trace of harshness, bitterness or flippancy when we speak of our Saviour and Lord."

There are no accidents in God's plan. Use all your chance encounters with people that you would not normally come across to speak of your dear Lord and Saviour. You can testify to them about what the Lord has done in your life and leave it open for them to ask questions. Point them to the one that your soul loves. People's questions open doors for us to witness.

From Bible Reference dot com.

"First we should set aside our hearts as the place where Christ is fully honoured as the Lord. Peter calls us to full submission to Christ. When we set apart Christ as Lord it will change us. Peter says that those who observe us will see the difference. That difference is hope. Even while suffering our hopefulness should be apparent. How can you be hopeful and be a witness for God in difficult circumstances? We must be prepared to give our defence and make the case for faith in Christ and reject cultural pressures to keep our beliefs to ourselves. Believers should openly share the good news of redemption through faith in Christ."

If we are living fully surrendered lives to our precious Saviour and love Him with our all then people will see Jesus the hope of glory in us and ask us questions.

Oh to reflect you my Lord and dearest one.
Oh, for chance encounters to speak of you
and point them to Jesus the Son.
May my life be so pure and beautiful that it causes a
thirst in those who from your grace has so long run.
Don't let my life put other's off you but shine through
me so they will know what gift on the cross was done.
Jesus my hope of glory.
May I ever be on alert to share your story,
So that those who are perishing in sin
may know your love for them.
So they will invite you in and dwell with you in all
eternity as one of your precious gems.

56

The Transfiguration

Matthew 17:1-3 *"Jesus taker Peter James and John... and bringeth then up into a high mountain. And he was transfigured before them and his face did shine as the Sun and his raiment was white as the light. And behold there appeared unto them Moses and Elijah talking with him."*

:5 *"This is my beloved Son in whom I am well pleased: hear ye him."*

I have always marvelled at this passage. Jesus taking three disciples up a mountain and revealing to them who He was in all His glory. Then two already long-departed saints - Moses and Elijah came down from Heaven to talk with Jesus. Think how you would have felt had you been on that mountaintop seeing Jesus in all His glory and two long-dead men coming down from Heaven.

Peter wanted to keep the mountaintop experience forever. He was in so much awe that he did not want to return to normality. He wanted to keep Jesus, Moses, and Elijah thereby building tents for them. Oh, he just did not want the glory to end. Yet as Peter was still speaking, God the Father's voice bellowed from Heaven that this was His beloved Son in whom He was well pleased. At that voice, the disciples were *'sore afraid'* and *'fell to their faces.'* Jesus told them to arise and not be scared. I love verse eight.

"And when they had lifted up their eyes, they saw no man save Jesus only."

When we experience the glory of the Lord in a mighty way we want to stay up there on the mountaintop where all is beautiful. The mountaintops of life where in our quiet times or at church we have brief glimpses of the glory of the King are not camping sites. We cannot stay there. We have to go right back down the mountain and into the valley to carry the light to all who are hurting at the foot of the mountain, for people in the valley are full of need and their greatest need being for our Saviour's redemption. We cannot live in a spiritual bubble where it is all glory - we must be willing to go through pain, suffering and hard trials, valleys not of our choosing to bring His glory to others.

The Scripture, *'This is my beloved Son in whom I am well pleased'* struck me. It challenges me to live a life so pure, holy, and love-filled that someday my precious Lord will say those words to me. He will call me daughter and tell me that He is well pleased with me. Oh for a pure, beautiful, Christlike heart that will one day hear the words *'Well done good and faithful servant'* when I enter glory. Are you with me? Do you long to hear those words too?

In verse 8 when they had lifted their eyes, they saw no man save Jesus only. Oh to ever lift my eyes in my lowest of valleys and see Jesus only. No one thrills the heart like Jesus. No one can dispel shadows of gloom that cloud our vision but Him. Determine to lift your eyes from your pain, agony and suffering today and place them on our glorious Saviour. Graham Kendrick wrote these words:

> To keep your lovely face.
> Ever before my eyes.
> This is my prayer.
> Make it my strong desire.
> That in my secret heart,
> No other love competes.
> No rival the one survives,
> And I serve only you.

57

Samuel Walker

I got a terrible shock once. My father was not long home from church when we got the news that Samuel Walker had died suddenly. Who was Samuel to me you may ask? Samuel was my Girl's Brigade Scripture teacher and afternoon Sunday school teacher. He majorly impacted my life. He was a man of God's Word. The effort and study that he put into every lesson that he prepared was out of this world. Some teacher's put no effort in. They read a pre-prepared sheet or just hand the class a Bible word search or something. Not Samuel! He made us learn huge chunks of the Word of God that remains with me today. We always got a prize for reciting full passages from memory! Samuel studied the Word in detail, and he taught it faithfully. Samuel's Scripture lessons shaped me into who I am today - a woman passionate for the Word of God.

Samuel was never in the public eye. He was a 'behind the scenes' man shaping young lives weekly with the power of God's word. I will never forget a series he did at G.B. on Song of Solomon. Oh, he deeply explained how it was a picture of Jesus and His love for the Bride - the church. It deepened my faith so much for I wanted to be a beautiful bride of holiness and love for God that Samuel talked about.

When I heard of his passing, I honestly could not believe it. Just eight days before his death I had phoned him for a chat. We got into a deep conversation about the Word of God and things that we were studying in Scripture. I'm glad I got to tell him one more time just what a brilliant Scripture teacher he had been and how he had shaped me into the woman of the Word that I am today.

1 Peter 5:2-4 *"Feed the flock which is among you... being ensamples to the flock. And when the Chief Shepherd shall appear ye shall receive a crown of glory that fadeth not away."*

Samuel fed his flock of children like a true Shepherd and led by example. He is now promoted to glory and has received his crown of glory for his years of teaching faithfully.

If you are reading this today and you teach children or teenagers in any capacity, then please be a Samuel. Truly study the Word for yourself so you have something solid to feed your flock with. Do not lose heart in what you are doing for the Lord's Kingdom! You are having a mightier impact than you realise! I wrote this poem about Samuel (or Sammy to us).

You were a man of the Word who faithfully
taught the truth to young flocks your whole life.
Your passion and zeal for the Word were infectious.
You taught the undiluted Scriptures
in a world full of sin's strife.
Every week you had a powerful lesson that blew us away
and took us deeper in our walks with our wonderful God.
You never watered things down or left any parts out.
You inspired, challenged, and encouraged.
You always left us awed.
Thank you for being that shepherd
who ever laid himself down for his flock.
Your life had 'Impact' with a capital 'I'.
Watching your life inspired
us to walk as Jesus would walk.
So precious faithful saint now in the
presence of the Lord you are adored.
You will be dearly missed by many
but I promise to continue in your example so that many
lives to our Saviour will be saved and restored.

58

Abandonment And Acceptance

I watched a true-life movie called, *'Leave Behind'*. It was about the life of a child called Hollis Woods. She had been found as a baby in a basket on a pavement. She spent most of her life in and out of temporary foster homes. No one ever really wanted her or accepted her, they just went through the motions of caring for her till she moved on to her next placement.

Hollis felt unwanted and alone in the world. When a family finally wanted to adopt her and love her as their daughter, she ran off afraid of getting hurt. She felt that they would eventually reject her. Meanwhile, she was placed in the temporary care of a former art teacher called Josie. Hollis loved her but knew she was sick. Josie was not just forgetful, she forgot where she was at times, she put dishes in the bin after washing them instead of the cupboard.

Hollis loved Josie and hid what was happening from her social worker. But her social worker did find out. So Hollis ran away, driving Josie's car to a cabin where she had stayed with the family that had wanted to adopt her. When both Josie and Hollis were reported missing the would-be adoptive parents were hysterical and were searching the country for her along with her social worker. They found them at the cabin. Hollis realised then for the first time in her life that she truly mattered to these people and accepted their love and became their daughter. Josie had developed Dementia and moved in with her cousin who was to care for her. Hollis often went to visit her even though Josie no longer could recall who she was. But the rejected, abandoned child who had spent her life in care now had a new name - Hollis Regan she belonged, she was no longer alone in the world.

Not everyone has grown up in the care system like Hollis, but many have experienced abandonment, rejection, extreme loneliness caused by others.

Isaiah 64:4 *"Thou shalt no longer be termed Forsaken, neither shall thy land anymore be termed Desolate: but thou shalt be called Hephzibah and thy land Beulah for the Lord delighteth in thee.."*

:5 *"As the bridegroom rejoiceth over the bride so shall thy God rejoice over thee."*

:12 *"Thou shalt be called, sought out, a city not forsaken."*

Maybe right now your life is a completely desolate place. You have been hurt and let down by people and you feel forsaken. Your heart breaks because you feel unloved. Maybe you have been in circumstances of great loneliness for so long that your life feels like a barren desert. The Lord is reminding you that with Him you are never abandoned, with Him you are never forsaken, with Him you are never desolate for He accepts you and loves you His precious child. All may fail you, but the Lord never will.

He rejoices over you the way a bridegroom rejoices over his bride! With Him, you are constantly loved and sought out and never forsaken. Plus you have the 'Beulah' promise. Beulah symbolises a place of great fruitfulness. This barren desert of pain, abandonment, loneliness and rejection will not last forever and until the Lord brings you out of this barren desert to a more fruitful, beautiful place - you have to lean on Him to carry you through. Some people's love is fickle and conditional but His love for you is unconditional. Your Lord will never leave you nor forsake you, He will ever be your dearest friend. You are fully accepted, beloved, and adored by the King of kings and Lord of lords.

Hold onto the beautiful fact that He is with you always in the most desolate place you have ever been in. You are not forsaken. You are not desolate, and you will not dwell in this place forever.

59

When Others Cause Us Pain

2 Timothy 4:14 *"Alexander the coppersmith did me much evil."*

Alexander was someone who caused Paul great pain and did him much harm. It seems likely that Alexander testified against the apostle and brought false charges against him or in other words spread vicious lies about him. However, Paul ends the verse in confidence saying that the Lord would repay him according to his works.

In other words, it was in the Lord's hands to bring justice. It was not up to Paul to react and repay evil with evil. It was not his place to retaliate and be equally nasty to Alexander. As a Christian it was up to Paul to forgive him, to release all bitterness to God, to walk away quietly and have no more to do with him and pray for him.

Romans 12:14 *"Bless those which persecute you: bless, and curse not."*

:17 *"Recompense to no man evil for evil."*

Paul's attitude to being harmed was the same one that Jesus commanded in Matthew 5:44

"But I say unto you, love your enemies, bless them that curse you and pray for them which despitefully use you and persecute you."

Matthew 6:14-15 *"For if you forgive men their trespasss, your heavenly Father will also forgive you. But if ye forgive not men their trespasses, neither will your father forgive your trespasses."*

If you have been greatly wronged by someone, if someone has hurt you, viciously attacked you, slandered you, tried to destroy you as Alexander did to Paul - forgive them immediately. Unforgiveness leads to bitterness in our hearts and blocks our relationship with God.

What forgive does not mean is that you must let every person who has harmed you back into your life as a bosom friend. Not so! You can pray for them, refuse to speak evil of them and if there ever comes a time when you hear that they are in great need then meet that need. You do not need to rebuild a relationship with everyone that has harmed you, that just leaves you vulnerable to satan's attacks through that person yet again.

But cast away all bitterness and unforgiveness immediately. For if you do not forgive, the Lord will no longer hear your prayers and the bitterness you feel will destroy you - even your physical health.

Dr Carlsten Wrosch says: "Persistent bitterness may result in global feelings of anger and hostility that when strong enough could affect a person's health."

Get rid of all Ill feeling towards the person who has harmed you. Leave them in the Lord's hands. He is the one that brings justice. Do not dwell on Alexander's of life - Be grateful to the Lord for those who love you, cherish you, encourage you and build you up. Do not let what 'Alexander' did to you cause you to press the self-destruct button. Forgive and be free within.

60

Full Surrender

I read a book by Grace Livingston Hill called, *'An unwilling Guest'*. In it, a rich girl travelled from New York to stay with her Aunt for the summer. However, a servant in her Aunt's household came down with smallpox so her Aunt had arranged for her to stay with neighbours. They were plain, hardworking and all Christians. The girl did not want to stay. It was not good enough for her and she hated having no maid. God used her stay in that house to bend her will to His and make her His child.

The Scripture that says, *'Not my will but thine be done'* really stuck out while I was reading this book. (Luke 22:42)

Against her will she stayed in a place that she felt was beneath her. But it was God's beautiful, perfect will and He worked it out beautifully.

Jesus prayed not my will but thine. The horror of what was to come to Him by death on a cruel cross made Him cry out to be delivered from it. But nevertheless He surrendered to the Father's will. The surrender - that prayer not my will but thine brought about the greatest gift of all. For our Saviour did go to that cruel cross and He purchased our salvation - our admittance to everlasting life in Heaven if we will only trust Him and accept Him as our Saviour.

We need to daily pray, 'Not my will but thine Lord'. We need to abandon our own wills, plans and ways and let our Saviour do beautiful things for His honour and glory through us. He cannot do much with a stubborn, unyielded heart but He can work greatly through us when we abandon our stubborn ways to let Him lead.

When you sing the song, 'All to Jesus I surrender, all to Him I freely give'. Do you truly mean the words that you are singing? The words are easy to sing but not so easy to live. You might be abandoning yourself to a path in life that you would not have chosen.

But there is freedom in surrender. There is freedom in letting the Lord have His way for He has beautiful plans that would not unfold otherwise if you had not fully surrendered. When we do not fully surrender, we miss God's best and miss becoming all He intended us to be.

I love the old hymn, *'Take my Life and let it be'*. Can you truly sing and mean these words?

Take my Life and let it be,
Consecrated Lord to thee,
Take my moments and my days,
Let them flow in ceaseless praise.

Take my hands and let them move,
At the impulse of thy love.
Take my feet and let them be,
Swift and beautiful for Thee.

Take my voice and let me sing,
Always only for my King,
Take my lips and let them be,
Filled with messages from Thee.

Take my silver and my gold.
Not a mite would I withhold.
Take my intellect and use,
Every power as thou shalt choose.

Take my will and make it Thine.
It should be no longer mine.
Take my heart it is Thine own,
It shall be the royal throne.

61

Paper Angels

I remember watching a true-life Christmas film called, *'Paper Angels'*. In it, families in America who were struggling financially went to the Salvation Army and they gave them paper angels for their children to write what they would like for Christmas on it. The paper angels were returned and hung on a huge Christmas tree in the middle of the mall. Then people who were better off could choose a paper angel from the tree and buy the child who otherwise was not going to get anything what he or she wanted.

It deeply touched me. What a beautiful loving thing for believers in the Salvation Army to organise. What beautiful love in action!

It made me think of the scriptures in Romans 12:10

"Be kindly affectioned one to another with brotherly love; in honour preferring one another."

:13 *"Distributing to the needs of the saints, given to hospitality."*

Love is a doing word. *'For God so loved the world that he GAVE...'.* His love moved Him to action. While Jesus was on earth He daily ministered to others' needs. Christlike love is a love that moves us with compassion. A love that is unselfish and makes us want to do all in our power to distribute to the needs of others and be given to hospitality.

The power of this unselfish type of love is the kind that causes others to see Jesus in us and makes them really want to know about our Saviour. It opens doors to lead souls to Jesus.

Think of different ways that you could expand your horizons and minister to the needs of others with kindly affection.

The paraphrase of 1 Corinthians 13:2 says, *'If I have not love I am nothing.'* Love is more than mere words. Words are easy to say but putting those words into the action of sacrificial giving is a different matter. It is a go out of your way to make a difference type of love that truly cares. It is going the extra mile to make a difference in others' lives for the glory and honour of our Saviour and for the extension of His Kingdom.

1 John 4:7 *"Beloved, let us love one another; for love is of God and everyone that loveth is born of God and knoweth God."*

If we claim to love God His love should shine through us in a way that makes us willing to minister to the hurting, comfort the weary, provide for those in need. Minister to orphans and widows in their distress.

There are so many organisations like the Salvation Army that are reaching out in practical ways to all classes of society that we can support. There are so many ways that we can be ready to listen out for the cries of those in need and meet those cries through practical kindness.

I remember the words of a song that I heard on a Christian radio station a few years ago:

I wanna live like there's no tomorrow.
Love like I'm on borrowed time.
It's good to be alive.
Won't take it for granted.
I won't waste another second.
All I want is to give you a life well lived to say thank you.

We are all living on borrowed time because every breath comes from God and we do not know when we will take our final breath. So let us all take the advice of this song and love like we are on borrowed time!

62

In These Days Have The Courage To Speak Out

Joshua 1:6 *"Be strong and of a good courage."*

I listened to a sermon by David Purse from Whitewell Metropolitan Tabernacle, Belfast. He gave a few facts that startled me. Recently a teacher in Oxford lost his job because in a class of all girls he said, "Well done girls." A simple statement with only praise intended. Yet one of the 'girls' had made it known to the school that she wanted to be known as a boy. This 'girl' went home and complained to her parents about these three words and as a result the teacher lost his job.

In another case a student training to be a social worker at a university in Yorkshire posted on his own personal Facebook page his views on Biblical marriage being between one man and one woman. As a result he was called before a panel at the university and was expelled from his course. Little did he know that the Dean of that university was a leading 'LGBT' campaigner.

Recently Asher's bakery won their court appeal after their refusal to bake a cake with the slogan on it 'Support gay marriage.' They had been accused of discriminating against the customer. But they were saying that they could not fulfil the order because it went against their beliefs as Christians.

It seems like the whole world has freedom of speech these days apart from Bible believing Evangelical Christians. We live in a world where there is total uproar if a Christian speaks out about the Biblical view of things. We are labelled 'narrow minded' and 'bigots' if we state what God's Word says on matters.

The early Christians were not exactly popular either. They were hated for what they believed and were thrown to lions, set on fire and all other kinds of torturous deaths were inflicted on them because they refused to say, 'I do not believe in Jesus.' They had the courage and bravery and guts to stand up for Jesus no matter what people would say or do to them.

As God's children in these wicked days where abominable things are happening all around us, we must *'Be strong and of a good courage.'* To continue to take our stand for our Saviour no matter how unpopular it is and no matter what people may do to us as a result.

We need backbone to stand up for Jesus as soldiers of the cross. How many times on social media have you come across something that you badly wanted to share? Maybe it was on the Biblical view of marriage or an anti-abortion post or something similar, but you do not share it because you fear the tirade of nasty comments you will get. Fear blocks your courage to speak out for the truth of God's perfect and precious word.

As for Joanne Peden, she shall serve the Lord. She will speak out even when it is unpopular, she will take her stand even if she is labelled narrow minded. She will fight for the Lord's name to be honoured no matter what it costs her because she loves Jesus and if He could give His life for me, I want to honour Him by giving my all for Him.

Are you with me Evangelical Christian? Now is the time to *"Be strong and of a good courage"* more than any other time in history.

63

When Life's An Emotional Rollercoaster

I watched a true movie recently. I cannot remember the name of it, but it was about four women's lives and their desires to have a baby. For one of them it was no problem. She had her child. For another, she learned that something was wrong with the child in her womb and her little one might not make it. In the end her child was born healthy. Another one of the ladies wanted a child so badly and could not conceive so it drove a huge wedge between her and her husband. Though eventually they adopted a beautiful baby girl. The last lady had put her career as her priority and the man she had dated for years did not want marriage and a child. She broke it off as it was not going anywhere. But she yearned so badly for a husband and a child. But eventually she had to accept her life as it was and be content.

Watching the ups and downs and real struggles of these four women was an emotional rollercoaster for me, never mind them!

Life can be an emotional rollercoaster at times. We yearn for things. We have desires in our hearts, yet they come crashing down so often.

Paul's life was not easy. He had been shipwrecked, beaten, imprisoned and yet despite his rollercoaster life he wrote:

Philippians 4:11 *"For I have learned in whatsoever state I am in therewith to be content."*

Content means in a state of peaceful happiness, fulfilled, satisfied, tranquil, untroubled, at peace.

What an amazing man of God Paul was! To be able to say it doesn't matter what has come against me, what has afflicted me, what has hurt me for I have learned to be content, learned to be fulfilled, tranquil and at peace in horrific surroundings! How do you learn to be content when circumstances are at their worst? Our initial reaction to troubled times is to be distressed, agitated, and troubled. I know my reaction to being in this bed and being sick is not one of contentment at times. For I strive! I try every so called 'cure' going and then I get distressed when they do not work. Paul is miles ahead of me in learning to be content in a stinking filthy, jail cell chained to a Roman guard. But he gives us the secret of his learning to be content in all things.

Philippians 4:13 *"I can do all things through Christ which strengtheneth me."*

Paul could not be content in his own might. It's when we try to be content in our own might that we so badly fail and become so badly distressed.

The secret of being content in all things is to learn to do so through the strength which the Lord wants to pour into you in abundance whatever your circumstances are. That is something that I am continually having to learn - when I strive in the flesh and my own might I get disappointed and troubled. More than ever before I'm learning to lean upon my strong Saviour, to ask Him to daily fill me with His strength, to let Him carry me in His strong arms when I feel unable to go on, to let Him be the strength of my life.

Isaiah 26:4 *"Trust ye in the Lord forever: for in the Lord Jehovah is everlasting strength."*

Let the Lord Jehovah be your everlasting strength. Lean on those strong everlasting arms and through all the emotional rollercoasters of life and you and I will learn to say like Paul that whatever state we are in, we have learned to be content.

64

Heartsickness

I read a book by Lynn Austin called, *'Until we reach Home'*. It was about three Swedish sisters who moved from Sweden to American to be near an uncle who lived there. Their parents had died and the thought of a new life in America was one that filled them with hope.

However it was not as 'nice' as their expectations had led them to believe. Their uncle did not want them, and they were forced to get cleaning jobs and live elsewhere. It turned out that their uncle had not paid their passage but rather three men who wanted wives. Once the girls refused to marry these strangers their uncle wanted nothing more to do with them. They had to work extremely hard to pay these strangers back without getting what they had been promised. Their hopes were dashed. Their expectations of the wonderful life that they would have in America vanished and they felt worse than they had done in Sweden. At that point they were completely disillusioned and totally crushed. Things did work out well in the end for these sisters, but it is this period of crushed hopes and utter disillusionment with life that I want to focus on.

Proverbs 13:12 *"Hope deferred maketh the heart sick but when desire comes, it is a tree of life."*

Are you in a place today that is the same as the three Swedish sisters? You have hoped and prayed for something and really believed it was about to happen but when it does not happen your hope turns into, I cannot cope, and you become heartsick and troubled.

David must have been in a place of total hopelessness when he penned these words, Psalm 102:11 *"My days are like a shadow that declineth, and I am withered like the grass."*

The word expectation means a strong belief that something will happen or be the case - anticipation.

When you are in a waiting period for a long time, maybe waiting for a spouse, waiting to have a baby, waiting for healing from disease and many other scenarios you can begin to get heartsick. I remember one year getting so many texts from so many people saying they believed that I was going to get healed at a certain healing service. My body made it to the meeting at great effort when I could get out only once a week. My hopes were through the roof. I was prayed over and anointed with oil and willed with everything that was within me that this was my time, that my hour had come. But sadly nothing happened. In fact in the weeks that followed my body deteriorated back to completely bedbound. The effects of pushing my body to that service when my body was already so weak caused major deterioration. I lay here feeling totally crushed. This great healing that I had expected to happen did not come and like the Psalmist I felt withered like the grass, totally heartbroken.

But God never leaves us in heartsick periods. By His grace He lifts us out and gives us courage to keep going and keep serving Him regardless.

So dear heartsick child of God today, please know this period is not forever. Your hope deferred is just for a season and remember that your sudden good break that will turn your life around could come at any time! That tree of life that will spring up, filling your life with that which is sweet and reviving, will blossom.

Take your heartsickness to our precious Saviour today and continue to wait on whatever you are waiting for in a place of deep love and service for God.

65

Use All Circumstances To The Glory Of God

I read a book by Lynn Austin called, *'A Woman's Place'*. In it, while all the men were away fighting in the second world war, the women had to step up and do the jobs the men had been doing to support the war effort. The women in this book were working on electronics for large ships. The four woman's lives that the book followed could not have been more different but through the witness of one of these woman who happened to be a Christian all the ladies found the Lord as Saviour.

Circumstances had thrown them together. Their common desire to support the war effort had thrown them together. If there had not been a war on, these four women would never have met.

Sometimes life's trials that we must endure opens doors of possibilities and opens our world to people that we would never have met before. We do not like the circumstances and we want it to be over. Yet while we are dwelling there the Lord wants to use us to bring His Gospel to people whom we would have never met under normal circumstances.

1 Peter 5:7 *"That the trial of your faith, being more precious than of gold that perisheth, though it be tried with fire, might be found unto the praise and honour and glory at the appearing of Jesus Christ."*

Peter is saying that this trial you are going through is in the Lord's eyes, *'more precious than of gold'*. If we face it with Godly contentment and see it as a divine opportunity to reach people who aren't normally in our circles with the Gospel then we will be found unto the praise, honour and glory of our Lord at His appearing.

You did not get that job you wanted and have been forced to take one that you do not like in the meantime! Not an accident! You have been thrown together with those people to carry the light. You did not get the grades for the university that was your first choice! You are not awfully keen on your second choice, but it is not an accident! God needs you there to share His story for the extension of His Kingdom. You take sick and find yourself in hospital. Of course you do not like being sick but you are there to share the Gospel with everyone in your ward, doctors, nurses, cleaning staff, tea ladies etc. Something major went wrong with your car. You are annoyed. It is going to be costly to fix but you can still use it for the Lord's glory by witnessing to your mechanic.

The key is to live with an eternal perspective on what matters most to God. Jude tells us what matters to God.

Jude 22-23 *"And of some having compassion, making a difference. And others save with fear; hating even the garment spotted by flesh."*

What matters most from a God perspective life is that we have compassion on others, share the Gospel with them to literally snatch them from hells flames so they can be safe in the arms of Jesus when they die. My elderly pastor used to say that we should be rescue ships within a yard of hell.

So if you are in a trial or circumstance today that you don't really like, try and see it through Heaven's looking glass, let nothing be wasted and let all that you're going through count in winning the lost to Jesus.

66

Something Borrowed, Something New

I watched a bridal programme called, *'Something borrowed, Something new'*. In it, a bride must choose between wearing her mother's or grandmother's dress (which the team makeover to modernise it a bit) or choose between a brand-new dress.

Some of the dresses beforehand looked quite funny! Some were awful looking but once they had undergone transformation, they looked like the most amazing dresses ever! They were completely new creations! In every case the bride must choose her mother's transformed dress over a brand new one.

2 Corinthians 5:17 *"Therefore if any man be in Christ he is a new creature (creation) old things are passed away, behold all things are become new."*

Once you have given your life to Christ you are a brand-new creation! All the guilt, sin, shame, and stains of the past are forgiven, and you are a new man or woman. Though the transformation doesn't all happen at once!

2 Corinthians 3:18 *"But we all, with open face be holding as in a glass the glory of the Lord are changed into the same image from glory to glory even as by the Spirit of the Lord."*

Our full transformation will not happen until we reach Heaven but every day that we live on earth and walk closely to Him - He will continue to transform us to be more Christlike - better reflections of His glory.

The word 'transformation' means a complete change in appearance or character of something or someone so that the thing or person is improved.

Think of yourself as an old broken-down house that needs extensive repairs. It takes time and patience but imagine what that old broken-down house would look like as a mansion! That is what the Lord is doing with us. Brick by brick, sin by sin, bad attitudes to good attitudes, bad thought life to good thought life, bad speech to good speech, desire for worldly things replaced with a desire for God honouring things. Little by little God the Master artist is chipping away at us to make us into the most Christlike, shining bright light, radiant with His glory!

New creations should abstain from all things, substances and places that bring the Lord dishonour. If you cannot proudly glorify God in a place, then you most certainly should not be there. When you are a bearer of the name of Jesus you need to not let any habit or worldly desire cause you to bring Him dishonour. He expects us to be Holy and pure, to daily confess sins and live lives that bring Him glory, not disgrace.

A song we used to sing at children's camps when I was a child went like this.

Little by little every day,
Little by little in every way,
Jesus is changing me.
Since I made a turn about faith,
I've been growing in His grace,
My Jesus is changing me.

He's changing me,
My precious Jesus,
I'm not the same person that I used to be.
Sometimes it's slow going,
But there's a knowing,
That one day perfect I will be.

67

Philemon

Philemon 4-5 *"I thank my God, making mention of thee always in my prayers. Hearing of thy love and faith, which thou hast toward the Lord Jesus and all the saints."*

From his prison cell, Paul with joy had heard of the love and faith that Philemon had for others and wanted him to know that it had not escaped his attention. Paul was proud of him. He thanked God constantly for he was always lifting him up in prayer.

Believer's Bible Commentary (page 2149)

"When Paul prayed for Philemon, he thanked God for his noble brother. We have every reason to believe that he was a choice trophy of the grace of God - The kind of man you would like to have as a friend or brother. There are two great qualities in Philemon's character that gave great joy to Paul - His Love and Faith. His faith in Christ showed he had the root of divine life and his love towards all the saints showed that he had fruit as well. His faith was productive. Paul goes on to talk in verses 6-7 about Philemon's sharing the faith and being an encourager and refresher to the other saints of God.

The sharing of your faith means the practical kindness that Philemon showed to others. We can share our faith not only by preaching (explaining the gospel) but also by feeding the hungry, clothing the destitute, comforting the bereaved and relieving the distressed. Paul prayed that Philemon's life of benevolence would lead many to acknowledge that all his good deeds came from Jesus Christ. News of Philemon's overflowing generosity and self-sacrifice travelled from Colossae to Rome bringing great joy to Christ's prisoner. How assuring it was to know that the hearts of the saints were being refreshed by this beloved brother and especially by his love. We can have limitless potential for good or for evil."

What an amazing child of God Philemon was, and the Lord is calling us today to follow in his footsteps. Like Philemon the Lord wants each of us to be choice, bright, shining trophies of grace. He is calling us to share our faith in every way possible from speaking the Gospel to reaching out in love and kindness to others in great need. He is calling us to constantly bring refreshing and encouragement to others. He wants us to use the limitless potential that He has given us for good and not harm.

'Philemon' type people through their kindness, self-sacrifice, and love accomplish more for Christ's Kingdom than they will ever know. Paul wanted to make sure he told Philemon just how highly he regarded him. If you have a 'Philemon' in your life that makes things brighter and a blessing then follow in Paul's example, thank God and pray for them daily and also let them know exactly what you think of them for they may be totally unaware of the impact that they are having.

The world needs more 'Philemon's'! Will you be one?

68

In Helplessness Lean On Jesus

I watched a true movie about a mother who had left her baby asleep for less than five minutes while she popped out to speak to the landlord about the lack of hot water. When she got in, she discovered her baby girl was gone. She got hysterical. Can you imagine that happening to you to have someone take your child? She went to the police, but the police pointed the finger at her and made her a suspect for killing the child. She was completely helpless and powerless. Eventually it was discovered that the child's father had taken the baby and put her up for adoption. What joy and relief she felt to be holding her child again after all the helplessness and despair.

In Psalm 69, David was in a place where he felt completely helpless and powerless. He writes:

Psalm 69:1-3 *"Save me O God for the waters are come in unto my soul. I sink in deep mire where there is no standing. I am come into deep waters where the floods overflow me. I am weary of my crying: my throat is dried, mine eyes fail while I wait for my God."*

David was certainly in a season where everything was spinning out of control for him. You can hear the desperation in his voice. Waters are come into my soul; I am weary of my crying! Statements of complete helplessness and defeat. He could not get himself lifted out of the situation he was in, so it made him feel like he was drowning.

Have you ever been there? Are you there right now? Everything has started to spin out of control and you too feel completely powerless. There is a sinking feeling in your stomach, and you feel like you are going under. Maybe this is the result of an out of the blue situation or maybe you have been in a painful situation for so long and it is only now that you can take no more. You feel desolate and barren.

The Lord sees your deep distress, He cares for you as much now as He does when things are sunny and bright.

Hosea 13:9: *"But in me is thine help."*

God has got you. He is holding you in His strong arms even when things do feel crazy and all you can do is cry. He will be your help. He will be the one to save you out of the deep mire. He will be the one to still your crying and restore peace to your heart. If He can turn night into day, He can bring light into your darkness once more. I found the lyrics to this Christian song online.

Holding You
by Matt Hammitt

Where will you find peace when you cry.
In these hard times it's not what you hold onto.
It's who is holding you tonight.
It's like staring down a wishing well.
The voice inside cries for help.
But you've never felt so helpless in your life.
And time becomes the enemy.
Cause you just got to wait and see,
While all the world is passing by.
You are safe in the arms of the Father.
Always safe in the arms of the Father.

You are never as helpless as you feel. Your Heavenly Father has got you and He's not letting go!

69

Young People Arise

1 Timothy 4:12 *"Let no man despise thy youth; but be thou an example of the believers in word, in conversation, in charity, in spirit, in faith, in purity."*

Young people you might feel because you are at school or university that you are not very brave when it comes to talking about the Lord. But if you have placed your trust in Him His precious anointing covers your whole life! You can be a powerful example to believers and non-Christians alike. The key is to walk closely with your Saviour, surrender all of yourself to Him, determine to not give in to the worldliness that you see all around you and God will use you mightily.

He will fill your lips with words that build up and don't tear down. He will remove from your conversations anything that brings Him dishonour like gossip.

He will fill your heart with a powerful love, tenderness, and compassion for others that you never dreamt possible!

He will make your spirit meek, gentle, and beautiful like His so you can reflect Him to the world.

The more you feed on His word, He will build up your faith to make you strong in sharing the Gospel with others. For if people have questions then you will be able to answer them.

Lastly, he will make you an example in purity. In the Sermon on the Mount Jesus says, *"Blessed are the pure in heart for they shall see God"*. Through your purity and Christlikeness others will see God in you. Ask the Lord to give you boldness and He will, in a way you never thought possible.

Although I am no longer young. I remember the days of my childhood and youth so well. I spent time with my beloved Saviour every day. I got to know His Word well. I was a little timid and shy though, so I had to constantly look to the Lord to give me strength to talk about Him. Even as a child, through His might and not mine I bowed on my knees with people and led them to my Saviour. That was nothing to do with me but all about the Lord showing up in strength when I needed Him most.

When I got to my late teens, I went to Bible College. I lived in Belfast through the week and came home on weekends for my part time job and church. The Lord laid it on my heart that He wanted me to give out Gospel tracts and church tapes and strike up conversations on the train. At first, I found it awkward. I was talking to compete strangers and that made me feel insecure. But for those three years travelling by train up and down every week the Lord always took over when my shyness threatened to stop me. It was all God and not me. Young people, you can do that too if you will dare to step out in boldness and let the Lord have His way. Again if you determine to walk closely by your Saviour's side, He will shine a light out of you for all others to see! It will be nothing of you but everything of Him.

I remember standing in Tesco during my time at college looking into the frozen food section. This woman who I had never met before came up to me and said, "You're a Christian aren't you?" I can just sense it. She wanted to talk. It turned out she was feeling suicidal and badly wanted to know Jesus. I stood there talking to her for over an hour. She then said that she would go home and make things well with her soul! I was completely in awe after it. I just could not believe what had just happened.

Child of God never underestimate the power of your God to work through you despite shyness, weakness, and insecurity. Just keep close to His heart and He will shine His beautiful light through you. Your life will be a lamp to those who walk in darkness.

70

Emerging From The Prison Cell

Isaiah 42:7 *"To bring the prisoners from the prison and them that sit in darkness out of the prison house."*

Prison today does not look like it was back in Bible days. Prisoners were bound in a dark dungeon and chained to a guard. Today prisoners have more freedom. They can walk around to keep fit, get an education and other online study courses. But what prisoners in Bible days and prisoners today have in common is that they are well and truly under lock and key with no chance of escape.

The prisoners were there because they committed a crime and being locked up was their punishment. In some cases today there are many 'prisoners of circumstances'. People who are in nightmare circumstances in which they feel trapped, suffocated and under lock and key. A prison is a place where one no longer has any freedom. Maybe your circumstances are so bad today that you feel like a prisoner. Then this verse is for you today.

The Lord sees you sitting in the darkness of your prison house. He sees how afflicted you are, and He is saying that He is going to bring you out of your prison. That is His promise to you today.

He's saying: "My child, I see your chains and I hear your cries that you utter to me in the thick darkness. Because you are so oppressed and tormented, I am oppressed too, and I weep for you amidst your pain. But beloved one do you not know that I am the one who sets captives free? I know just what you are in chains too and I am the one who can free you from those chains. I will shatter each chain in pieces, and you will emerge from the darkness of the prison house once more."

Imagine what that will look like! Coming out of darkness into spring-like beauty where everything is new and fresh and where you will have total liberty.

I will end with this poem by Sarah Magoon, *'Freedom in Christ'*.

Jesus the jail breaker,
Life maker,
Sorrow taker:
Chains of destruction broken right off.

Jesus the soul saver,
Path paver,
Life flavour,
Chains of corruption,
Broken right off.

Jesus the rock shaker,
Tomb breaker,
Soul waker:
Chains of inferno,
Broken right off.

Look to Jesus your chain breaker today and look to Him to free you from captivity. You alone know what your captivity is. You alone know just what it is that makes your heart race with fear. Give it all to Jesus today for He alone can do that which no other can do.

71

Healing

I read a book by Beverly Lewis called, *'The First Love'*. It was different from her other books in that it was about a girl called Maggie who had suffered from an extremely painful chronic illness since she was eleven. Maggie was pure sweetness and full of joy. Despite her suffering, she was always looking for ways to make others' lives brighter. Her heart shone like a lone bright star. Maggie struggled though. She thought because of her illness that she would never have a chance to marry and fretted greatly about this. However, a young man did fall in love with her and marry her despite her illness. One night her new husband prayed for her and she was healed completely. Her affliction was forever gone.

Though unlike Maggie so many people do not receive their healing this side of Heaven. They must wait till glory to be free of their afflictions!

Yes, the New Testament is full of healing stories and yes, I believe Jesus can heal today. But for some reasons that we will only discover in eternity - not everyone gets healed. People die daily from illnesses like cancer, M.S., M.E. etc. Some of them were Godly people and you could not say of them that they lacked faith, yet God chose to take them home to heal them.

I have noticed a lot of false prophets twisting the scripture in Isaiah 53 as a 'name it, claim it' verse to prove everyone will get healed if they have enough faith. But it is a total perversion of the passage. *"By His stripes, we are healed"* does not mean everyone with sickness is going to get healed. If it meant that then no one would ever die! There would be no funerals! If you read this Scripture in the context of the passage you will see that the healing means spiritual healing and Salvation! Because of what Jesus did on Calvary our sin-sick souls can be forgiven and healed from a lost eternity if they will but accept Jesus as Saviour.

One thing I liked in Beverly's book was where Maggie was talking to someone about healing and they said, focus more on knowing the healer and not getting the healing. For whether He heals you or not, you have Christ and that is the greatest gift ever!

Habakkuk 3:17-18 *"Though the fig tree shall not blossom, neither shall fruit be in the vines, the labour of the olive shall fail and the fields shall yield no meat, the flock shall be cut off from the fold and there shall be no herd in the stalls. Yet I will rejoice in the Lord. I will joy in the God of my salvation."*

Basically, He is saying, Lord even if you do not do what I want you to do and I find myself in a barren place then I will still rejoice in you. I will still take joy in you the God of my salvation. He is saying no matter what comes I will still praise you even when circumstances are at their worst! What incredible faith!

Dear child of God, maybe like me, you desire to be healed. Healing can come this side of Heaven. The Lord has done it so many times before but even if healing doesn't come until I am with Him in glory then I am going to follow the example of Habakkuk and rejoice in my salvation even in the worst of times. Come what may, He is my Saviour still and I will always love Him whether He grants my request for healing in the way I desire most or not.

72

When Your Heart Gives Way To Fear

I remember once as a teenager going to a funfair with a friend. There was a ride that we had lined up for ages but as soon as I got on it fear gripped my heart. I just had to get off! I bolted off at lightning speed leaving my friend on it alone! Something about it just felt dangerous to me. Something about it made me afraid.

Fear is something that grips us all at times in our lives. Sometimes it can be anxiety or sometimes it can be so crippling that we cannot function properly because we have let it take over.

Fear can limit us and stop us from accomplishing all that we could for God. Faith says, 'Yes you can', yet fear says, 'No you can't'.

Scripture has a lot to say about fear.

Isaiah 35:4 *"Say to them that are of a fearful heart- be strong, fear not, he will come and save you."*

John 14:27 *"Peace I leave with you, my peace I give unto you, not as the world giveth, give I unto you. Let not your heart be troubled neither let it be afraid."*

Psalm 34:4 *"I sought the Lord and he answered me; he delivered me from all my fears."*

Fear affects the physical body. The body freezes up, the heart rate quickens, blood vessels in your extremities constrict and you might have a fearful emotional reaction like a blood-curdling scream. Living in fear of circumstances or fear of the future affects your physical health.

The Lord is saying to you today, "My child, I see you have a fearful heart, I'm telling you to be strong for I am here. Lean hard upon me and release your fears to me. For if you hold onto them dear child, they will paralyze you mentally and spiritually and they will start to affect your physical health too. For bottling things up in your spirit is blocking your closeness with me for fear and faith cannot live in the same heart. Child surrender your fears to me so I can fill you with my perfect peace. Release it, let it go, place it in my hands for it is too big for you to handle. Let me have it all so I can fill your mind with supernatural peace and calm. Remember how I called the troubled waters in my word? I also can calm the troubled waters in your heart if you will let me. I can take your troubled heart and still it once more. Seek Me and I will answer and deliver you from all your fears. You are my beloved; I hate to see you so distressed. Release it all dear one for I will bring calm once more." I will end with a poem by Deborah Ann Belka:

Fear Thou Not

As the storms of life rages on,
And your hopes are all but gone,
When your faith is tossed about,
And in it's wake you're left with doubt.

Find comfort in the storms centre,
His peace will greet you as you enter,
And you'll hear His whispers above the sea,
Fear thou not for I am with thee.

When in the midst of a test or trial,
You find yourself in complete denial.
When your trust has been rocked and shaken,
And you're tormented as soon as you awaken.

Find comfort in the face of tribulation.
His love has come to give you a new revelation,
And His whispers will set you free,
Fear thou not, for I am with thee.

73

The Wilderness

Psalm 107:4-6 *"They wandered in the wilderness in a solitary way... Hungry and thirsty, their soul fainted in them. They cried unto the Lord in their trouble, and he delivered them out of their distresses."*

We have probably got no concept in our hearts of what it is like to wander in an actual wilderness and suffer from physical hunger and thirst.

A wilderness is described as an uncultured, uninhabited, and inhospitable regions. Or a neglected or abandoned area. Other words for it are the wilds, the wastes, badlands etc. A wilderness is not a place we would want to go for a holiday, yet the children of Israel dwelt there for forty years.

We do not know much about physical hunger and thirst in our land. I remember when I was a teenager doing a 24-hour fast to raise money for World Vision. I was so glad to see a big plate of chicken and chips when it was all over as I was ravenous. I cannot imagine how hard it must be for people in poor countries who go day and weeks without food, it is heartbreaking!

The children of Israel cried unto the Lord in their trouble and He delivered them out of their distresses. The word distress means extreme anxiety, sorrow or pain, anguish, suffering, agony, affliction, torment, heartbreak etc.

We may not be able to relate to being in a wilderness or feeling hunger and thirst in a physical sense, but we may be in a spiritual wilderness where we are barren and dry. We may be in a place of deep distress where we feel nothing but extreme anxiety and heartache.

Life can put us in wildernesses at times. We can find ourselves in circumstances, not of our choosing. There is the feeling of walking around in circles and having nowhere to turn too. No end seems to be in sight and our spirits start to faint. We become distressed because we are trapped in a place that we cannot get out of.

You might understand a place like that whether because of an illness, a marriage, a seemingly unsolvable problem, worry over a sick child and the list could continue. Your spirit feels like it is in spiritual famine for you have coped for so long that you have burnt out all your inner resources. So you hunger and thirst for God to come and let this dry spell be over.

You will not dwell in your wilderness forever. It might feel like it, but it is not a permanent place. This road that you are on though painful is taking you to a better place in God than you have ever been before.

The season of distress you are in now will not be always. You may feel like there is no way out when darkness clouds your mind and your little light goes dim.

Dear child of God keep calling out to the Lord always in all your distresses and trust Him to come to your help in His precious timing. It troubles our Saviour to see you troubled. He does still deliver!

74

Be Alert!

I read a book by Grace Livingston Hill called, *'Daphne Deane'*. In it, a so-called minister had taken over their church and wanted to date her. However, even though he had the title minister, he preached things that were against God's word and believed compromise with the world was just fine. Daphne did not want anything to do with him despite how persistent he was in continually seeking her out. Eventually, he left town for a larger church taking with him for a wife a woman who was not a Christian. Daphne by her strong adherence to God's word had been saved from marriage to a false prophet.

> Matthew 24:24 *"For there shall arise false Christs and false prophets and shall shew great signs and wonders insomuch if were possible, they shall deceive the very elect."*

> 2 Timothy 4:3-4 *"For the time will come when they shall not endure sound doctrine; but after their own lusts shall they heap to themselves teachers having itching ears. And they shall turn away their ears from truth and be turned unto fables."*

Many believers have turned to false prophets who preach what they want to hear and be told that they can live in an unholy way as they like. These false prophets omit to preach the full Gospel, the Blood, Salvation, sin, and Hell and replace it with 'talks' that feed the flesh only. They have distorted the Word of God and made it say what they want it to say. They talk about life on earth and having health, wealth, prosperity as if this life is all that there is and not a long eternity to prepare for.

Anything in the Bible about holiness of life or anything that would make people uncomfortable they omit. Just giving feel-good talks with twisted scriptures taken out of watered-down versions as their only backup.

They make millions of pounds each year selling this false gospel. People would rather flock to hear them than listen to a preacher who preaches the whole Word of truth, even the bits that rebuke and convict.

These false prophets will one day have to answer to God for what they have done in being wolves in sheep's clothing. Sadly too many children of God are being deceived by them as they are not reading and studying the Word of God for themselves therefore leaving themselves spiritually clueless and ripe prey for those who distort the Word.

Child of God, the point of this more sobering devotion today is to make you aware of just how many people want to lead you away from the truth to a watered-down message that is not the Biblical message at all.

So be alert, do not be prey to satan's deceit. The only way to be truly alert is to take time each day to properly read your Bible and study it. God's children need to be prepared and loaded up with truth now more than ever before.

Please do not let yourself be deceived by these people. The Bible is not a bag of 'pic-n-mix' that you can enjoy the bits you like and throw away the ones you do not. Every sentence in the Word is for you. Do not be fooled in these last of the last days before Christ returns by those sent to deceive. Be ready for them with the sword of God's Word firmly rooted in your heart and mind. Also, remember that not everyone who performs signs and wonders is of God. The devil has been mimicking and imitating God's miracles from the days of Genesis to deceive.

75

Looking Upwards When Everything Is Spiralling Downwards

Acts 7:55 *"But he, being full of the Holy Ghost, looked up steadfastly into heaven and saw the glory of God, and Jesus standing at the right hand of God.*

:50 *"And said, behold, I see the heavens opened and the Son of Man standing at the right hand of God."*

I was studying this passage on the stoning of Stephen for his faith and these two verses struck me.

Just before they stoned him to death, he got a glimpse right into the glory of God the Father on the throne and God the Son at His right hand! He was looking steadfastly up into Heaven when this vision occurred. He was about to depart this scene of time and face a horrific death. Yet he never looked inwards and panicked, he looked upwards and was rewarded with the blessing of seeing God and the very place he was about to depart too. What a glorious way to exit earth, being filled with a glimpse of his eternal home beforehand.

Had that been me, I probably would have missed that great vision for fear would have seized me and my focus would have been on the rocks that were about to come flying at me! We have this permanent record in God's Word to give us a glimpse into Heaven too! He went to his death having seen his eternal home first!

Stephen had been a deacon who was mightily used of God in performing miracles and in preaching the Word of God. Zealous Jews had secretly induced false witnesses to accuse

Stephen of blasphemy against Moses and God. To spare himself all he had to do was deliver a compromising speech, but he would rather die than betray his sacred trust! Admire his courage!

He did not compromise, he put his life wholly in the hands of his Lord whom he loved.

Are you like Stephen, determined to use all your gifts that the Lord has given you to further God's Kingdom? For when you determine to do so and not compromise with the world in any way, the Lord's glory and anointing will be powerfully upon you and He will use your life in wonderful ways.

Maybe circumstances in your life are not spiralling downwards as badly as things were in Stephen's life but you are in a difficult place right now. Physical rocks are not being thrown at you but rocks from the enemy of your soul to discourage, to defeat you, to stop you being so powerfully used of God are coming at you in full force right now. Child of God, I've felt those rocks coming at me many times and I'm sorry to say I have focused so much on what the enemy was throwing at me that I failed to look up and see the glory of God in the midst of it and let the Heavenly vision of my dear Lord's presence comfort me.

Like Stephen when all hell is breaking loose, look up and focus your eyes on God. I remember a choir that use to sing this song:

> Focus my eyes on you oh Lord.
> Focus my eyes on you.
> To worship in spirit and in truth.
> Focus my eyes on you.

Look up dear child of God! Do not focus on people or what is coming at you or what you are going through. Look up and let the comforting presence of God sustain you.

76

Long Way Back

I watched a true film called, *'Long Way Back'*. It was a true film from 1978. In it, a healthy teenage girl boarded her usual school bus home. However, on that day there was a detour and sadly the bus broke down on a railway line when a train was approaching. Many were killed but Celia lived. But she had a major brain injury and had to have a leg cut off. At first, on coming out of the coma, Celia could not speak or communicate in any way. It was a slow process before she could speak again and an extremely slow process before she could walk again.

It was a long way back to any kind of normality, but Celia had a great determination that her new limits were NOT going to conquer her. When she returned to school, she expected to be a top-grade A student again, but her brain injury meant that she could not recall information anymore and her grades plummeted. She had come to a place where she had to come to terms with the fact that her limits had changed her and when she came to terms with that then she was free to be her new self.

It was a moving film. It documented every part of her journey. It really did speak to me.

Maybe you are in a place where you are far more limited than you wish to be. Maybe not through illness but other circumstances. Unlike Celia, I have never fully accepted my limits and find them crippling and suffocating but through Jesus, I have had the strength to go on and keep serving Him despite my limits.

James 1:12 *"Blessed is the man that endureth temptation (trials) for when he is tried, he shall receive the crown of life, which the Lord hath promised to them that love him."*

Revelation 2:10 *"Fear none of these things which you shall suffer... be thou faithful unto death and I will give thee a crown of life."*

John 16:33 *"In the world ye shall have tribulation, but be of good cheer; I have overcome the world."*

No matter how limited you feel, you are not going to be overcome. The enemy simply cannot defeat you for you are an overcomer in Him. Keep being faithful to God through your hard pressing, keep serving Him! He has promised a crown of life in Glory to His children who have refused to let life's limits make them give up. I love the verse to this hymn *'Deeper Deeper'*.

Deeper, deeper though it cost hard trials.
Deeper let me go.
Rooted in the holy love of Jesus,
Let me fruitful grow.

You are not limited in God's service though it cost hard trials! He is still taking you deeper into Himself and causing you to be fruitful! Never forget it! God's army needs the weaker vessels as well as the stronger ones!

77

Precious Shepherd And Comforter

Psalm 23:4 "Yea, though I walk through the valley of the shadow of death, I will fear no evil; for thou art with me, thy rod and thy staff they comfort me."

I am thankful that in my beloved Lord I have found a Shepherd who tends to me, cares for me and nurtures me as well as being my precious comforter. Jesus is our Good Shepherd. A shepherd tends to his flock day and night. He would gather his flock into the sheepfold at night for their protection. The shepherd would then sit in the sheepfold opening ready to guard his sheep against harm. He had a genuine, loving concern for what belonged to him.

When we are passing through what seems to be our lowest valley and darkness surrounds us, our precious Shepherd is right there, holding us and comforting us. I wrote this song years ago and included it in my first book:

Shepherd of my soul, hide me under your strong arm.
Shepherd of my soul without you I'm lost and alone.
Here I am precious comforter, afraid, weary, and worn.
Shepherd of my soul, protect your child I pray.

I am so thankful for the Shepherd of my soul who has always been there for me and never left me comfortless. His tender touch, His closeness, His strength is what has kept me going through years of illness.

The shepherd would have used his rod and staff to protect his sheep from danger. If wolves appeared the shepherd used the rod to scare them off. If his sheep were straying off the right path, he would gently pull them into safety. Also at night as each sheep entered the pen for protection, he gently tapped each one as he counted that they were all there.

Jesus cares when you are hurting, just like the shepherd gently tends his injured sheep. I love the verse in John 11:35 *"Jesus wept."*

That showed how greatly He grieved for His friend's death and for all the others whose hearts were broken over this bereavement too. That shows how much He deeply feels for you when you are breaking. When you think that you cannot go on one more day, He weeps for you His precious child because He is well acquainted with suffering. Run into your Shepherds arms this day and ask for His comfort. Like a child in His arms, He will cradle you and hold you close until the storm passes by. I will end with this beautiful poem by Deborah Ann Belka.

When my spirit is weighed down,
From tension that is all around...

My Good Shepherd,
Brings to me,
Those still waters.
Where peace flows through.

When my Spirit,
Feels weary and spent,
From all the cares,
Today I've met...

My Good Shepherd,
Leads me to those calming waters,
Where peace runs true.

When my Spirit,
Feels out of control.
It's in those still waters,
Jesus calms my soul.

78

The Dead Battery

Years ago when I was healthy, I was struggling to deal with something that had happened. So on a Sunday afternoon between church services I got to my knees in my bedroom, but I just could not pray.

It was raining heavily outside so I could not go to my usual place up through the fields to pour out my heart to the Lord. So, I got into my car and drove for miles pouring out my heart to the Lord the whole way. I was miles away from home when I pulled my car into a tiny car park.

I studied God's word and continued to pour out my heart and then wrote what I felt the Lord's responses were from His word into my journal. A lot of time had passed since I stopped my car. I looked at the clock and realised I needed to head home to get ready for the evening service. However, the car would not start! It was dead. I tried to ring for help, but my mobile had no signal at all. Another car had pulled into the car park not that long before I was going to start for home. It had two adults in the front and two bored-looking teenagers in the back.

When they saw I was struggling, one of the women came over. She told me that I had been sitting with my lights on! How dumb was that! That is what had caused the battery to die. She said that her thirteen-year-old son was good at getting cars going and would I let him try. Sure enough, without jump leads or anything, the young boy got my car started. I took my kind angels address and later sent them vouchers to thank them. After the car was going, I drove it straight home and did not dare stop it again! It was a fast ride home!

I could not help but think how the Lord had sent those people as angels for I had been truly stuck. There was not even a filling station nearby that I could have walked to for help.

Is your life like a dead battery? You cannot find any fight or hope, and everything seems dead and bleak? I read about a character in a book who had been severely injured in WW2. He had given up the fight. He saw nothing to live for as he thought that the girl that he loved belonged to another. But then she showed up as a nurse in France where he was and like the angel by his side, her presence gave him the courage to fight for he now had something to live for. (from the book, *'The Search'* by Grace Livingston Hill)

When God sees that the fight has left one of His dear children and that their hope batteries have died, this is what He does.

Psalm 34:7 *"The angel of the Lord encampeth round them that fear him and delivereth them."*

Psalm 91:11 *"For he shall give his angels charge over thee, to keep thee in all thy ways."*

Also in 1 Kings 19, when Elijah was afraid, severely depressed and running for his life, an angel appeared to him and provided food and water for his journey.

Child of God, the Lord is fighting for you and so are all His ranks of Heavenly angels. He sees when we cannot take it anymore and has promised to send His angels all around us to bring help in our need, comfort, peace, reassurance that He is there. You might not even be aware of God's angels. But they are there to protect you from the dark forces of the evil one.

Like my car dead battery incident, He might even send angels to you in human form. He will continue to minister His comfort, strength, and love to you till your fight and courage and hope have been renewed. This is not a permanent season dear discouraged one - God will help you fight. His angels surround you even now!

79

The Search

I read a book by Grace Livingston Hill called, *'The Search'*. It was about two different individuals who were searching for God during WW2. John, a soldier fighting in the war in France, knew that he faced death every day and was searching to make things well with his soul. The Salvation Army was also stationed in France and they served the soldiers coffee and warm doughnuts. One night, one lady made the way of Salvation very clear and many soldiers bowed and accepted Christ as Saviour. John, however, had a massive blockage in his heart that hindered him - A spirit of great hate and bitterness towards another man.

Bitterness and anger towards another human soul are massive blockages to knowing God. We cannot know a loving forgiving God and hate another at the same time. Eventually, John realised that his hate and bitterness were separating him from knowing the Lord and he finally let go of the bitterness and made things well with his soul by accepting Jesus as Saviour.

Jeremiah 29:13 *"And ye shall seek me and find me when you search for me with all your heart."*

If you do not know the Lord and truly want Him to be your Saviour, seek Him with all your heart. If there is hatred, bitterness or anger in your heart cast it aside then bow the knee and pray: "Lord, I know I'm a sinner. I ask you to forgive me for all my sins. I thank you for dying and rising for me so I can be your child and not go to a lost eternity. Lord, I believe, now make me your child, and let the rest of my life bring you glory. Amen."

If you have prayed that prayer and sought the Lord with all your heart and want Him as Saviour of your life, He will come into your life and the angels in Heaven are now rejoicing!

As for those of you who are already Christians, this is still important to you to remove all bitterness, anger, and hate. If you are living with hate for another person in your heart, then you can be sure that the Lord will not hear your prayers. Your heart is too full of bitterness for it to be full of Jesus.

1 John 4:20 *"If a man say, I love God and hateth his brother, he is a liar: for he that loveth not his brother whom he hath seen, how can he love God whom he hath not seen."*

It is impossible to claim you love God and hate someone else at the same time. Scripture tells us to bless those who curse us and pray for those who have harmed us - not build up a barrier of hate in your heart. Scripture is clear that you cannot love God and be full of hate at the same time.

Giving our hearts over to bitterness means we have resisted the prompting of the Holy Spirit to love. If we are truly earnest about seeking God, He will reveal the sinfulness of bitterness in our hearts and compel us towards seeking His healing and forgiveness. Bitterness can be remedied if we recognise our failings, repent and humble ourselves to receive a renewed spirit from the Lord otherwise bitterness consumes our heart and becomes a barrier between the Lord and ourselves.

Ephesians 4:31 *"Let all bitterness, and wrath and clamour, and evil speaking be put away from you with all malice."*

Get rid of it all for it is poison to your walk with God. Do not let it be a blockage in your heart between you and God anymore. Bitterness only makes prayer a struggle. *"If we regard iniquity in our hearts the Lord will not hear us."* It will make your life resemble darkness rather than light. Cast it all away and be free to know God wholly.

80

The Rescuing Hand Of God In Troubled Times

Psalm 140:1 (NIV) *"Rescue me O Lord from evil men. Preserve me from violent men."*

2 Samuel 22:3 (NIV) *"My God, my rock, in whom I take refuge. My shield and the horn of my salvation. My stronghold and my refuge; my Saviour, you save me from violence."*

I read a Grace Livingston Hill book called, *'Exit Betty'*. In the book, the girl had been tricked on her wedding day, not to the stepbrother she had consented to marry but to the violent abusive stepbrother who wanted her only for her money then threatened to have her put away in a mental asylum. As Betty walked down the aisle and saw the evil man at the front, she knew that she had been tricked by her stepmother. As she walked on, she felt more and more horrified so when she got to the front she pretended to faint.

For a moment, the doctor and the stepmother stepped out of the room. Betty seized the opportunity and fled. Running wildly out the back door in all her bridal finery she met a girl who was standing outside and pleaded with her to help her escape which the girl did. She took the bride to her apartment and helped her flee to the safety of the girl's mother. While staying with the lady called 'Ma', Betty found the Lord as her Saviour. She had not only been rescued from the hands of an evil man, but she had also been rescued from a lost eternity when she placed her trust in Jesus.

The two Scriptures quoted at the start struck me as I thought about this book. Maybe like Betty, your circumstances are so dire that you feel the need for the strong rescuing hand of God to intervene. You could be in an oppressive situation that is causing you to fear. Just like He helped Betty, He will help you. He will be your God, your rock, your refuge, your shield, your stronghold, and your refuge. The one who saved from all violence and oppression.

In Betty's circumstance, God sent the right person at the right time to help with her rescue and he will do the same for you. He often uses people as His hands and feet on this earth to help those who are afraid and troubled to get to a better place - a place of safety - where their souls are no longer troubled and afraid. He does and will rescue! Hold tight to His loving hands and let Him bring you, His beloved child, to a place secure, restorative, and a joyful wherein you will dwell.

We are also called to be like 'Ma' in the book. She cared for the weary and troubled and cared for their souls. So many people suffer in life without any knowledge of the Lord's great salvation plan and how to know Him. It is our job to have hearts of compassion that not only reach out to be the Lord's hands and feet but who also are not afraid to speak to people of their great need for Jesus as Saviour. I love the words to this song.

He rescued me from the darkest night
and brought me into His glorious light.
To know His presence is my delight.
Hallelujah He rescued me.

What beautiful words! Today weary soul if you are amid your darkest night cry out for rescue. And remember to be a 'Ma', one who cares enough for other's souls to point them to your Saviour.

81

Deborah

Judges 4:4 *"And Deborah a prophetess.... she judged Israel at that time."*

The Lord called her to go to Mount Tabor and take with her ten thousand men to fight Jabin's army and was promised full deliverance.

Deborah responded:

:9 *"I will surely go with thee: notwithstanding the journey that thou takest shall not be for thine honour; for the Lord shall sell Sisera into the hand of a woman and went with Barak to Kadesh."*

Deborah was a woman of strength who heard from God and believed Him. Her courage awakened the people, enabling them to throw off foreign oppression.

At the time she was a judge her people had sunk into despair because of their idolatry. They had forgotten God and His promises. Deborah's great joy was that the Lord turned the enemy's strength on its head, bringing power to the weak and blessing the land with peace for forty years.

Deborah's bravery is achievable when we put our whole trust in God and His promises. She is a brilliant example of someone willing to be used of God.

Psalm 20:7 *"Some trust in chariots and some in horses, but we will remember the name of the Lord."*

Deborah was on my heart this week because she did answer the call of her beloved Lord and obey His voice.

Sometimes the Lord asks us to do things that we do not feel we have the courage or the bravery to fulfil the task. But the Lord is reminding you today that He equips those that He calls and your obedience even when you feel afraid could lead to others being brought forth from darkness and into the light.

Dare to have the courage to step out. The Lord will be your battle shield. Do not let feelings of inadequacy, insecurity, inferiority, or worthlessness pull you down as they are lies from the enemy to stop you fulfilling what the Lord has asked you to do. The Lord asks us to do things that will bring great encouragement to His people and Salvation to lost souls, so no matter how big or small the task, take the plunge and look to God to be your help.

We cannot do anything for the Lord with our own strength. But we can do great things with His might, power, and spirit.

Life is a battleground. Maybe you do not even feel like you have the courage to take your next breath and keep living in your painful circumstances, never mind try to serve God at a time when you are at your weakest. But that is the time when you are most fruitful, for when you are weak God shows His strength and you marvel at His grace.

Keep fighting the good fight weary one. Keep listening for the Lord's voice and do what He says in obedience and in His strength Be a Deborah. A person of courage and bravery for the glory of His name and extension of His Kingdom.

82

God is Still On The Throne And He Will Remember His Own

I read a book called, *'Ladybird'* by Grace Livingston Hill. In the book, the girl's mother had just died. Before her mother died, she told her to flee the dangerous community that her late father had settled them in. A community of outlaws and dangerous men. Fraley fled for her life with the evil men close on her trail for many days. After so many long days running, she climbed a tree to sleep in as she thought it would be safe there. She was extremely hungry and had not eaten in days. A man appeared and asked her if she thought that she was some kind of bird being perched in a tree. He invited her down and shared his abundance of food with her. When she was out of resources and was struggling with hunger, God sent someone to bring her food.

It reminded me of the story of the Israelites in the desert. They too had nothing to eat and God sent them food straight from Heaven - manna and quails.

Exodus 16:4 *"Then the Lord said unto Moses, Behold I will rain bread from heaven for you and your people shall go out everyday and gather a certain rate everyday.*

:35 *"And the children of Israel did eat manna forty years - until they came unto the borders of the land of Canaan."*

Maybe today you are in a place of great need. Your need may not be a lack of food but dire circumstances.

Philippians 4:19 *"But my God shall supply all your need according to his riches in glory by Christ Jesus."*

God has not changed. God is still the God who can miraculously meet your need in ways you did not expect. He sees our deepest needs, He sees our tears, sorrow, pain caused by something you are lacking, and He will provide for you. I came across this hymn which ties in perfectly.

In some way or other, the Lord will provide.
It might not be my way, it might not be thy way.
And yet in His own way the Lord will provide.

At some time or other, the Lord will provide,
it may not be my time, it might not be thy time.
And yet in His own time the Lord will provide.

Despond then no longer; the Lord will provide.
And this be His token - no word He hath spoken,
was ever yet broken. The Lord will provide.

Author Anon

Our gracious loving Lord sees the need that is weighing you down and He is still on the throne and always remembers His own. A parent would not let their child go without something that they badly needed and in the same way our Heavenly Father is not going to let you down. Do not fear for miraculous manna will appear! The miraculous answer to your needful prayer will be answered in the Lord's own time.

83

Though Waters Roar

I read a book by Lynn Austin called, *'Though Waters Roar'*. At one point in the book, it talked about a great flood that had swept across part of America and many lost their lives. Had it not been for the selfless actions of one man who lost his life getting others to safety the death toll would have been much higher without.

It reminded me of the historical happening of the Titanic. There was an estimated 2224 passengers and crew aboard, and more than 1500 died. While the ship was sinking the orchestra was playing *'Nearer my God to Thee'*. It was a night of devastation and heartbreak as many were engulfed in the deep waters. I have always felt it was so sad. When the movie came out about it, I didn't watch it. I would have cried too sore because I often wonder how many of those 1500 people who lost their lives had made things well with their souls before going into eternity. Did they go to Heaven or hell? My only hope is that they cried out to the Lord for salvation before going under for Jesus is our only safety.

We do not drown in the trials of life because of His presence in our hearts and nothing can separate us from being His child. The greatest tragedy that could happen on this earth is never a tragedy for the child of God because once things are well with our souls, life's trials cannot drown us. He has promised to be near and be a comforter. Life ending is a release into an eternity of everlasting bliss.

Isaiah 43:1-3 *"Fear not, for I have redeemed thee, I have called thee by name. When thou passest through the waters, I will be with thee; and through the rivers they shall not overflow thee. When thou walkest through the fire, thou shall not be burned, neither shall the flame kindle upon thee. For I am the Lord thy God."*

There may be times in life that you feel you are drowning. There may be times when you feel the current pulling you under. There may be times you are gasping for air wondering how you will make it through. But we have this powerful promise that when we pass through deep waters then the Lord Himself is right there beside us as we press through. In the deepest river of trial, He has promised that you will not be consumed.

Even walking through the fires of life we will not be burnt because our Lord is seeing us through our most painful times. We are going THROUGH not remaining in the river to drown. Our lifeguard is holding us firmly and carrying us to dry ground. Rivers and seas can be unpredictable. Life can be unpredictable but when Jesus is Saviour of our lives, we do not have to fear what life throws at us.

A lady called Ruth Johnston wrote this poem at a time of great sorrow and pain.

Drowning
Head swirling, Saltwater burning my eyes,
I feel out of control, Breathless,
Frantically gasping for air,
My thoughts everywhere.
All that surrounds me is crashing.
My world is crumbling. Will I ever be free of this volatile sea?
My heart screams a prayer, to him who is always there.
Father God! Please save me.
From this relentless raging sea,
That is pain and change. That is life without stability.

If you feel like Ruth then the solid rock, the anchor of your life is with you even now through raging trials! You are NOT going under! God is going to bring you through.

84

And God Heard Her Cries

As some of you know I have an eye disease called Keratoconus which means that I can only see out of specially made lenses. I cannot see out of glasses as my eyes are oval instead of round so all glasses do is magnify the blur.

I was nineteen when I was diagnosed and found it scary especially when the doctor said as the disease progresses in later life, I will no longer be able to get my contacts in and be legally blind. The words terrified me. How could this happen? One week I could see fine out of my glasses for short-sightedness and the next I am struggling at my part-time job to see the digits on the till.

All is calm when I can get my lenses in for then I have sight. But everything goes wrong if I take an eye infection. It means I cannot get my lenses in; therefore I cannot see. These infections take weeks to clear up which leaves me unable to read, write, watch things, go online etc. It is part of my healing prayer that the Lord will heal my eyes completely as well as my physical suffering.

However, last week I got a scare. My eyes were hurting me all day and thick yellow gunk was pouring out of them. So before I took my lenses out that night in desperation and fear I contacted my prayer warrior friend. I told her that I knew without a doubt that it was the start of an infection and I was terrified to go weeks without sight. My prayer warrior friend contacted others who pray hard.

I had a rough scary night. I cried sore to God to not take my sight. I was on edge. I quoted reassuring scriptures repeatedly to try to calm myself down. Then I finally went to sleep.

When I woke my eyes were FINE! No pain, No yellow gunk. I could get my lenses in and see! Oh, how I praised and thanked my precious Saviour for hearing my cries. I am trapped in a body that does not work and if I had to lie here all day without books, things to watch etc I would break down. I have been in that place before many times and it has been horrific.

Maybe that only seems like a small thing to you. But it was a massive thing for me. I write this in praise, honour, and glory to my beloved Lord for not letting me suffer more than I could bear! It was a mini-miracle.

I still believe God for full healing in my life whether He heals me on earth or takes me home to heal me but for now, I praise Him for sending me a mini-miracle when I was extremely distressed.

Psalm 50:15 *"And call upon me in the day of trouble: I will deliver thee, and thou shalt glorify me."*

Psalm 17:1 *"O Lord, attend unto my cry, give ear unto my prayer."*

If you are in a place of great distress today, call upon the Lord and He will hear your cry. Ask someone else who you know to be a praying person to pray for you too. There is power in prayer especially the more people that are praying. Those cries go to the Lord's throne room.

Do not be afraid or troubled child of God today. The Lord sees your need. He sees what is causing you stress and He will not let you go through more than you can bear. Your soul may be weighed down today but Jesus your burden-bearer wants you to cast your cares on Him.

85

Jesus Frees From Addictions And Chains

I watched a real soul-stirring true movie on called, *'Not my Kid'* from 1985. It was about this fifteen-year-old girl from a well-respected family who had become a drug addict. She had been covering it up and lying to her family for years. When she was supposed to be in school, she was out stealing to get money to buy drugs. Her parents finally found out when one day under the influence of drugs she violently beat up her younger sister.

It was then that it all came to light. The father, an expert surgeon could not cope. He was used to being able to fix things. He hated the powerlessness that he felt to be able to help his daughter. Her mother also, a stay at home mum, blamed herself for not noticing anything.

Both parents blamed themselves. They tried their best to help Kelly but more and more she drifted from them so bound by the chains of addiction that they became more and more powerless. So one day they tricked her. They told her that they wanted her to view a private school nearby so she would be away from her drug sources. But they took her to a drug rehab centre for teenagers. For weeks she was angry and hostile. She would not admit that she had a problem. But finally, she broke down and admitted that three years before when she was just twelve, she had an abortion. After that, she felt so guilty for murdering her child, that she turned to drugs to get a high to numb herself to the guilt feelings. The counsellor said that by admitting that she had a problem was a breakthrough and the first step to recovery. It ended happily.

After months in rehab, her chains of addiction and shackles fell off. She was no longer a slave to something that controlled her, she was free. It ended with her being whole again, running into her family's arms with total joy on her face. It was a hard film to watch. I cried a lot through it as I deeply felt for her parents and little sister, but it brought me much joy too to see her free of her chains.

This whole movie made me think of the passage in Scripture where Jesus raised Lazarus from the dead. He emerged from the tomb alive but not free as he was bound up with grave clothes.

> John 11:44 *"And he that was dead came forth, bound hand and foot with graveclothes and his face was bound about by a napkin. Jesus saith unto them, loose him, and let him go."*

Maybe like Kelly and Lazarus, you are bound by addictions and chains today. Chains that only you know about. Chains that you have kept well hidden from those you love. I do not know what your chain is today, but wouldn't you love to be free of it? Does it hinder your walk with the Lord and what you can accomplish for Him?

Brother or sister, whatever that secret thing is in your heart that is stealing your liberty, surrender complete control to your Lord. Cry out to Jesus the one who has conquered death and has limitless power. He's right there with you now waiting to loose you from your graveclothes.

86

Called To Bear Fruit

Proverbs 12:12 *"The root of the righteous yieldeth fruit."*

John 15:16 *"Ye have not chosen me, but I have chosen you, and ordained you, that ye shall go and bring forth fruit, and that your fruit shall remain."*

It is almost harvest time. The time where we celebrate trees producing fruit and the land producing fresh produce. Without harvest and the fruits of all the farmer's labours reaping the rewards of their hard work, we would have little to eat. Trees and land that do not produce any products are labelled as barren and they do not serve their purpose.

Luke 10:2 *"The harvest is truly great, but the labourers are few: Pray ye therefore the Lord of the harvest, that he would send forth labourers into the harvest."*

The need in the harvest field for the bringing in of the souls of men is so great but the labourers who care where their fellow men and women spend eternity are so few. It is truly the 'selfie' generation where people are too caught up in their own lives to reach out to others. The Bible does say that in the last days, *'Men will be lovers of their own selves'*. 2Timothy 3:2

How long has it been since you last tried to reach out to an unsaved person? Could the Lord label you as one of the labourers in the greatest harvest of all, the souls of men or would He label you a lover of self that doesn't care? I feel that the Lord is laying this on my heart so He can speak to someone who once had a passion for souls but has now lost it.

Live with a Heavenly vision and live to be an active passionate soul winner who will bear much fruit for the extension of God's

Kingdom. There are still many people who have never heard the Gospel message. The greatest calling on your life is to care for their souls. Do all in your power to be a witness.

A poem I read years ago went like this. It greatly challenged me. It is written from the perspective of a person who has gone to a lost eternity and is speaking to their Christian friend on earth.

My Friend

My friend, I stand in judgement now.
And feel that you're to blame somehow.
On earth I walked with you day by day.
And never did you point the way.

You knew the Lord in truth and glory.
But never did you tell the story.
My knowledge then was very dim.
You could have led me straight to him.

Though we lived together here on earth.
You never told me of the second birth.
And now I stand condemned this day condemned.
Because you failed to mention him.

You taught me many things that's true.
I called you friend and trusted you.
But I've learned now it's too late.
You could have saved me from this fate.

We walked by day and talked by night.
And yet you showed me not the light.
You let me live and love and die.
You knew I'd never live on high.

Yes, I called you friend in life.
And laughed with you through joy and strife.
And yet on coming to the end...
I cannot now call you friend.
By D.J Higgins.

87

Lessons From The Sunflower

Sunflowers have been adopted as a symbol of happiness, strength, a love of the sun and because it is always said to turns its face toward the sun, it is considered to be a symbol of faith. Their main meaning is said to be loyalty. Also, no flower can lift your spirits as the Sunflower can. Bright, cheery, and bold, the Sunflower is a warm and caring gift.

I loved the comparison of the Sunflower being a happy flower because its face is always towards the sun. It reminded me that if we as Christians would keep our eyes fixed on Jesus - the Son, then we would not be so overwhelmed with our burdens and trials.

Hebrews 12:2 *"Looking unto Jesus the author and finisher of our faith."*

Always keep your eyes towards the Son because when we lift our eyes off Him discouragement, defeat, and the enemy's voice creep in. Our heads will droop and our spirits sag.

I know personally that whenever I get my eyes off Jesus and unto circumstances that hopelessness sets in. But when I keep them on Him, I have hope, strength and courage to press on through sore trials.

Proverbs 15:13 *"A merry heart maketh a cheerful countenance; but by sorrow of the heart the spirit is broken."*

When our hearts are full of the joy of the Lord, it radiates from our faces. Happiness is dependent on our circumstances, but joy is having the Lord in your heart and He remains despite the circumstances. When our spirit is broken all we can do is to ask the Lord to revive and refresh our weary hearts. In the meantime focus on having a spirit of thankfulness despite your downcast heart for that greatly honours the Lord.

I also liked how the Sunflower is a symbol of strength. We do not have to weather the storms of life in our own strength for God has promised to be your strength!

Psalm 46:1 *"God is our refuge and strength, a very present help in time of trouble."*

Your spirit might be sagging today but the Lord will not let you completely break. He WILL be your strength! That greatly comforts me. I do not have to hold myself up through the grief of illness for the Lord is already doing so. I can truly sing the words of this song. "You are my strength when I am weak. You are the treasure that I seek. You are my all in all. Seeking you as a precious jewel, Lord to give up I'd be a fool, you are my all in all." What a strong, mighty, and powerful God we serve who breathes life into His children to help them carry on when they think they can't.

Proverbs 20:6 (NLT) *"Many will say they are loyal friends but who can find one who is truly reliable?"*

In this life, people will let us down. Even people we thought would be friends for life can hurt and abandon us. But the truest most loyal friend we can have is our beloved Saviour. He will always stand true when others let us down. He will never walk away. He calls us to display the same loyal devotion that He has for us towards Himself that we might daily walk closely to Him and let Him be our everything.

Be a Sunflower for Jesus. Keep your face towards the Son, let Him be your joy when your spirit is broken, let Him be your strength and love Him and others with the same love, loyalty, and devotion that He shows you.

88

Refrain From Judging Others

I read a book that was called, *'The Outcast'* by Jolina Petersheim. In the book, a girl called Rachel had a child outside wedlock. Yes, sex outside marriage is a sin that breaks the Lord's heart. But if that person truly repents for his or her sin, walks away from repeating the action and returns to the Lord, He will freely forgive.

However, in the community in which Rachel lived, the people's judgement of her was harsher than God's. People looked at her with hate and scorn and made it clear they did not want her in the village, so she was an outcast, a reject, a person whom others hated. It made me think. God alone is the judge. It is not our job to condemn others for we will all individually have to stand alone before God and give an account of our lives at the end of the day.

Matthew 7:1-5 *"Judge not, that ye be not judged. For with what measure ye judge, ye shall be judged and with what measure ye mete (use) it shall be measured to you. And why beholdest thou the mote (speck) that is in thy brother's eye, but considerest not the beam (plank) that is in thine own eye... Thou hypocrite, first cast out the beam out of thine eye, and then thou shalt see to cast out the mote out of thy brother's eye."*

The problem today is that people are so focused on other peoples faults that they fail to see their own. Gossipy tongues wag, 'Did you hear about what she/he did?' And they follow on with the juicy details. When you are judging the lives of everyone around you - you are not in close communion with God yourself.

1 Corinthians 11:28 *"But let a man examine himself."* :31 *"For if we would judge ourselves, we should not be judged."*

This was in the context of taking communion. It went on to say he or she who drinks the cup unworthily heaps judgement on himself. If you take that cup in your hand knowing you have unrepented sin in your heart do not drink it. Do not heap judgement on yourself.

We are to daily examine ourselves and daily repent for 'the little foxes are spoiling the vine.' Get your eyes off other people and get them on yourself. You could have sins in your heart like pride, greed, selfishness, a harsh gossipy tongue, bad language etc. The Lord is making it clear that we need to examine ourselves closely and to repent daily to stay in close fellowship with Him. He does not mean that we are to be self-condemning, just quick to recognise and repent of our sins so that He is truly our everything.

"If Jesus is not Lord of all, He's not Lord at all."

With all our sins and imperfections we are not put on planet earth to be harsh judges of others. We were placed on earth to be witnesses for Him and bright lights shining for Him. It does not mean we should water down our message either or tolerate sins that Scripture speaks out against. You still need to be a vessel of truth who stands on His word.

But what you are not to be is a hard-hearted, critical gossiper who constantly condemns and puts others down. It is the Lord's job to convict consciences and bring them to repentance. Our job is to obey His Word, walk closely with Him and clearly show His glory and love for others in this dark, sin-stained world.

Do not set yourself up as judge and jury over others. That is God's job, ours is to continually examine ourselves and live lives that are an example to others of how God wants us to live and love.

89

Possessing All In Jesus

I read a book called, *'The White Lady'* by Grace Livingston Hill. In it, a girl who thought she had a fortune was informed by her lawyer that the money was all gone through bad investments her late father had made. Up until that point, she had lived a life of extreme luxury, full of parties, concerts, and social occasions. But it all vanished, and she realised she must now make a living somehow. She left town and went to a quiet little village where no one would know that she had lost her fortune.

For the first time in her life she realised that although she had possessed everything for years in the way of wealth, expensive possessions, social standing, many admirers, she now felt an emptiness inside. A hollow hole in her heart haunted her. She stayed with her grandmother's sister and while staying there saw that even though her Aunt was poor, she glowed with joy. The joy that came from having the Lord as Saviour - the greatest prize. Eventually, after finding a church in the small town, she settled in Constance gave her life to the Saviour. She realised how empty her life had been without Him. She realised that she had never really been content until now. Her possessions and wealth were things that she could not take with her into eternity, all she could take was herself, a soul made right with her Saviour and ready to meet Him.

> Matthew 6:19-20 *"Lay not up for yourselves treasures upon earth, where moth and rust doth corrupt and where thieves break through and steal... But lay up for yourselves treasures in heaven."*

Jesus is saying that there is no security in material things. Any type of material treasure can be destroyed or stolen. You will not be able to fit all your earthly possessions and money into your coffin. What is more important is Jesus and living a life that pleases and honours Him. When Jesus is our treasure, we will commit our resources, our time, our talents, our money to His work in this world. When you serve Him with your all, you lay up treasures in Heaven. The Lord's 'well done', rewards with various crowns.

Putting things into perspective, all that matters at the end of the day is Jesus and having made things well with our souls so we can spend eternity in Heaven and not a lost sinners hell.

1 Timothy 6:6-7 *"But godliness with contentment is great gain. For we brought nothing into this world and it is certain we can carry nothing out."*

:10 *"For the love of money is the root of all evil; which while some have coveted after, they have erred from the faith and pierced themselves through with many sorrows."*

Contentment consists of satisfaction with the necessities of love. Coveting money leads to envy, strife, dishonesty, greed, and selfishness.

What's more important to you today? Accumulating more wealth and possessions or truly starting to build up treasure in Heaven by devoting yourself in service to the Lord in the faithful service of building His Kingdom.

Only one life, twill soon be past.
Only what's done for Christ will last.

Life is but a vapour, as the years go in quickly. Determine to spend the rest of those years not in 'getting' but in sacrificially giving yourself to win the lost for Jesus. Make it your priority for the rest of your days to be treasure in God's eyes and if you have never accepted Him as Saviour make things well with your soul while there is still time.

90

God Shields His Children From The Attacks Of The Enemy

I read a book by Grace Livingston Hill called, 'Astra'. The name means 'Star' which I thought was beautiful. Astra was a beautiful, godly girl who had fled from her mother's cousin's house where she had lived since her father died (her mother was also gone). It was a very oppressive environment and Astra was treated harshly. When the family was at a wedding, she fled back to the place where she had grown up to consult her lawyer about her funds. She was to receive a massive inheritance from her late father's will when she turned twenty-one in a few days. However, the husband of her mother's cousin came after her planning to harm her and keep her fortune for himself. However, the Lord sent someone to protect her and the oppressor's evil plans were foiled. It made me think of these two Scriptures.

Isaiah 54:17 *"No weapon formed against thee shall prosper."*

Isaiah 59:19 *"When the enemy shall come in like a flood, the spirit of the Lord shall lift up a standard against him."*

The enemy does attack God's children at times. He can use people against us as weapons to harm us or come in like a flood to try and drown us. The enemy attacks those who are walking close to their Saviour's side, those who are in a deep close relationship with Himself, those who honour His word and have a passion for winning the souls of men and building up the saints.

Oh, he can attack! He can make you feel defeated and discouraged. That seems to be his favourite fiery dart to throw.

However absolutely no weapon that satan and his demons throw at you will be successful in destroying you for the Lord has promised to protect you.

No attack against your faith and integrity as a child of God can ever destroy you. No evil shall defeat you. Even if you lose your life here on earth for your love for God and willingness to stand for righteousness and His own name's sake, you will regain it in eternity.

No wonder it is a part of the Lord's prayer to *'deliver us from evil'* for the Lord knows satan will do all in his power to tear down the saints of God and stop them from extending God's Kingdom. Pray for the courage to overcome evil for good and do not be afraid for the Lord has promised to never leave thee nor forsake thee.

When the enemy comes in like a flood, the Spirit of God will make him flee. Even under attack, He wants us to keep raising our standards or in other words, keep flying the colours of Jesus for all to see and stand firm in faithfulness to Him and holiness. To raise your standard under attack will require boldness and faith in the face of opposition.

Even if it feels like the enemy has almost won, God is saying - no way! His armies are ready to do battle for you and are just hidden from your sight, ready to fight for you and they far outnumber any foes.

Trust till the danger is past. Keep asking God to deliver you from evil. Do not be afraid to proclaim 'Get behind me satan' when you feel powerless and always remember with God as your protector no weapon formed against you shall prosper.

91

From Weeping To Worship

Lamentations 3 *"He hath brought me into darkness... he hath broken my bones...he hath made me desolate... He hath filled me with bitterness... And I said my strength and my hope is perished from the Lord."*

What a place of thick darkness Jeremiah was in! Darkness, desolation, bitterness! His strength and hope were gone. In a deep depression, he voices his innermost feelings to God.

Have you ever been in the same place as Jeremiah was? A girl who contacted me a while back, who we will call Sarah, told me her story. Sarah's world had fallen apart. Every ounce of hope drained from her. Haunted by what she had been through, she could no longer cope. She loved God but the thick blackness in her spirit was weighing her down more and more every day. Then she snapped. She bought a pile of pills and sat down on the floor with two jugs of water. She swallowed six pills and then the presence of God filled the room and she felt like the Lord was holding her, stopping her from her self destruction. She lay on the floor with unending tears. She knew that her Lord was there in her darkness. She went from feeling like her life was over to worshipping her Lord through the tears for His presence was so strong. She rose comforted and determined to press on with her precious Lord by her side.

Jeremiah's feelings were like Sarah. He perfectly describes what it's like for your mind to be extremely sick with depression. Like Sarah, Jeremiah also went from a place of complete weeping to a place of worship.

When he got his eyes unto the Lord his hope was revived and he began to worship. He gets his eyes on the Lord's mercy, compassion, and faithfulness.

That is what happened to Sarah. When she felt like she had been consumed and devoured, the Lord in His great mercy and compassion saw His weary child about to break and that very same day she was worshipping Him for His love and faithfulness.

No matter what you are going through today, the Lord in His mercy, compassion and faithfulness will not let you be consumed. He is right there in your midst. He adores you and will comfort you and eventually restore you to a place of joy. You are deeply loved and held in the hands of the King of kings and Lord of lords.

One of my favourite hymns is 'O Love that wilt not let me go'. Its writer, George Matheson, had the pain of going blind. He asked his beloved fiancee if she would still marry him and her answer came like a dagger to his heart. "I do not want to be the wife of a blind man" were her words and she left him. But despite his great sorrow, anguish and weeping he turned his words to worship and penned these words.

> O Joy that seekest me through pain.
> I cannot close my heart to thee.
> I trace the rainbow through the rain,
> And feel the promise is not vain.
> That morn shall tearless be.

In his agony, he turned to God and worshipped Him for being the one love that would never let him go. He found joy amidst the pain and through it all he did not close his heart in anger to God. Despite his harsh circumstances and great sorrow he was still able to say 'I trace the rainbow through the rain!' What amazing faith!

If today you are like Jeremiah, Sarah, or George and feel nothing but the agony of heart, despite your tears, worship the Lord. He is still the God that sends rainbows during the rain.

92

Jo-Ann

1 Corinthians 10:13 *"There hath no temptation taken you but such is common to man: but God is faithful who will not suffer you to be tempted above that he are able; but will with the temptation also make a way of escape that ye may be able to bear it."*

That verse came to my mind after watching a true movie about a girl called Jo-Ann. The girl was born into a family that forced their daughter to sell her body to support the family. When the child was born - her grandfather tried to get rid of her by placing her at the side of the road. But later they heard cries on the doorstep. Someone had left little Jo-Ann back with a gold cross around her neck and a note that said, "God is watching and so am I". They had no choice but to bring the child back in. But Jo-Ann suffered nothing but abuse from the batterings of her grandfather, the absence of a mother who was out all the time selling her body and she had the cruellest words constantly spoken over her all the time.

But Jo-Ann found neighbouring people called Two Tall and Honey. She went there all the time. They eased her burden in the middle of her nightmare life and loved her like their own. Honey was Jo-Ann's constant encouragement, comfort, and support. However, the time came when the trial became worse than a living hell. Jo-Ann's mother had taken off and now her grandfather wanted her to fill her mother's shoes by earning money the same way as her mother had. He said he would kill her if she did not do it. Jo-Ann fled to Honey and Honey and her hubby gave her all the money in the world that they had saved and got her to escape the town with a dependable, kind stranger who drove her out of harms way. When things were at the state of complete breaking point God provided a way out in the nick of time. Jo-Ann had a lovely life after that. She married the soldier who had driven her to safety and raised a beautiful daughter who she loved the way Honey had loved her. God did not let His child break. She went through agony but the Lord did intervene with a way of escape from her continual trial.

The Lord provided a Honey for Jo-Ann during her trial. When the raging seas rolled she had someone in her life that encouraged her through it and helped her to bear it.

God is faithful and He will not let you go through anything that will break you in pieces. He knows exactly how much we can handle and He is our 'Honey' through it all. Our comforter, our encourager, the one who loves us, the one to whose arms we can flee every time we get distressed! During darkness, He is our light and He'll send us special encouragers throughout our journeys to help us find the strength to endure and bear it!

I know throughout my years of illness He has been my 'Honey' through it all. His arms have been the arms that held me when I cried and didn't think I could bear it anymore. His voice through His word has been my continual support system and encouragement as He whispers hope into my soul. He has used many people as His hands and feet to lift me when I am struggling. He has also promised to provide a way of escape. The day of my release from captivity has not come yet but it will!

The day of your release from captivity will come too. You might be suffering intensely today due to the trials of life but remember God is always good and faithful. Run into the arms of your precious comforter in the darkness. Listen for His voice through His Word and accept the ministrations from Angels in human form that God sends to sustain you. Hold on to the words He will *"make a way of escape".* You might not be able to see the wood for the trees now but you can trust the Lord to make a way where there doesn't seem to be a way.

93

The God Of The Unexpected

I was reading a book by Grace Livingston Hill called, *'The Story of a Whim'*. In it, a group of girls found an old piano in a house they were helping to clean. Unknown to them the house had previously been owned by extremely poor people. One of them found a forwarding address and out of kindness sent the piano to the address with a box of goodies filled with other things and also Sunday school books so her recipient could start a Sunday school wherever she now lived. They only knew that the recipient was called Christie and assumed her to be a female with not very much.

Christie turned out to be a man! A man who did not know the Lord. A hardened man who liked alcohol and to gamble. But he wrote back to Hazel thanking her and just let her continue to think he was a female! They corresponded back and forward and became dear friends. Hazel explained the way of Salvation to Christie after learning her new friend did not believe. Christie came to know the Saviour and did set up an outreach Sunday school. But as the letters continued he knew he was falling in love with this girl who still assumed she was writing to a female penpal!

Then out of the blue Hazel turned up at his house. She was so shocked that she had been sharing her heart with a man that she took off and had an accident, falling off her horse. She felt like the whole friendship had been a lie and everything he had told her had been a lie. She refused to see him but her friends went to visit his Sunday school and after hearing him pray they knew he was a real genuine believer and hadn't lied to Hazel about becoming a Christian.

Eventually, the random correspondence led to the two getting married! It made me think. God can truly work in unexpected ways at times. Through the girls' random act of kindness, she met her future spouse! It made me think of these scriptures from Exodus 6.

:1 *"Then the Lord said unto Moses. Now shalt thou see what I will do to Pharoah; for with a strong hand shall he let them go and with a strong hand shall he drive them out of the land."*

:7 *"I will bring you out from under the burden of the Egyptians and I will rid you of their bondage. And I will redeem you with a stretched out arm."*

The Israelites had grown so used to their bondage that they truly despaired. They could not see that during their struggle God had an unexpected rescue plan for them! The seemingly impossible. I do not think they could have imagined the rescue plan God had for them using His servant Moses. A curse of plagues and a hasty escape as Pharoah's armies chased them. They were at a dead end. A full sea separated them from safety.

Exodus 14:10 *"And they were sore afraid, and the children of Israel cried unto the Lord."*

It was an unexpected answer to prayer for God to answer by separating the whole sea so they would have a path to cross to safety! Can you imagine the look on their faces? That same sea did not part long enough to let Pharoah's army pass. They drowned while God's people went on to safety.

We pray but sometimes God can surprise us when we least expect it. The season of life the Israelites were in was no different from any other season. It was full of pain, harsh treatment, meagre rations, full of struggle, and deep anguish. I am sure they kept praying for God to deliver them but I'm sure they were shocked at the miraculous and unexpected way that He did so!

94

Divisions And Strife

I was listening to an online service where the Pastor was talking about treating others cruelly by our words. Not necessarily to their faces but behind backs. One group of Christians were fighting with another group of Christians in the church. Both parties were guilty of saying the cruellest things behind backs and it brought the Pastor deep grief. For here he and other Christians were busy trying to build the church and reach out to the lost, while these other fleshy carnal Christians were tearing down the church by their disunity.

He mentioned a time when his mother and father, himself and his aunt and uncle went together to visit an out of town Aunt and Uncle. While they were there the Aunt who had travelled with them praised her sister for everything from dinner to the way her home looked. Yet on the way back in the car, the same woman started a rant about how the food tasted like dog food and the decoration of the house looked a mess. To her sister's face, she'd been nice but behind her back she slandered her. There is nothing right about this kind of behaviour. You are proving yourself to be fake and you are dishonouring God with a cruel tongue.

Paul addressed the same problem in 1 Corinthians 1:10 *"Now I beseech you, brethren, by the name of our Lord Jesus Christ... That there be no divisions among you."*

:11 *"For it hath been declared unto me by them which are of the house of Chloe, that there are contentions among you."*

These scriptures speak out about contentions and arguments between Christians.

Proverbs 15:18 *"A wrathful man stirreth up strife but he that is slow to anger appeaseth strife."*

Proverbs 20:3 *"It is an honour for a man to cease from strife: but every fool will be meddling."*

Proverbs 29:22 *"An angry man stirreth up strife and a furious man aboundeth in transgressions."*

2 Timothy 2:24 *"And the servant of the Lord must not strive; but be gentle unto all men, apt to teach patient."*

While we are on earth we will not see eye to eye on everything. At times you must agree to disagree to keep the unity of the Spirit. Behaving in a quarrelsome way, slandering, stirring up strife, being full of anger and taking it out on others will have the effect of tearing down all your church's efforts to reach the lost. You and your hate sect are tearing it down brick by brick and the devil is loving it. When God's people aren't getting on, God's work comes to a halt.

So like the messenger from the house of Chloe to Paul, my message to you is to stop the infighting. Stop the contentions. Stop the strife. For if you don't stop you will continue to do great damage to the work of God. You cannot say you truly care about the souls of others and are deep in prayer for their Salvation if you are using your tongue like a flame of fire to burn every good work down.

Get your passion back for God, get out of that old dishonouring to God gossiping attitude, set out to make peace with those you have been slandering, forgive, encourage, build others up, be gentle, put away anger and instead of using your tongue the wrong way use it to see precious souls who are heading to a lost eternity won for Him. Be God's united army, ready to tear down the walls of the enemies darkness instead of tearing one another down.

95

God Makes All Things New

I read a book called, *'All Things New'* by Lynn Austin. It was based at the time of the American Civil War which was fought from 1861-1865 that broke out as a result of a long-standing controversy over slavery. As a result, slavery was abolished and four million slaves were freed. The reconstruction era (1866-1877) followed the war with the process of restoring national unity and granting civil rights to freed slaves.

The book featured a family called the 'Weatherlys' who were from the South and did not want slavery abolished. They felt it was their right to buy and own black human beings. When their side lost the war and they returned home to the South they found it hard. Old mindsets take a long time to die. They still felt it was their right to have slaves running their cotton plantation. The brother Daniel and his friends formed a rebellion group killing ex-slaves who they no longer possessed and burning down the ex-slave's new school. They even tried to kill the man who ran the office for finding slaves new jobs and helping them get started in their new way of life.

The mother also struggled with old mindsets about people not being created equal. She still classed people by their social standing, wealth, background etc. She was trying to live in the mindset of the old way and marry her daughters off to wealthy plantation owners whom they did not love.

Jo was the only one who started to adjust, to see how wrong their lifestyle had been. She became friends with Alexander (the man from the office that was helping the freed slaves). He helped her to understand things biblically about no man or woman being anyone's possession. She began to adjust. She started doing the former unheard-of things for a woman of class. Practical chores like planting food in the garden, washing dishes, sewing clothes etc. Things that outraged her mother. The mother was still of the mindset that these were black people's jobs.

But eventually, old mindsets did change. Jo fell in love with Alexander who had fought on the other side of the war, who was not even in her social rank! That would never have been allowed before the war! Slowly everyone began to see that this new way of life was better than the old ways. It was not just the slaves who became truly free after the war, it was the people of the South too who had been in bondage to destructive mindsets. The whole book reminded me of these scriptures.

Isaiah 43:19 *"Behold, I will do a new thing, now it shall spring forth, shall ye not know it? I will even make a way in the wilderness and rivers in the desert."*

Revelation 21:5 *"Behold I make all things new."*

Maybe the place you are in right now is like a wilderness, a dry place. You feel dead inside and do not know if your cries have reached God's ears.

In this Isaiah passage, the Lord is saying He is about to do a new thing in your life, and it will spring forth out of the blue, is a scripture I treasure.

Maybe your battle is not a physical illness but deep grief, depression, worry over a child or family member, a difficult marriage etc. But no matter where you are God has heard your cries as well as mine. It may feel like it is taking forever but the Lord has promised to do a new thing! Like the slaves, we will emerge from darkness into light. God is going to make a way in our wilderness and rivers in the desert. It shall surely come. It will spring forth suddenly and we will stand in awe at the marvellous way the Lord has answered our prayers and made things new for us.

96

Our Lily Of The Valley.

Sometimes when I receive flowers lilies are among them. It caused me to do some research into the lily flower. The lilies main meanings are royalty, humility, purity, and fruitfulness. Greek and Roman brides were often given a crown of lilies in the hope of a pure and fruitful life. If a lady in Victorian times was given a lily, she knew it was from someone who adored her. Chinese people give them to others who have lost loved ones because they believe them to relieve heartache. With its three petals, the lily is often considered a trinity symbol holding the representation of the three virtues - Charity, Hope and Faith.

Song of Solomon 2:1 *"I am the Rose of Sharon and the Lily of the Valley."*

Jesus is royalty. He was mightier than kings and emperors, yet He was humble. He compared Himself to a humble flower. He is royalty yet humbled Himself to die on a cruel cross. Jesus calls us to be humble. Humble means having or showing a modest or low estimate of your importance, meek, respectful, unpresuming, submissive, and free from vanity.

Jesus calls us to walk in His shoes. To not be puffed up, to put others needs before our own. If we are puffed up with pride, we will put others off coming to Him but if we walk in His humble shoes many will be attracted to Him through you.

Proverbs 11:2 *"When pride cometh, then cometh shame but with the lowly is wisdom.*

Proverbs 22:4 *"By humility and fear of the Lord are riches, and honour, and life."*

Walking in lowliness and humility of mind brings great favour in the Lord's eyes. He cannot bless the puffed up but promises honour to the humble. Jesus was also the perfect picture of purity for He never once sinned. He was clean in His Father's eyes.

The whiteness of lilies denotes holiness. It is said of the bride, the lamb's wife (the church) that she shall be arrayed in fine linen, clean and white. For clean linen represents the righteousness of the saints. (Revelation 19:7-8)

We are called to a pure life. One that honours our Saviour not one that is filled with the garbage of the world. He wants us free from putting vile images into our minds, clean from anger, bitterness, swearing and a list of other sins. Only when we have a pure heart can we truly expect to know God in prayer and be classed as a vessel of honour (2 Timothy 2:21) in His eyes. The line to the old hymn goes, "When the bridegroom cometh will your robes be white, pure and white in the blood of the lamb." Will they? If Jesus returned to earth this week would He find us in pure white, sin-free garments or would He be disappointed?

Matthew 5:8 *"Blessed are the pure in heart for they shall see God."*

True pureness of heart brings intimate friendship with your King. Are you 'lily-white' like your 'Lily of the Valley'?

Jesus is exceedingly fruitful. It is observed that one lily root puts forth fifty bulbs. He is the root from which the church has sprang! He is calling His children to be fruitful in bringing souls to Him and fruitful in living a God honouring life.

Genesis 1:28 *"Be fruitful and multiply."*

He wants us to truly care about being fruitful for Him, truly caring for the souls of men. So remember today, your 'Lily of the Valley' is humble, pure and fruitful and He wants us to follow in His footsteps.

97

Not Forever The Victim

I watched a true film about a girl who moved to New York in the hope of becoming a model. She made it big time but there was a problem, a stalker would not leave her alone. Eventually, the stalker determined to destroy her life. So he got two of his friends to attack her with razor blades. They destroyed her face leaving it covered in deep scars. He took away from her the ability to have a career in modelling any longer. What the girl said at the end of the film struck me, "He may have taken my face, but he didn't take my life. I do not see myself as a victim. I see myself as a survivor and have my whole life in front of me."

The girl went on to work with victims of awful crimes in a counselling centre for the rest of her life. Her story made me recall these scriptures.

2 Corinthians 4:8-9 *"We are troubled on every side, yet not distressed, we are perplexed but not in despair. Persecuted but not forsaken, cast down but not destroyed."*

Paul was declaring himself not to be a victim but an overcomer. He was saying... yes on every road we turn we are troubled but not distressed, perplexed but not in despair, persecuted but not forsaken, cast down but not destroyed.

Believer's Bible Commentary (page 1835)

"Troubled on every side means that he is constantly pressed by adversaries and difficulties, yet not completely hindered from uttering the message freely. Perplexed but not in despair. From the human standpoint, Paul did not know there could be a solution to his difficulties and yet the Lord never allowed him to reach the place of despair. Persecuted but not forsaken. At times he could feel the hot breath of the enemy on the back of his neck, yet the Lord never abandoned him to his enemies. Cast down but not destroyed means that Paul was many times wounded in action. Yet the Lord raised him to go with the glorious news of the Gospel."

You will not forever be cast down! You are an overcomer and even though things are awful at the minute you will not be a victim of your circumstances forever. You will rise victorious! Paul did and so will you! You will live again and no longer be in a place of constant bruising.

1 John 5:4 *"For whatsoever is born of God overcometh the world and this is the victory that overcometh the world even our faith."*

You will not be overcome, you will overcome. You will not be the victim you will be the victor and God will use all the hard knocks that have come against you greatly for His glory.

98

Greater Things To Come

Habakkuk 1:5 *"For I will work a work in your days, which ye will not believe, though it be told you."*

In other words, you are not going to be able to dream that it is possible, the way I will work things out.

I read a book called *'Brentwood'* by Grace Livingston Hill. In the story, the girl knew she was adopted and always felt an emptiness and sadness about why her birth mother had rejected her. When both her adoptive parents passed away, within months of each other, she found a letter addressed to herself from her adoptive mother explaining that her real mother had wanted her. The adoptive father had manipulated the situation to get what he wanted - a baby for his wife.

As the birth mother's husband was near to death and the child's twin sister was born extremely sick, he told the birth mum that if she gave up the other twin to them, he would pay for her husband's medical care. He also told lies about how the sickly twin would die without expensive surgery which he would pay for. The poor woman was desperately sick herself and gave in to the blackmail so her husband and the other child could live. A year later the real parents tried to get their child back, but the adoptive parents would not allow it.

Hesitantly, Marjorie went to meet her birth parents. She had never been told anything about them and what a reunion it was! The girl who felt rejected and unwanted all her life could not have dreamt possible how much she was loved and wanted. She would never have dreamt God could work things out that far exceeded her wildest dreams.

The beauty of the story made me think of the verse in Ephesians 3:20

"Now unto him that is able to do exceeding abundantly above all that we could ask or think."

Maybe the season of your life today is extremely dry and bleak. In this season, I am fighting chronic illness every day and wondering if I am ever going to get a chance to live again. I am writing this from a place of faith that the Word of God has given me.

- I will work a work in your day that you couldn't even dream possible!

- I am the one who can do exceeding, abundantly above all that I could ask or think!

Powerful statements!

We cannot always see how a situation is going to turn out but God can! And He is reminding you and me of His mighty power to do things that our minds could not even conjure up!

Child of God if you are struggling today, if you really cannot see the wood for the trees, if you feel desolate and hopeless then this word is for you. Leave your situation at His feet and believe that these scriptures are promises to you and trust Him to work things out in His time.

Child, in darkness, I see your pain.
Though you can't see it now
it's for yours and others gain.
Watch and see what I will do.
Let those dead dreams once again reign.
Your barren dry season
will be turned to one of abundant rain.

99

Amazing Grace

I finished a book called, *'Eve's Daughters'* by Lynn Austin. It had such a strong message throughout it of the amazing grace of our Lord and Saviour. It spanned four generations of women from great grandmother to great-granddaughter. It was Grandmother Emma's story that struck me the most. In her youth, Emma sinned. She felt like her sin was too big for God to forgive so she lived an anti-God life until she had a defining moment at eighty years old when she finally ran into her Saviour's arms, repented and was restored unto Him.

There was a scripture quoted in it that clearly showed the gracious mercy of Jesus in a situation that others considered unforgivable.

John 8:3-4 *"And the scribes and Pharisees brought unto him a woman caught in adultery. Master this woman was taken in adultery in the very act."*

According to the law of Moses, both the man and the woman were to be stoned to death. They were bringing her to Jesus to trap Him and get Him to contradict the law of Moses. If they could succeed in that then they could turn the people against Jesus.

Jesus did not instantly reply. He stooped down and started writing in the sand. There have been many theories as to what He was writing but I favour this one. He was writing out a list of the sins of the people standing around Him. For when He did speak, He said, *"He that is without sin among you, let him cast the first stone."*

Again He began to write on the ground. Convicted by their consciences they all left, and it was just Jesus left standing with the woman.

:10 *"Woman, where are thine accusers. Hath no man condemned thee? To which she replied no and Jesus said he didn't condemn her either.*

:11 *"Jesus said unto her. Neither do I condemn thee: go and sin no more."*

Jesus in His wonderful grace saved her from being stoned. He also forgave her and told her to no longer continue in sin. Jesus does not approve of sin in any way but once He has forgiven you, He asks you to no longer live in sin.

What is Grace? It is the love of God shown to the unlovely: the peace of God given to the restless, the unmerited favour of God. Grace is the opposite of 'Karma' which is all about getting what you deserve. Grace is about getting what you do not deserve and not getting what you do deserve. Grace was Jesus sacrificing Himself on a cross in your place so that if you ask His forgiveness and ask Him to be your Saviour - you will not go to a lost eternity. There is no system of works to get to Heaven - Jesus paid the price in full. It is by His grace that we live every day as Christians. It is by His grace that says you are forgiven, go and sin no more when we repent of things that have come between us and our Saviour.

His love and grace are so deep and merciful. Think of that adulterous woman left alone with Jesus. By law she deserved death but Jesus forgave her and set her free. It is by this wonderful Grace that He sustains us in times of sickness, pain, and grief. I would be lost without His endless Grace to carry me through.

If you do not know Jesus as Saviour, then do accept His gift of Grace today. If you are a Christian who constantly condemns and judges yourself and beats yourself up, then STOP for if He in His Grace has forgiven you then you don't need to torment yourself with self-condemnation!

100

The Lesson From The Quilt

I read a book called, *'The Beloved Christmas Quilt'* by Wanda Brunstetter. It was an Amish book. It told the story of a quilt that had been passed down through three generations from grandmother to granddaughter. Each had their trials in life to face. To begin with, Luella wanted to marry a man sixteen years older than herself. It was a love so deep, but her parents banned it as they said he was too old for her. But after weeks of seeing her heartbreak and agony of heart over this, they finally agreed to let their daughter marry the man she loved.

The next story featured Luella's daughter Karen and her marriage problems and dealing with a child with a disability. The third story featured Karen's eldest daughter Rose-Anna who was to be married but her groom ran out on her on their wedding day. Through all these trials they found great comfort in the scripture that was sewn into the quilt.

Psalm 31:3 *"For thou art my rock and my fortress, therefore for thy name's sake lead me and guide me."*

In this psalm, David was deeply distressed. He asked the Lord to be his rock of refuge for he knew only his God was steadfast and immovable in a time when he felt like he was falling apart. He cried to the Lord to be his fortress in which he could hide through peril. He knew God was his only defence and security.

A fortress is a castle or other well-protected place which is intended to be difficult for enemies to enter. In other words, a source of support. God was being his fortress, his defence and protector in his time of darkness. Hiding in God his fortress, meant no harm could come to him.

The image of God as a rock emphasises God's strength. A large rock is strong and solid, just like the Lord. Thus a rock can provide security. You can hide under a rock while being pursued by enemies or use it as a cover to avoid the heat of the day or a soaking rainstorm. Thus a rock can be your salvation. (Psalm 62:2)

Charles Wesley once described God as a rock of refuge like this:

> Other refuge have I none.
> Hangs my helpless soul on thee.
> Leave, O leave me not alone,
> Still support and comfort me.

I thought these were such beautiful words. In seasons of distress and anguish, we can run into the arms of our rock and fortress, the Saviour who wants to cradle us, shelter us, and protect us and bring us through the storm.

David went on to ask for leading and guidance from God in his anguish. He truly believed God's promise to deliver the righteous even in his time of turmoil.

As we pilgrim through a barren land that brings times of great sorrow and confusion the Lord has promised to lead us and guide us no matter what situation we are in. We are weak but through it all, He is mighty and is holding us with His powerful hand.

If your life is a very troubled and confusing place right now then run into the arms of the one who is the rock and fortress. Trust Him to keep you safe until the storm ceases and to provide the answers and the leading you need amidst anguish.

One thing is for sure, if you place it all in His strong arms, He will always come through for you, in His time.

101

The Prodigal Girl

I finished reading a book by Grace Livingston Hill called, *'The Prodigal Girl'*. Like the story of 'The Prodigal Son' she was in complete rebellion against God, yet what struck me in both stories was the deep love of their father's, welcoming their rebellious offspring home with deep unconditional and deep forgiving love. Both these stories reminded me of the book of Hosea.

In the book of Hosea, he married Gomer. (1:2) *"Go take thee a wife of whoredoms."*

She bore him three children. Gomer was unfaithful and despite this Hosea sought her in great love and bought his wife back from slavery and degradation. The book of Hosea is a parable - showing God's love for His sinful people.

Imagine marrying a woman who was given to whoredom at the Lord's command. Imagine Hosea going to a public market to buy back his faithless wife from her sin. Like the nation of Israel, she was unfaithful to Jehovah, she ran after other lovers (idols). But God bought her back. God's people were destroyed for lack of knowledge, they had abandoned the law of God - they gave into unfaithfulness, unkindness, irreligion, swearing, lying, killing, stealing, and adultery to name but a few. They were God's prodigal children.

4:16 *"For Israel slideth back as a backsliding heifer."*

God was still loving them and calling them back to Himself. God cannot tolerate sin, but He continues to reach out to and love His children until they return to Him in repentance for their sin.

6:1 *"Come and let us return to the Lord and he will heal us."*

8:14 and 9:1 *"For Israel hath forgotten his maker... thou hast gone a whoring from thy God."*

They had deeply corrupted themselves. Despite their wicked ways, chapter fourteen shows His patient mercy and call for them to come back to the one who loves them without measure.

14:1 :4-5 *"O Israel, return unto the Lord thy God, for thou hast fallen by thine iniquity. I will heal their backsliding. I will love them freely, for mine anger is turned away from him. I will be as the dew unto Israel, he shall grow as the Lily and cast forth his roots as Lebanon."*

What radical Love! God's people had committed the most horrendous sins. Yet when they returned to the arms of their loving Father and repented of their sins, He promised to heal their backsliding, love them freely, and turn His anger from them. The picture of restoration is beautiful. Can you imagine a love like that!

Maybe you are a prodigal child of God today. You were once on fire for the Lord, but rebellion and sin have taken you away. His call to you is to return unto me and I will heal your backsliding and love you freely and restore a right relationship between you and I. What boundless love to think that even though He cannot tolerate sin, He is standing watching out for you to return to Him with loving arms of mercy and grace. Child of God who has gone astray, please return to the arms of your loving God even now for He is waiting for you with arms of love open wide. Run into those Heavenly arms of love even now for the lover of your soul patiently awaits.

102

Asters

For my birthday I was bought a pair of blue earrings that were in the shape of the flower blue Asters. Asters are a daisy-like flower that has grown wild since ancient times. They represent patience, love, elegance, and daintiness. With their wildflower beauty and lush textures, they have been considered an enchanted flower. In ancient times it was thought that the perfume from their burning leaves could drive away evil serpents. Asters come from the Greek word 'Star' and its star-like flowers have been found in a rainbow of colours - white, red, pink, purple, lavender and blue with mostly yellow centres. Its meaning of 'star' brings to my mind a verse from Daniel.

> Daniel 12:3 *"And they that be wise shall shine as the brightness of the firmament (the expanse of the heavens) and they that turn many to righteousness as the stars forever and ever."*

Or in other words, those who lead many to Salvation will shine forever brightly like the stars. Stars in the night light up the canvas of the sky. So, God wants us to light up the dark canvas of the world.

Like Asters the Lord wants us to be bright shining flowers for His glory who will lead many to a saving knowledge to Himself. Do you care for the souls of others? Do you go out of your way to be a witness? Do you care about where your friends, relatives, workmates, college mates, etc spend eternity? Have you tried to make the way clear even if it is uneasy? Dare to be a bright star for God who leads many to know Jesus as Saviour.

Patience is also a meaning for Asters. It is not easy to have patience when you have been in a waiting season for a long time.

We can get impatient and frustrated and want God to do things in our time.

Habakkuk 2:3 *"For the vision is yet for an appointed time, but at the end it shall speak, though it tarry, wait for it, because it will surely come, it will not tarry."*

No one likes waiting in traffic, in supermarket queues, in dentists/doctors' offices etc. But what is harder, is waiting for something that the Lord has promised you will come to pass. The Lord is saying even though it feels to you like it is tarrying too long, wait, for it shall surely come! Patience is one of the fruits of the Spirit and means forbearance, endurance, and composure. Keep looking to God to bring to pass what He has promised and in your waiting room time know that He is still working for your good!

Asters are a symbol of love. The famous love passage of 1 Corinthians 13 truly tells us how to love one another as Jesus does.

Love never gives up.
Love cares for others more than self.
Love doesn't want what it doesn't have.
Love doesn't strut, doesn't have a swelled head.
Love doesn't force itself on others.
Love doesn't fly off the handle.
Love doesn't keep score of the sins of others.
Love doesn't revel when others grovel.
Love takes pleasure in the flowering of truth.
Love puts up with anything.
Love trusts God always.
Love always looks for the best.
Love never looks back but keeps going till the end.

Loving like this will cause our hearts to be moulded into the image of Christ and then we will become true bright stars who shine for His glory and lead many others to Christ.

103

In The Most Horrific Times,
God Is Still There

I finished a book by Colleen Coble called, *'The View from Rainshadow Bay'*. The book was about a series of murders that were happening in the area. It was a dangerous time and the killer had made it clear that another woman was his target. As it unravelled, all the killings were in aid of feeding one man's greed. A man who was well known in the community and whom people never suspected. One of the main characters kept saying that God was in control through it all.

Horrific things do not happen because God wants them too. But He has given man free will to either choose Him or choose sin. Sadly most choose the latter and great calamities and horrific times happen in this land and all over the world. I am thinking of all the school shootings in America were people took the lives of so many schoolchildren. In one book *'Rachel's Tears'*, her parents give an account of how it made them feel when they lost their daughter in a school shooting. They were confused, they asked God why their beautiful sixteen-year-old daughter was snatched away from them.

Excerpt from her mother: "I remember being in so much pain. I went home to a sleepless night, haunted by the memory of a beautiful girl who had been the joy of my life. I wept till there was nothing left but dry sobs. That night I could not see the positive impact her life and death would have on millions of people. All I could see was a huge hole in my future that could never be replaced. There are some things worse than physical torture or death. Losing a child is one of them. But God preserved me when I felt I was falling apart."

Some days she felt the absence of God so strongly that like the Psalmist she had to cry out:

Psalm 13:1-2 *"How long, O Lord? Will you forget me forever? How long will you hide your face from me? How long must I wrestle with my thoughts and everyday have sorrow in my heart."*

Maybe you have lived through something awful or are going through something awful now. Let me encourage you that when all around you, you sense nothing but confusion and have so many unanswered questions, God is still there in the midst. He will never leave you comfortless even when tragedy is so great that you question Him.

Let these scriptures encourage you:

Psalm 9:9-10 *"The Lord also will be a refuge for the oppressed, a refuge in times of trouble... thou Lord hast not forsaken them that seek thee."*

Psalm 27:5 *"For in the time of trouble he shall hide me in his pavilion... He shall set me upon a rock."*

Job 5:11 *"To set up on high those that be low, that those who mourn might be exalted to safety."*

He is in your oppression. He remains in times of trouble. He sees your mourning and will exalt you to safety. Even if you are confused and in pain, He is your still your Saviour.

104

What We Can Learn From Honeysuckle

I just read a book called, *'Honeysuckle Dreams'* by Denise Hunter. What struck me is that even though it was an unusual choice, the bride wanted to have honeysuckle in her bridal bouquet because of its meaning.

Honeysuckle signifies happiness. It also means a sweet disposition which might relate to the sweet-smelling aroma that the flowers have. Honeysuckle's main meaning is devoted affection.

Among the French, giving honeysuckle to a partner represents generous love. It also represents tenderness. Honeysuckle vines are extremely hardy and difficult to kill once established in a garden. This attribute contributes to the honeysuckle's meaning of devotion and lasting bonds.

What beauty! What inspiration! There are so many spiritual parallels and lessons from scripture.

Devotion means, love, loyalty, faithfulness, trueness, admiration, and care. Affection means, fondness, tenderness, and warm-heartedness.

Romans 12:10 *"Be kindly, affectioned one to another with brotherly love, in honour preferring one another."*

Ephesians 4:32 *"And be ye kind one to another, tenderhearted, forgiving one another, even as God for Christ's sake hath forgiven you."*

Ephesians 5:1 *"And walk in love as Christ also hath loved us and hath forgiven us."*

Hebrews 13:1 *"Let brotherly love continue."*

The Lord is calling us to be Honeysuckles for His glory. To be of a sweet disposition and put away all bitterness of spirit, complaining and gossip. He wants us to treat one another as if we were ministering to Him alone in devotion and affection. We live in an age where too many people are too caught up in their own lives to care about others, but God is calling us to be different. We are to be kind and affectionate one to another with brotherly love, putting others needs before our own. We are to be kind, tender-hearted, and forgiving. We are to walk in love. We are to be devoted to one another. He wants His children by their fruits to be shining lights in a dark world for Him.

To become like Honeysuckle requires great effort on our part, just like Jesus went to extreme measures for us. It means being an encouragement, lifting others, doing all in your power to meet others needs despite the busyness of life. If you begin to selflessly pour out, Jesus will begin to selflessly pour in, your cup will run over, and you will be reaching people that you never dreamt you could reach. Demonstrating the devotion, lovingkindness, and affection of your Saviour paves the way for miracles. You could be someone's angel of blessing in their desperation. Years ago the young people at church sang this song:

I surrender to You.
Lord, I'm giving all I am to You.
You have captivated me.
And I come to give my devotion.

When you surrender all to your Saviour and in practical ways by touching the lives of others, He will use your hands and feet to meet an abundance of needs! He needs all your affection and devotion and sweetness. You are His Honeysuckle child!

105

Maris - The Testing

I read a book called, 'Maris', by Grace Livingston Hill. Maris was a girl who had let her walk with the Lord fade and had gotten into a relationship with an extremely wealthy young man who had no interest in God. They were to be married that June but something awful happened - her mother took ill. She lingered on the brink of death for weeks. Her younger sister took sick too and her father was not overly well with burn out from overworking. Maris threw herself into caring for her family. She told her fiancé Tilford, that they would need to delay the wedding as she could not get married with her mother on the brink of death.

In those circumstances, she sadly discovered Tilford's true colours. He was angry and said that he didn't care whether or not her mother lived or died, he said that the engagement ring on her finger was proof that she was his possession and he would not accept a cancelled wedding. He was unsupportive, harsh, demanding and so Maris broke things off. In the weeks that followed with all the pain and suffering under her roof, she began to walk with her Saviour once more and went from strength to strength in Him. Her friend told her that perhaps God allowed these dire circumstances to turn her eyes back on her Lord again and to see how desperately she needed Him.

As I read the book, I felt so happy that Maris was no longer in Tilford's care. For a man to treat a woman as his possession does not show true love, it shows a controlling and abusive mindset. The testing that came upon Maris worked for her spiritual good and His glory.

1 Peter 1:5-6 *"Who are kept by the power of God through faith unto salvation... wherein ye greatly rejoice though*

now for a season, if need be, ye are in heaviness through manifold temptations. That the trial of your faith, being much more precious than of gold that perisheth though it be tried by fire, might be found unto the praise and honour and glory at the appearing of Jesus Christ."

There was a purpose to Maris's testing. Through it all, she was kept by the power of God but He did have her in a season of heaviness through great trials, that after her faith had been tried with fire she would emerge so beautiful, like that of a sparkling diamond. It was just for a season. This pain and suffering were not a permanent dwelling place for her.

Do you know that refiners use fire to purify gold? When all the impurities are gone you are left with 24-carat gold. In Maris's case, her test was to burn away impurities so she could return to and be found as pure gold in her Saviour's eyes. Jesus said we need not fear the fire, because God, the refiner, watched the process so closely that He keeps track of the exact number of hairs on our head.

Not everyone who is going through a trial is because they have let their love for God cool. Job was the Godliest man on earth, yet he suffered so much. I knew so many Godly saints that were always on fire for God before severe Illness set in.

Like Maris, you are going to come through this trial! You are adored and loved by the King. If suffering comes, do not be afraid for the Lord is using it so He can shine forth with His glory even greater than before.

Like Maris - this heaviness is *'but for a season'* and through it all the Lord is leading you! Yes, I said 'through' this is not a permanent dwelling place. Take courage, God's hand is still mightily upon your life and you will emerge like 24-carat gold!

Job 23:10 *"He knoweth the way that I take and when he hath tried me, I shall come forth as gold."*

106

Vessels For God To Pour His Comfort Through

2 Corinthians 1:3-6 *"Blessed be God... the God of all comfort which comforteth us in ALL our tribulation that we may be able to comfort them which are in trouble, by the comfort where with we ourselves are comforted of God. For as the sufferings of Christ abound in us so our consolation also aboundeth by Christ. And whether we be afflicted, it is for your consolation and salvation."*

Stacey Marie "Our suffering allows us to be a support for others. So often we go through these things with limited support but God allows us to shine our light by being there emotionally for others who are going through a hard time and might not have support in a similar situation to the way we haven't had it."

Through all my years of illness amid distress and affliction the Lord has sent comfort to me. At times when I thought I was left 'comfortless' because so many 'friends' walked away wanting nothing to do with a sick friend, the Lord met with me. Many a time I have sensed His supernatural presence as I have wept in His arms in the middle of the night.

Paul also was abandoned by many whiles in prison, but he was determined to share with others the comfort he had received from the Lord in his moments of anguish. He passed on the encouragement and comfort to others in need. He did not just keep it to himself. Paul believed that he had been afflicted for others encouragement, even Salvation. Others would see how God had given him a special grace to endure the hardest of times and come to know his Saviour. Paul always seemed to be able to trace the rainbow through the tears.

Before I took sick amidst the busyness of life, I would have written many encouragement cards. After I took sick and read this passage, I determined in my heart that I was going to let the Lord use my affliction for the encouragement of fellow believers and the Salvation of those who are yet without Him. I determined I was not going to drown in self-pity but follow in Paul's example. I have done all in my power to give, to find ways to share the Gospel and be a channel of blessing and comfort for my Master. The chorus to an old hymn goes:

> Make me a channel of blessing today.
> Make me a channel of blessing I pray.
> My life possessing, My service blessing.
> Make me a channel of blessing today.

Maybe your life is extremely painful right now - but your suffering is not without purpose. The purpose of your suffering is that though you are broken you will be a spilt out, sacrificial, comforter and soul winner.

Just because you are in the valley of hardship does not mean that you are no longer needed or no longer useful in the Lord's service. This might be the most fruitful time of your life. The only thing that can block you from being a channel of blessing is your selfishness, not being able to see past yourself and your needs so you stop caring for others.

Let Jesus spill out of you amidst your suffering and use you as a fresh river spring from Him - your source, your precious comforter and just watch what He will do!

Determine now to let God make you fruitful in the land of your suffering.

107

Joanna

Luke 8:2-3 *"And certain women which had been healed of evil spirits and infirmities, Mary called Magdalene... And Joanna the wife of Chuza, Herod's steward, and Susanna and many others which ministered unto him of their substance."*

A few years ago, in my quiet time, the healing of Joanna encouraged me at a black time in my life. I felt strongly at that time that if the Lord could heal Joanna, He also could heal me.

Joanna is my closest biblical namesake, for like John and Joanne it means God is gracious or the Lord gives graciously. Her healing gave me hope in my suffering, of a day when I too will be free from the shackles of illness.

Joanna was a woman of high rank in Herod's court. She responded to the Lord's healing touch by giving herself totally, supporting His ministry and following Him wherever He went! Little did she know that her kindness to the Lord did not go unnoticed or unrecorded. Little did she think as she shared her possessions with Jesus, that Christians of all subsequent ages would read of her generosity and hospitality!

Even though if Herod had caught wind of Joanna being a Jesus follower, unlike Nicodemus she made no effort to hide her admiration for Jesus and provide for His needs from her purse. Even if it had cost her life, Joanna pledged complete allegiance to her Lord. She also had the joy of being one of the women at the empty tomb to witness Jesus risen from the dead. Joanna discovered great joy that day! She went to the tomb to grieve and instead her sorrow turned into great joy.

These are the lessons I see from Joanna's life.

1: Determine to be one of life's givers, not takers. Even if you have not experienced a breakthrough in your situation, continue to serve God through the pain. Give, bring others joy and minister to needs. Proverbs 11:25 says, *"The liberal soul shall be made fat."* Joanna has gone down in history for her generosity in her Master's service, determine to do likewise.

2: Joanna was fearless in her devotion to her Master even though it may have cost her life. We live in the Laodicean church age where no one wants to stand for Biblical truth anymore. An age of compromise with the world. Dare to be a Joanna and stand firm on God's word and speak out for Him even when it's unpopular for the Lord will reward your courage and fearlessness greatly.

3: Her Sorrow was turned into joy.

Psalm 30:5 *"Weeping may endure for a night, but joy cometh in the morning."*

Think of Joanna's agony of heart when she saw her beloved Saviour and healer dying on a cruel cross. Imagine her inner anguish! Yet she was one of the first to witness the empty tomb and share in the precious miracle of our Lord's resurrection. What is causing you great pain and sorrow today? What is causing your pillow to be wet with tears? What is causing you sorrow of heart, depression, and despair? Then let me encourage you, dear friend, that in God's time you will see your sorrow turned into joy. The Lord knows how long you have suffered, and He loves and cares for you. He will bring you joy again after your long season of pain. Do not lose heart, you are so precious to Him.

108

Liberty Versus Bondage

Galatians 5:1 *"Stand fast therefore in the liberty wherewith Christ hath made us free, and be ye not entangled again with the yoke of bondage."*

I once knew a girl that inspired me so much faith wise. She was devoted to her Saviour. She adored Him. She knew His word inside out and every conversation with her was about God. She prioritised spending time each day with her beloved Lord in prayer and Bible study. She did not tolerate anything that hinted of worldliness or compromise by going hand in hand with satan into places that she could not take her beloved Lord with her. Her fire and passion for souls was a bright shining light that inspired all around her. I knew nobody more devout and solid faith wise than this girl.

But then gradual differences began to show every time we met up for coffee. She stopped reading her Bible and praying every day saying it was too legalistic and she wanted to be more of a free spirit. Then she started to skip church and go to pubs with non-Christian friends. Pubs, nightclubs, and alcohol were once things she was extremely against. Then she hit the club scene and started sleeping around (Note all sex outside of marriage is called fornication and greatly grieves God's heart. His design for intimacy was to be in a stable marriage relationship. Anything outside it is Sin). The girl now avoids all contact with all Christians. The changes were gradual - like the song says, *'People never crumble in a day'*. I grieved deeply over this beloved girl going from liberty in Christ to total bondage and enslavement with the world.

Bondage means, the state of being a slave, oppression, domination. When worldliness starts to take over, people choose to run with satan and the world over walking with their Saviour and they lose their liberty. No man can serve two masters - you are either wholly God's or wholly satan's. There is no in-between.

1 John 2:15 *"Love not the world, neither the things that are in the world, if any man love the world, the love of the Father is not in him."*

1 Corinthians 10:21 *"Ye cannot drink the cup of the Lord and the cup of devils: ye cannot be partakers of the Lord's table and the table of devil's."*

You cannot be at bars and nightclubs on a Saturday night and then come to the breaking of bread service on Sunday mornings and take the Lord's cup after spending the night drinking satan's cup. It is either or - no in between.

You cannot sit on the fence. You are either a Jesus follower or a satan follower. There is no middle ground. Your freedom to know Christ and be saved cost Him His life so why give in to the flesh and go back to bondage.

Have you lost your first love - our precious Saviour because you have gone lukewarm with compromising with the world? You go through the motions of church and maybe have others fooled about your spiritual state but in your secret heart, Jesus is no longer Lord of all and if Jesus isn't Lord of all, He's not Lord at all.

Your first love is calling you back into His arms today to repent and be wholly restored to Him. He wants to light your fire that once burned bright and clear with a purity of heart, devotion, and passion for souls again. He is calling you to liberty from sin and to be no longer bound in a yoke of bondage. He gave everything for us, and he is calling us to surrender everything to Him. Whose side are you leaning on? The Saviour's side or satan's side? Do you delight His heart or bring Him sorrow? Choose ye this day whom ye shall serve.

109

A Sacrifice Of Thanksgiving

1 Samuel 7:12 *"Then Samuel took a stone and set it between Mizpah and Shen, and named it Ebenezer, saying 'thus far has the Lord helped us."*

In this passage, the Lord heard the Children of Israel's cry for to deliver them in battle.

:9 *"Samuel cried unto the Lord for Israel and the Lord heard him."*

So, in thanksgiving for the Lord's deliverance, he laid down a memorial so the people would not forget what the Lord had done. Ebenezer means *'stone of help'*. The Israelites had suffered defeat at a different place called Ebenezer and it seems like Samuel deliberately reapplied the name to record the first Israelite victory over the Philistines.

There have been many times where I have laid before God, my Ebenezer, out of thanksgiving for His help in keeping me from defeat.

I can recall many memorials in my mind that were seasons of great joy. Every time I remember them, I thank the Lord. Every time of joy before illness, I have hidden in my heart as a memorial! Through all the pain of illness, I have still thanked God for being my help. Thanksgiving and praise in both seasons of great joy and seasons of great sadness. The Lord loves His people to have thankful hearts!

Psalm 9:1 *"I will give thanks to you Lord with all my heart. I will tell of your wondrous deeds."*

Psalm 100:4 *"Enter his gates with thanksgiving and his courts with praise."*

1 Thessalonians 1:18 *"In everything give thanks: for it is the will of God in Christ Jesus concerning you."*

I remember with fondness and thanksgiving the 'on a high', joyous times in my life. The night of my baptism is one of the best. The joy at exam results. The days spent in the fields for hours seeking God and receiving mighty promises from Him.

The friendships He has blessed me with. Graduation day getting my theology degree. Seasons of rejoicing with friends over engagement, wedding, and baby news. Precious times with family. Leading precious souls to my Saviour at the church youth club, CEF camps, and outreach from Bible College.

Oh, how I praised Him in those high times! But even now in suffering, I can still bring Him a sacrifice of thanksgiving and praise. I can thank Him for being my daily help. I can thank Him for His precious word that I adore. I can lift my voice in worship along with the online services. When I feel really low due to all the suffering, I thank Him for my care from my family, the friends who love me, food, water, warmth, the books I read, the cups of tea that I enjoy. I can thank Him for an endless list of things. For in the joys and the sorrows my God has been good to me and continues to be good to me and be my ever-present help even on days when I feel like I'm walking through the valley of the shadow of death.

My name means God is gracious. He has never stopped being good and faithful and He will never stop! I do not like the land of suffering at all. I want to be healed and better. But no matter what, I will continue to choose thanksgiving, to choose praise, to choose to be grateful and not hard-hearted or bitter. Choose to raise Him up today no matter what your circumstances.

110

The Masterpiece

Ephesians 2:10 *"For we are God's masterpiece. He has created us anew in Christ Jesus, so we can do the good things, he planned for us long ago."*

The word 'Masterpiece' means a work of outstanding artistry, skill, or workmanship or in other words, a wonder, sensation, triumph, showpiece, gem, or prize.

I read, *'The Masterpiece'* by Francine Rivers. It was a very complex, yet intriguing book based on the lives of two people - Grace and Roman. One had come from an abusive background where she daily had to witness her father beat her mother, until one day he went too far and killed her. Immediately afterwards he killed himself leaving Grace orphaned at seven. Roman also came from a terrible background with no father, and a prostitute mother. He also was taken into foster care aged seven.

There were lots of twists and turns in the book but Roman ended up as a great artist. But the true Masterpiece was not Roman's work of art that he presented after he got saved, the masterpieces were Grace and Roman's lives and how God made so much beauty out of so much mess. There was a great deal of many broken pieces in each life to put back together again but God, the Master artist, painted so much beauty for His glory and honour upon the canvases of Grace and Roman's lives.

I had a China doll that fell off my dresser and smashed into pieces. It was too damaged to glue together again. It had to be thrown out. In our lives, we can be like smashed up China dolls at times but with God, He can not only put all your broken pieces back together again, he can make what once was broken into a Masterpiece, a greater work of art than it was before.

No matter how black the canvas of your life looks, no matter how many broken pieces of you are shattered across the floor, God still says you are His Masterpiece! You! Yes, you! You are His wonder, showpiece, gem, triumph, and prize who despite all you have been through still reflects the glory of your beloved King. Think about that! As His showpiece, you reflect your Saviour to the whole world. He has you on display for He knows that when others look at you, they will see Jesus and come to know Him as Saviour. Let the words of this poem by Deborah Ann Belka sink deep into your soul and encourage your heart.

You are unique.
You are one of a kind.
God moulded your heart,
Your soul, your mind.

You are unique.
God created every part.
He put you together.
Right from the start.

You are unique.
God designed all of you.
He shaped you into.
His beautiful masterpiece.

You are unique.
Marvellous in every way.
That's why you should sing to Him,
Your praise today.

Feeling low? Crushed? Disheartened? Life's circumstances bleak for you right now? Be encouraged dear friend for no matter how many broken pieces you have - you are still a Masterpiece created by your Lord to serve mighty purposes for His honour and glory on this earth!

111

For The Love Of Her Daughter

I watched a true-life film called, *'For the love of her daughter'*. In the film, the couple's sixteen-year-old daughter was diagnosed with Leukaemia. It was a rare form that needed a matching bone marrow donor for a transplant. Without it, she would only have three years to live. The family were all tested and none were a match. They put out appeals for strangers to be tested and many came forward. Sadly, none were a match. In desperation, the woman suggested to her husband to have another child to see if the new child could be a match.

The media caught wind of it and considered it unethical to have another child for his/her bone marrow. So the press would not leave them alone. The mother did a press conference to say she would love her new child as much as her older two, but she had to do all in her power not to let her daughter die. In the end, the new baby girl called Marissa was a match and her older sister was cured of cancer!

That family went to great depths to make sure their daughter did not die. That is the same extreme love your Lord has for you. There is nothing in His power He would not do for a son or daughter in crisis. After all, He demonstrated His love by sacrificing Himself on a cross for the Salvation of all who will place their trust in Him.

His love for you is a love beyond measure, a love that knows no limits. If an earthly mother or father would go to such extreme lengths out of love to save their daughter, think of the even greater lengths of love our Heavenly Father goes to for us. He is always loving, always giving, always there!

1 John 3:1 *"See what kind of love the Father has given to us, that we should be called the Children of God."*

Romans 5:8 *"For God commendeth his love towards us, in that, while we were yet sinners Christ died for us."*

Zephaniah 3:17 *"The Lord your God is in your midst, a mighty one who will save, he will rejoice over you with gladness, he will quiet you by his love, he will exalt over you with loud singing."*

1 John 4:7-8 *"Beloved let us love one another, for love is from God and whoever loves has been born of God. Anyone who does not love does not know God because God is love."*

There are many more verses, but these show the extreme measures that the Lord went to for us. He died for us when we were completely undeserving of it to make us His children. He rejoices over us and quiets us with His love. We are deeply flawed, we have done nothing to merit such love, yet He lavishes it on us freely. Because God is love, we are to follow in His footsteps and sacrificially love others to extreme measures.

Reading these scriptures made me think of the two world wars. Men went to battle and laid down their lives for others so that future generations would be free and not be under a dictatorship.

What can we do in the next few days to show extreme love to another person? Maybe someone battling depression, physical illness, bereavement. Do something to follow in the footsteps of Jesus to show His love radiating from you which will draw others to Him.

112

Christ Our Cornerstone

"Christ alone, Cornerstone. Weak made strong by the Saviour's love. Through the storm, he is Lord, Lord of all."

> Isaiah 28:16 *"Therefore the Lord says: Behold I lay in Zion a stone for a foundation, a precious Cornerstone, a sure foundation."*

In every stone building, one stone is crucial. It is laid first and it is to ensure that the building is square and stable. It is the rock upon which the weight of the entire structure rests on.

Scripture describes Jesus as the chief cornerstone of our faith. As the chief cornerstone, Jesus ensures the stability of the whole system of our Salvation.

> Matthew 21:42-44 *"Jesus said unto them. ' Have you not never read in scriptures: The stone which the builders rejected has become the chief Cornerstone, this was the Lord's doing and it is marvellous in our eyes."*

Jesus came to His own and instead of embracing him, they stumbled over Him and ultimately nailed Him to the cross.

> Acts 4:12 *"Neither is there salvation in any other, for there is no other name under heaven given among men among men whereby we must be saved."*

Jesus is our cornerstone, our solid foundation, the rock that holds everything together. He may have been rejected by His own, but He is still offering Salvation and complete assurance of Heaven to those who give Him their lives.

As I thought about this I thought Lord, all these years of illness. All the times when I felt like I was falling apart and could not take one more day. You have been my strong rock of refuge, my sure foundation, my cornerstone that keeps me ploughing on. You have never let me fall apart because you have been holding me together all this time in sickness and in health.

Maybe you are reading this and are in dire straits today. You have taken more than you can take of your current situation then remember Jesus is your cornerstone and He will not let you crumble. Remember the line from the hymn, "On Christ the solid rock I stand. All other ground is sinking sand."

Psalm 18:2 *"The Lord is my rock, my fortress and deliverer, my God is my rock in whom I take refuge, my shield and the horn of my salvation, my stronghold."*

Your Lord, your rock, your fortress, your deliverer is holding you up right now. Just run into His arms for refuge and pour out your weary, bottled up heart to Him. He loves you and cares for you and wants to hold you close. He is our solid foundation through the storms of life.

113

The Seemingly Impossible Can Become Possible With God

I read a book by Beverly Lewis called, *'The Road'*. In it, it gave a very bleak illustration where the parents of ten children were killed in a road accident. The siblings were split up amongst other families in the Amish community. But there was no place or work for the eldest Lena Rose. She was sent to her father's second cousin who lived 500 miles away. The whole time that she was away, she yearned for home. She was especially heartsick for her five-year-old brother Chris. But while she lived 500 miles away, she fell in love but told him that it could never work for she had to go home. An opportunity opened for a schoolteacher job back home and Lena Rose was reunited with her siblings. Though she was content, there was an ache in her heart for her left-behind love. She could not have foreseen that he loved her so much that he uprooted and moved 500 miles to be with her and he asked her to be his bride to which she happily consented.

What kept coming through from the book was that God is working behind the scenes to make a way where there seems to be no way. He co-ordinates things so well that sometimes it hits us like a surprise even though we have been praying for it.

There was a point where Lena Rose lost heart. There have been many times on my journey with illness that I too have lost heart and I have cried out the words of Psalm 22:1 *"My God, my God why hast thou forsaken me?"* I cannot see the bigger picture of what He is working at behind the scenes, but this I do know, there is nothing beyond His control and there is nothing that He cannot do. Our God is the one who parted a whole sea so that His children would be saved from their enemies. Our God is the one who kept Daniel safe overnight in a den of lions and he emerged unharmed. Jesus raised the dead, healed the blind, healed the lepers, and healed those afflicted with all kinds of untreatable ailments.

> Job 5:8-9 *"I would seek unto God, and unto God would I commit my cause which doeth great things and unsearchable, marvellous things without number."*

> Psalm 77:14 *"Thou art the God that doest wonders, thou hast declared thy strength among the people."*

> Luke 1:37 *"For with God nothing shall be impossible."*

Yet there are days when my faith is flat as a pancake but that does not change the fact that my God still does marvellous things. He is still the God that does wonders. He is still the one that has declared that with Him nothing shall be impossible. Some days we might feel spiritually flat but what can never change is that God is fighting for us behind the scenes!

I heard a children's song from a holiday Bible club. Some of the words went like this.

> You are the God who holds my future and my dreams,
> and I am holding on to your promises.
> So I am holding on.
> You never let go of me.

Keep holding on to the promises that the Lord has given you and do not get disillusioned for the Lord holds your future and your dreams and will bring things to pass in His time.

114

The Survivor Tree

I read Karen Kingsbury's book entitled, *'To the Moon and Back'*. It was largely centred around the Oklahoma bombing of 1995. I did not even know that there had been a terrorist attack before 9/11. I did not watch the news as a child! But after reading Karen's book I was inspired to look more into it.

The Oklahoma bombing took place on the 19th of April 1995. It was a terrorist truck bombing on the Alfred P Murrah federal building. The bombing happened at 9.02 a.m. and killed at least 168 people, injured more than 680, and destroyed one-third of the building. The blast destroyed or damaged 324 other buildings within a 16-mile radius and destroyed or burned 86 cars.

The Survivor Tree was part of the buildings original landscape that survived the blast and the flames that followed it. It now stands proud in the Oklahoma National memorial. It is a ninety-year-old American elm. It is a symbol of resilience or in other words, strength, hardiness, toughness, and the ability to recover quickly from difficult situations. After all, it did withstand a 4000-pound truck bomb going off right beside it.

The bomb was so big that its shock wave exploded parked cars nearby and the tree caught fire. Pieces of glass and metal shot out and stuck in the old Elm's base. Most of the branches were cut off by flying debris. When the dust settled all that was left was a smouldering blackened trunk.

In the weeks that followed the people cleaning up intended to cut the old tree down. They figured it was dead. But they left it standing because of the glass and metal lodged in its bark. From the way the pieces were positioned, local investigators were able to determine what they needed to know about the location of the bomb.

Then something amazing happened. On the first anniversary of the blast, they saw sprigs of green coming out of the bark. The tree was ALIVE! The glass and metal were removed, and the tree was nursed back to health. A year later it was growing branches again and it now stands in all its beauty as if nothing had ever happened.

This quote from the book about the Survivor Tree touched me. "It's proof that with God there is always a way to survive."

It made me think. We have all endured our own blasts of life. Blasts so bad at times that we thought we would always be living in the ruins and the ashes. But with God, we each have His strength, His hand upon us to get us through agonising times.

With God, we are all survivor trees. Not victims of whatever life has thrown at us and with God the season for the newness of life will come to each of us again. Even if it does not feel like it at this minute.

Hebrews 12:3 *"For consider him that endured... lest ye be wearied and faint in your minds."*

If you have become faint and weary with all the enduring, then look to Jesus. Look at the torture He went through for each of us, yet He endured the cross without complaining or giving up. Jesus conquered death and rose again so that if we place our trust in Him, we can be in Heaven with Him for all eternity. Look to Jesus. In Him you are even more than a survivor, you are, *"More than conquerors through him that loved us."* (Romans 8:37)

You are more than a survivor! You are a winner, a victor, a hero! No matter how burnt out you feel now, keep enduring, stay in the fight for a day of great hope and beauty for life's ashes awaits you. You WILL get through this and be like the Survivor Tree with people marvelling at God's strength in you for they will see that only with God on your side did you survive!

238

115

The Spice Box

I read a book by Grace Livingston Hill called, 'The Spice Box'. The book did not go into detail about what a spice box was, so I studied into it.

In Judaism, a spice box is at its simplest an ornate box usually made from wood. One example of a Jewish Spice Box is one that takes the shape of a flower, complete with wooden petals, stems and leaves. It is used to keep fragrant spices in. The wondrous smells of the fragrances would act as a reminder of the good times had during Shabbat. The sweet smell of the spices tries to counteract the sadness one feels as the holiday departs. A favourite spice is cloves because of their pungent smell that can last for a long time.

It got me thinking of the Scripture,

2 Corinthians 2:15 *"For we are unto God a sweet Savour in them that are saved and in them that perish."*

We like spice boxes are the refreshing fragrance of life itself if we are walking with our Lord. That aroma will rise into the lives of others around us. The fragrance of our close walk with God and Christlike character will encourage other Christians in their walk with the Lord. Helping their aroma be more fragrant in a dark world and it will also rise in the lives of non-Christians making them wonder what the difference is in you, causing them to seek the Lord for themselves. We must walk closely to our Saviour's side. If we do not do so and walk hand in hand with satan and the world instead of God that will cause a bad odour to arise that puts people off coming to know Jesus as Saviour.

Song of Solomon 4:16 *"Awake O North wind and come thou south, blow upon my garden that the spices thereof may flow out."*

We are to be more than the spice box containers of fragrance, we need to open the lid and let those spices be released.

"The winds in this verse represent the trials of life. The purpose of these trials is that the fragrance of the garden may flow out, witnessing to those around us of the character of our renewed lives. They will show you that we are different people.

The spices are patience, prayerfulness, joy peace and a well-controlled temperament. They give us a platform of character from which to witness." ('The mutual love of Christ for His people' by Peter Masters)

Has the lid of your spice box been opened by the trials of life? Ask the Lord to breathe afresh on you so that the spices of patience, prayerfulness, joy, peace, and a well-controlled temperament will be released, and you will bear much fruit seeing souls brought to your Saviour.

If you are in a trial no matter how useless you feel continue to let the Lord flow through you and serve Him in all ways possible that your fragrance released upon this world will be mighty and you will impact lives you could not even have dreamt possible of touching.

God's little spice box - go release your fragrance today so that a perishing world will come to know our Saviour.

116

When You Feel All Is Lost

I was never used to failing at anything. In school I got A*'s, A's, and B's in exams so when I got my provisional driving licence at seventeen, I assumed I would pass in no time but alas I didn't take to it! I worked every Saturday in a shop for £15. £13 went to the driving instructor. £1.50 was the Lord's tithe and I had a whole 50p leftover! That went on for two years! I had over ninety lessons. After failing the test for the third time I came home collapsed on my bed and gave up. I cried my heart out. I was so frustrated at myself for not being able to master it. I told my parents I was never trying again. I was beaten and a complete and utter failure. They told me that you are only a failure if you give up! So after much persuasion I took six more lessons and finally passed my test the fourth time, by that stage I was nineteen and my provisional licence was about to expire! Two long years of constantly trying and constantly failing but in the end, I got there!

I will never forget that day sobbing on my bed having completely lost heart. I was disillusioned and had lost all my fight, all my get up and go. It was complete hopelessness and despair and feeling like a complete failure.

Do you feel like that today? Have you persevered and endured at something till you are at the point where you have thrown in the towel in utter defeat and all you can say is, I can't do it anymore!

Well dear child of God. Winston Churchill once said, "Success is not final, failure is not fatal: it's the courage to continue that counts."

From somewhere deep inside your heart, today ask God for the courage to continue. Stay in the fight. You are not beat!

2 Timothy 4:7 *"I have fought the good fight, I have finished the race, I have kept the faith."*

1 Corinthians 9:24 *"Do you know that in a race all the runners run, but only one receives the prize? So run that you might obtain it."*

James 1:12 *"Blessed is the man who remains steadfast under trial, for when he has stood the test he will receive the crown of life which God has promised to those who love him."*

Keep fighting the good fight, keep running the race, remain steadfast under trial for there is a crown of life waiting for you. Pick that towel back up off the floor and do not let the enemy defeat you anymore.

The words to this song, by James Nelson, really encourage me in bad times.

It's not over. It's not finished.
It's not ending, it's only the beginning.
When God is in it, all things are new.
I know it's darkest just before the dawn.
Might be the hardest season you experience.
I know it hurts, but it won't be long.
You're closer than you've been before.
Look to the sky, help is on its way.
It's not over. It's not finished. I
t's not ending it's only just beginning.

117

The Lord of Goodness and Mercy

Nehemiah 13:22 *"Remember me O my God and spare me according to the greatness of the mercy."*

:31 *"Remember me, O my God for good."*

I have always loved these scriptures. There are countless scriptures which talk about the Lord's goodness and mercy. I have chosen these because Nehemiah had just accomplished an amazing task for God and yet the book closes with him on his knees. His accomplishments had not made him feel prideful, he still daily depended upon the goodness and mercy of the Lord that he loved.

I read a story about a girl with Cystic Fibrosis and she knew she was going to pass away. But her life's dream was to marry. She was only eighteen, but her boyfriend loved her so much and wanted her dream to happen. So everyone in that community pitched in to make her dream come true. A bridal shop gave her a free gown, a florist free flowers, a baker a free cake. The hospital staff decorated the hospital chapel and her big day dawned. She was wheeled down the aisle, struggling to breathe yet I have never seen a more radiant smile! She was witnessing the birth of her dream. She was seeing the goodness of her Lord in the land of the living. But she passed away forty-eight hours later to be with her Lord in glory. She died content and happy after witnessing the goodness of her Lord in the land of the living.

The word goodness means, uprightness, honourability, dignity, trustworthy, pure, kind, compassionate etc. The word mercy means, compassion, or forgiveness shown towards someone, charity, generosity, liberality.

Throughout scripture, the goodness and mercy of our loving Saviour shines through time and time again. It reminds me of this hymn,

> The King of love, my shepherd is,
> whose goodness faileth never.
> I nothing lack if I am His,
> and He is mine forever.

You might be so focused on your troubles that you can no longer see the goodness and compassionate mercy of the Lord in your life. Look closer for it is around you always. The clothes on your back, the food in your belly, the roof over your head etc. are signs of His loving care.

I feel like the Lord is saying this today: "My child you have been in such a bad place for so long that your spiritual vision has got blurred. I am still your loving, good and merciful God and I want you to ask me to show you my goodness and mercy afresh in your life for I am more than willing to shower you in it. Bathed in my goodness and mercy there's nothing in this life you cannot face. Let me your compassionate Lord reign afresh in your life."

There are many days that the severe Illness I live with gets me down and I cry sore. There are many days when I cannot see the light at the end of the tunnel, and I get spiritually short-sighted. But on my worst days, I see His goodness and mercy even more for in His love and compassion He comes to me to rock me like a child in His arms. He comes to me through the uplifting words of my closest friends who I reach out to when I feel like I am drowning, and their gracious words are Heaven sent.

Every day in every way I have a good Father! And I am loved deeply by Him, faults, failings, and all. His goodness and mercy follow you ALL the days of your life on earth and then for all eternity. My prayer for you is, "Remember every dear child of yours each day for good O Lord."

118

Abigail

1 Samuel 25:3 *"Now the name of the man was Nabal; and the name of his wife Abigail: and she was a woman of good understanding and of a beautiful countenance, but the man was churlish and evil in his doings."*

If you have read the whole story, Abigail is generous, quick-witted, courageous, and wise. Though she was in a mismatched marriage to a horrible man whose name means fool she did not get bitter in her Spirit or look for ways to show revenge.

David and his men had been taking care of rich Nabal's sheep for some time. He asked Nabal for some food and provisions but Nabal refused. David became enraged and told his six hundred men to gird up their swords! This meant to David to slaughter and go to war. But Abigail intervened. She heard what her husband had done and made haste and took the provisions herself, thus saving many lives. David said of her (v 32), *"Blessed be the advice and blessed be thou which hast kept me this day from coming to shed blood."* Not long after, Nabal died and David married Abigail.

1- Abigail must have felt suffocated having been paired with this man. Her father likely thought that with his wealth, Nabal was a catch, little realizing the man's domineering attitude might one day endanger his daughter's wellbeing. Her marriage to Nabal was one of difficulty and hardship. But through it all she kept her walk with God strong. Maybe you are in a marriage or relationship that is not what your couple image on social media portrays. You feel unloved, put down, constantly criticised. You feel like your husband feels no joy in you at all. 1 Peter 3:1 urges a wife who is in a mismatched marriage, *"That they may without words be won by the conversation of their wives."*

The emphasis here is on the wife's winning her husband by living Christ daily before him. I am sure Abigail did that but saw no fruit for her labours due to the man's hardheartedness. But she kept going. Suffering friend today who is in a mismatched marriage either through marriage to an unbeliever or your husband has backslidden, keep praying for him and keep living Christ daily before him. God released Abigail from her situation but not every situation is the same. He might bring release in your relationship by you praying and living as a true reflection of Jesus before him as many marriages have been restored that way. But can I add if you are in a domestic abuse situation and are daily facing battering's please get out while you can. Also, could I say to those who are in a relationship with an unbeliever or backsliders not to marry them for the Word says, *"Be ye not unequally yoked".*

2- Abigail was courageous and kind. The Lord honoured her for her consistency and her willingness to continue the right path no matter how difficult. God honours those who are faithful even when faithfulness brings hardship and pain.

2 Timothy 3:2 *"Thou therefore endure hardship as a good soldier of Jesus Christ."*

You might be in an awful situation that's not marriage-related. You have endured and endured and endured some more. Keep going! The Lord honours faithful people who despite living through heartbreaking situations still love Him and honour Him and keep going through the pain. God might not intervene in your situation like in Abigail's, but He promises to honour and bless those who keep honouring Him. He is still with us and will never leave our side, giving us His supernatural strength to keep going. Keep being courageous for God is smiling down on you with pride.

3- You are the Father's Abigail. You bring His heart joy. You are His beloved and the apple of His eye and His pearl of great price. You also bring others joy! Keep bringing others joy even when your situation is no picnic and God will bless your life abundantly!

119

The Pink Panther Pyjamas

Many years ago, in my healthy days, I did five Child Evangelism camps in a row one summer. Though I mistakenly only packed one pair of blue pyjamas. At the end of the first camp, I washed them in a sink and they soon dried being hung out of a window. Then I moved on to a second camp with a group of people I was most familiar with. Near the end of the week, I had an accident. I sprained my ankle and when I fell, I got a huge bleeding gash in my leg. Even though I had plasters on it when I woke the next morning the blood had seeped through and stained one of the PJ's legs.

I tried to wash it out, but it would not budge. So, I had one afternoon between that camp and the next one which was also to be in the same small town. I was in a pyjama dilemma. So I set off into the tiny town that only had two clothes shops. One for kids and one for elderly people! I stood in the old-fashioned shop looking at nightdresses that were so old fashioned that they belonged in a scene from Little House on the Prairie! I just could not bring myself to buy it! I went across the street to the kid's shop and they had an age thirteen set of pink panther shortie pyjamas. I knew I would feel highly embarrassed wearing them in front of a group of people new to me!

The first night all us female leaders changed into our nightwear to lead the children in their quiet times. When I came out of the room everyone was laughing! At the leader's meetings before that camp, I was extremely nervous in a new group of people and was extremely quiet and did not speak much. They said they were laughing because at those meetings I appeared very serious, that their expectation of who I was totally altered at the sight of those pyjamas! They were the perfect ice breaker, for now I felt like my real self around everyone who could laugh and join in. I was not the stranger anymore and we all became very close.

Their expectation of what they thought I was like totally changed as they got to know me over the next few weeks.

It made me think about the word Expectation. The word means, a strong belief that something will happen, assumption, belief, prediction, trust.

Proverbs 29:18 *"Where there is no vision the people perish."*

Or in other words, where there is no expectation or hope in a person's life that they wither up inside and die.

Have you lost your vision, your expectation, your hope for a day to come when your circumstances will no longer be as severe? Do you love the Lord, but you are slowly dying on the inside? Then ask the Lord to renew your spiritual vision. Ask Him to fill you with the expectation and hope of Him changing things for you will perish in despair if you do not.

Psalm 62:5 *"My soul, wait thou only upon God for my expectation is from him."*

Wait precious child of God. You might have lost all expectation and hope, but the Lord is reminding you otherwise. Wait upon Him and you will see what a beautiful season of joy He will bring to pass in your life.

120

Your Desert Becoming Like The Garden Of Eden

Isaiah 51:3 *"For the Lord comfort Zion, he will comfort all her waste places, and he will make her wilderness like Eden and her desert like the Garden of the Lord; joy and gladness shall be found therein, thanksgiving and the voice of melody."*

This scripture has always been such a hopeful comfort to me for many years. Do you find yourself dwelling in a wasted place today? Are you in a dry, weary, apparently never-ending wilderness? Imagine what living in an actual desert would be like. You would be scorched by the heat of the sun, in great thirst, alone and with nothing to see but endless horizons of sand and dust.

You could have ended up in this desert due to the circumstances of life. Something extremely painful and heart-wrenching has happened to you that has made you feel numb.

Everything has gone bleak through circumstances that one has no control over. You are gasping for breath as you panic and lose all sense of comfort. God knows where you are, but He is not going to leave you there parched and desperate.

First, He has promised to comfort you. You might not sense Him amid your feelings, but He is still there, comforting you the way a mother would comfort a child. He is holding you close and rocking you gently.

Second, He has promised to comfort all your waste places. When I imagine waste places, I think of old rundown buildings that are total eyesores. I know many times my life has felt like a waste place - a rundown, desolate, old place that is completely useless. But God has promised to comfort these waste places. He has promised to build up that which was torn down, to rebuild, and make you even more glorious than before. Did you ever watch sixty-minute makeover? They call in a team of experts to makeover their house. Rooms that previously had looked worn down and tatty now looked amazing, bright, cheerful, and new.

Third, the Lord has promised to make your wilderness like Eden and your desert like the Garden of the Lord! What a beautiful promise. Eden was the most beautiful place on Earth. Only God can transform a wilderness into something as spectacular as the garden of Eden and He has promised to do it for you. I remember when I was young and wanting to makeover my late Granny's garden. It was a total wilderness overcome with briars, thistles, long grass, weeds! The only good thing that grew there was rhubarb. After a week of faithfully spending twelve hours a day working hard, everything in that garden still looked the same - a complete wilderness!

So I got discouraged and gave up. I declared it a lost cause. Maybe your life feels like a lost cause. Take heart, your life that looks like a total mess, a total wilderness will be transformed in the perfect timing of the Lord to resemble the most beautiful, fruitful garden that ever was! It will be beauty beyond your wildest dreams. You will not even be able to imagine or comprehend how God could turn it around!

Fourth, joy and gladness shall be found therein, thanksgiving and the voice of melody. Maybe for so long, the pain has been so intense that you have almost forgotten what it is like to experience joy and gladness. Well, the promise that the Lord has for you today is to expect joy and gladness and the voice of melody. You truly may feel dead inside but cling tight to these promises to give you some hope in your Spirit of what the Lord is going to do. He will make all things new! That is what He has promised to do.

121

Letters To Emily

I watched a true film that was quite hard to watch. A woman had not long given birth to her daughter. Not long after, crisis struck. She had pain in her back, but she put it down to the ordeal of having a C-section and put off going to the doctors. When she did go to the doctor, they found she had terminal cancer and not long to live. She and her husband were devastated. The woman had little strength and deteriorated fast, but she pushed herself hard every day to write as many letters to Emily so that one day she might know her mother and how much she was loved. She desired so much that her daughter would one day know her through her writings.

It made me think of Philippians 3:7,8 and 10

"But the things that were gain to me, those I have counted loss for Christ. I count all things but loss for the excellency of the knowledge of Christ, my Lord, for whom I have suffered the loss of all things and do count them but dung that I may win Christ... that I might KNOW him and the power of his resurrection and the fellowship of his sufferings."

What an example Paul is to us of complete surrender to a life of knowing Jesus intimately. He was not satisfied with a superficial profession, he daily wanted to know Jesus more. Just as Emily came to have a deeper knowledge of her mother through reading her letters, Paul wants us to come to a deeper knowledge of our Saviour. I too like Paul desire to know my Jesus more deeply with every passing day. I am not content with yesterday's manna; I want to know my beloved afresh with every passing day. But like Emily's mother, it involves sacrifice. The total surrender of our will to His. The total abandonment of every 'little sin' that would drive you further away from Him. A passionate desire to hear from Him every day in His Word, taking time daily no matter how exhausted we are to walk with Him in prayer. Constantly desiring to be His mirror images - that will reflect a glorious, risen King to a dying world and being obedient to His call to spread the Gospel.

I have lost a lot because of my illness - the ability to work, to serve God physically on the frontlines, the chance to meet someone and marry, bucket loads of friends that did not want a sick friend etc. but nothing can ever take away knowing my beloved Lord deeply. He is my everything, the one who holds me when I cry, the one who never leaves my side.

If your walk with the Lord has become stale and stuck, make this the day you surrender all afresh and make it your daily goal to become more intimately acquainted with your Saviour, whom you will spend all of eternity with. Whatever idols or blockages are in your way of knowing Him then cast them away for knowing Jesus is all that matters.

As I thought of all this a hymn, we sang in my childhood church came to mind. The words fit this devotion perfectly.

O for a closer walk with God.
A calm and heavenly frame.
A light to shine upon the road,
That leads me to the lamb.

Return O Holy Dove return.
Sweet messenger of rest.
I hate the sins that made thee mourn
And drove thee from my breast.

The dearest idol I have known,
Whate're that idol be.
Help me to tear it from thy throne
And worship only thee.

122

The Unfolding Plot

I had never been to the cinema until I was twelve years old. That was my birthday treat! The movie that was showing was 'The Flintstones'! Like every other movie or book, it had an unfolding plot that eventually all worked together for good - even though there was a bleak part in the middle. Movies and books are all the same. They have scenes and chapters that look bleak!

It made me think, our lives are unfolding plots in God's grand scheme of things. Just because we hit a bleak chapter does not mean that things will remain this way.

Job 42:2 *"I know that you can do all things, no purpose of yours can be thwarted."*

Proverbs 16:4 *"The Lord works everything to it's proper end."*

If you look at every story you have ever read in Scripture so many of the characters have bleak chapters but time and time again God worked everything for good. The book of Job shows intense, horrific, suffering yet God ended that chapter and blessed his latter life more than the former.

David was anointed King of the land, yet he spent an extremely bleak period of his life living in caves and running from Saul who wanted to kill him. But again God's purpose was not thwarted, and he became King. God brought His purpose for David's life to pass.

Look at Esther, as a God-fearing Jewess, I am sure the news that she was to be taken to live in an ungodly King's quarters and be his wife, shook her up. It was not something godly Esther would have chosen for herself! Yet again behind the scenes, God was working for good in that He used His child in that place to save all her people from being killed. Again, God's purpose prevailed.

Paul certainly would not have chosen to live in a filthy, horrid, Roman prison cell and be chained. But if Paul had not been in that prison cell, we would not have a big chunk of our New Testament today. Paul through his writing from that prison cell is 'dead yet he speaketh.' Again, God was working behind the scenes of Paul's life for the extension of His Kingdom and the edification of His children.

What chapter are you stuck in today that is bleak and black and horrible, so horrible that you feel it will never end and you have not a clue why you have to go through this. Dear brother, dear sister even though you cannot see it now God's hand is still on your life and He is still working behind the scenes for good. This is NOT a permanent chapter in your life - God's purpose WILL prevail.

There is a song, 'Sovereign over us' and one line in the first verse goes: You are working in our waiting. The rest of the chorus goes as follows:

> Your plans are still to prosper,
> you have not forgotten us.
> You're with us in the fire and the flood.
> You're faithful forever, perfect in love,
> you are Sovereign over us.

God is in complete control even though it feels like your life is spinning out of control. He is working in your waiting and He is sovereign over your situation. Keep drawing near to the Author, our Lord Jesus Christ and remember that this chapter is not permanent!

123

Unfeigned Faith

I recently watched one of the episodes of, '*Little House on the Prairie*'. In it, Nelly fell off her horse. When she came round from her concussion, she pretended that she had no feeling in her legs. She used her fake paralysis to manipulate her parents so she could get whatever fancy toys she wanted. She also did it to manipulate Laura Ingalls who had previously owned the horse into doing all her schoolwork. It showed Nelly the moment her parents left the house how she jumped out of bed and danced around the room with her dolls. Finally, Laura caught her doing this and the deceit was out in the open. How anyone could sink to such levels of deceit, to fake not being able to walk to manipulate others, I will never know.

But that episode brought to my remembrance a short talk I had given to the youth at church many years ago.

2 Timothy 1:5 *"I call to remembrance the unfeigned faith that is in thee, which dwelt first in thy grandmother Lois, and thy mother Eunice; and I am persuaded that's in thee also."*

The word unfeigned means, not pretended, sincerely felt, or expressed, genuine, true, and not deceitful.

When Paul thought of Timothy he was reminded of genuine faith. His faith was sincere, true and did not wear a mask. This kind of faith had also dwelt in his mother and grandmother. It was a genuine faith that Timothy would maintain despite all the trials he might have to face.

There are those arisen in this generation who are wolves in sheep's clothing. They profess to have a Christian faith but hide behind a mask. They can fool their ministers and those in leadership, but they have arisen to deceive and cause havoc. They will say they are one thing but live a life that contradicts what they say. When the mask is off, they will run to all the worldly places of the day, places wherein satan is glorified and they will cause danger to new believers. New believers might look on their deceitful example and follow the wolf instead of the shepherd - hence wreaking havoc in the Kingdom of God.

Scripture says in Matthew 7:16, *"By their fruits ye shall know them."* Genuine believers will stand out against the fakes by their display of the fruits of the spirit in their lives. Their sincerity and pure shining love for the Lord. They will be exactly what they profess to be with no deceit in them. As Jesus said of Nathaniel, *"Behold a man in whom there is no guile."* (John 1:47) No guile means no slyness, no deviousness, and no craftiness.

The challenge to myself and you today is to ask the Lord to give you this pure unfeigned faith in these evil days. For when we have it, people will see our genuinely and see that we don't profess one thing and live another way and that the fruits of the Spirit are evident in our lives so much so that others see Jesus within us and come to a saving knowledge of Him.

I feel that the Lord is saying: "My child, I want you to be a clean, shining vessel in these dark days. I love those and I am especially close to those that are of a pure heart, who walk closely with Me, who live pure lives that are a reflection of Me and desire what I desire - the saving of precious souls while there is still time. Stay close to Me your Shepherd and I will protect you from the wolves. Go out into this world and be fruitful for my Kingdom, precious one. Stay close, ever close to Me the Lord who loves you."

124

King Josiah

The name Josiah means God supports; God heals. I remembered teaching the children at C.E.F. camps about this King.

> 2 Kings 22:2 *"And he did what was right in the eyes and walked in all the ways of David his Father and did not turn aside to the left or the right. He raised money to repair the temple and the High Priest Hilkah found the book of the law."*

Josiah sought God and truth first over everything, unlike the evil kings before him who had turned the people away from the Word of God and introduced idolatry and occultic practices. In his time as King, Josiah made sure that the temple was cleansed from all objects of pagan worship and the idolatrous high places were demolished. He restored the observance of the Passover and removed mediums and witches from the land.

> 2 Kings 23:25 *"Before him there was no king like him who turned to the Lord with all his heart and all his soul, nor did any like him arise after him."*

Sadly today, the word of God is being cast aside more and more. We need more Josiah's to arise in this generation to stand up for truth again. The Word of God in our society today is being diluted and used as a type of pic-n-mix to prove anything goes. So many false teachers have appeared on so-called God channels who do not promote the Gospel but have a hidden agenda in preaching a new age prosperity gospel that is not the Biblical one. This new one only brings glory to satan. I read one of those new-age T.V. preacher's books and in it, he said that we can bring anything to pass that we want by imagining it in our minds and it will visualise and become reality. This is so dangerous it promotes the occultic thinking that we are all 'gods' of our own universe and can command anything we want into being. Their gospel is not that you need to be saved by the blood of Jesus to be rescued from Hell. Their version is that God wants you to have your best life now and have all the wealth, health, and prosperity possible just by thinking it and commanding it into being. These preachers believe the sick want to stay sick as they could command their healing into being if they wanted too and they have no sympathy for the sick and the dying.

Josiah's life showed the power one person can have to turn a nation back to truth, back to the undiluted Word of God. It shows he lived a life fully committed and obedient to God and was blessed for it. By the time he became King, the scriptures had been long neglected and Josiah's heart was smitten by the people's failure to honour God.

Are you willing to be a Josiah and do all in your power to turn this nation back to the true, undiluted, Word of God? Are you willing to obey no matter what the cost and stand on the truth of His Word even when no one else does? Are you willing to stand up for Jesus and be true soldiers of the cross in these last days where the Word of God predicted that even some of God's children would turn away from Him?

We need to carry the Gospel light to the next generation and never let compromise reign in our hearts. Let us all start praying for this nation to return to truth. For revival to break out, for men and women and children everywhere coming to know our Saviour. It is an age of abominable practices so come on brothers and sisters let us use everything within us to carry the light before it's too late.

125

Bringing Ashley Home

The bonds of love between siblings are usually extremely strong but I have never seen a bond of devotion and love ever before in two siblings as I saw in a true-life film called, 'Bringing Ashley Home'.

When her wild young sister who suffered from Bipolar disorder and drug addiction (Ashley) goes missing, Libba her sister pours all her energy into finding and bringing her home.

As the years went past Libba refused to give up hope at the cost of her marriage and career. Libba finds her calling in life creating a much-needed resource centre for other families whose loved ones had fallen through the cracks. The name Libba means 'consecrated' to God and even though the Libba in this story was not a Christian, she had wholly set herself apart and consecrated herself in pure, unswerving devotion to finding Ashley. The name Ashley means, 'Lives in the Ash grove.' Though in this case the girl was lost to the ashes of drug addiction and alcohol. The organisation that Libba set up is called, 'Outpost for Hope'. It is still running today. This organisation through its constant efforts has reunited so many lost people to their families.

> Deuteronomy 15:11 *"There will always be poor people in the land, therefore I command you to be open handed toward your fellow men who are poor and needy in your land."*

The poor and needy extends not just to those in financial poverty. The poor and needy are the alcoholic, the drug addict, the homeless, those in any chains of addiction. We are called to be consecrated and devoted to reaching out to the lost and broken of this land no matter what it costs us personally. The word devoted means, loyal, faithful, true, steadfast, constant, committed, devout, dedicated, very loving.

God wants us to be steadfast, loyal, Libbas who are busy in their Master's service and never give up no matter how hard the task is.

Hebrews 6:10 *"And do not forget to do good and to share with others for with such sacrifices is God pleased."*

Child of God, make your Heavenly Father proud. Arise and shine and be the Gospel light that so many in this broken dying world needs. The Lord will reward you and with such sacrifices, He is well pleased.

I did not listen to pop music as a child, teen or adult but one night Mum let me watch 'Stars in their Eyes'. A young girl came out dressed up like Olivia Newton-John and sang a song called *'Hopelessly devoted to you'*. That night as I knelt in prayer, I told my Lord I wanted to be hopelessly devoted to Him. That is what our Saviour wants us all to be - hopelessly devoted to Him. Are you willing to heed the call and be hopelessly devoted to your Saviour? When you do start, keep going, do not get discouraged and give up your faithful work. Never give up your efforts. Never give up on people that feel unreachable and hopeless to reach or win.

When you feel like the world's at it's end.
Or when your heart seems to break.
Never give up hope because life holds a beautiful plan.

Libba, despite her heart breaking over losing a sister, determined to never give up and turn her heart-breaking situation into a rescue mission for others. Let us follow in her shoes and let our lives be a rescue mission to the perishing and lost.

126

The Photograph

A school friend of mine posted on social media a photograph of our entire year at Coleraine High school. I looked at all our faces and we all looked so young and happy, full of dreams and hopes. It triggered so many happy memories, especially being voted in as prayer secretary of the Scripture Union! The love, encouragement and acceptance I felt from the other girls were out of this world, after all, I was just a blow-in to the school, just coming there in lower sixth to do my A-levels after spending five years at another school.

I loved those Scripture Union days. I loved being the prayer secretary. I loved being the motivator of others to truly pray passionately and seek God's face, making Him a top priority. I was so young yet so in love with Jesus. Of course, due to taking sick, the hopes and dreams that that smiley face younger version of me held dear were snatched away. But just because life had not gone my way does not mean that I blame God, on the contrary, I love Him more.

I desire to be a motivator. The dictionary defines 'motivator' as a person who promotes interest or enthusiasm for something, who urges, who inspires. It is the goal of my devotion today to motivate God's children to truly pray. Not just a small prayer as you fall asleep at night where you are so tired that the words are mumbled and you are just doing it out of a sense of duty but to set aside time each day to commune passionately as friend to friend with your Saviour and make seeking His face your top priority.

Acts 1:14 *"These all continued with one accord in prayer and supplication..."*

1 Thessalonians 5:16 *"Pray without ceasing."*

Colossians 4:2 *"Continue in prayer and watch in the same with thanksgiving."*

There is power in prayer!

1. Following the release of Peter and John the believers prayed for boldness. As a result, the whole place was shaken, and they were all filled with the Holy Spirit henceforth empowering them to witness.

2. Peter prayed at Joppa and Dorcas was raised to life. As a result, many believed in the Lord.

3. When Peter was imprisoned the Christians prayed for him earnestly and God answered by miraculously delivering him from jail.

4. On the Island of Malta, Paul prayed for the governors' sick father. The result was that the patient was immediately healed.

I could list many more, but these examples have already proved my point - prayer changes things. God might not always answer us in the way we want but that does not mean He is not hearing us. Maybe you have grown discouraged in prayer because you cannot see anything changing. Then do not stop. Press on. Keep drawing near to the Lord's heart.

Ask the Lord to restore your passion for prayer today. You need a constant divine connection to be a powerful stream from the source! In my own life, even though I am not healed yet, I have seen answers to prayer that I never dreamt possible. So get to your knees and intercede. The souls of a never-ending stream of people are depending on you to keep praying that they will be rescued from darkness into light. Don't grow weary in well-doing (prayer) for you SHALL reap if you faint not.

127

Onesiphorus - The Refresher And Uplifter

Means 'One who brings profit'

2 Timothy 1:16 *"The Lord give mercy unto the house of Onesiphorus, for he oft refreshed me, and was not ashamed of my chains."*

Paul had been in prison a long time for preaching the Gospel. Yet despite his chains, he did all in his power through letters to churches to build them up. However despite how great a man of God Paul was, in his time of need most people abandoned him. They did not bother to go see him in his prison cell or reach out to encourage him. Paul said:

2 Corinthians 12:15 *"I will very gladly spend and be spent for you, though the more abundantly I love you, the less I be loved."*

Even though people had forgotten him, Paul loved on. These words from my Believers Bible Commentary sums it up beautifully (page 1867). "Here we have a beautiful glimpse into the unquenchable love of the Apostle Paul for the people of God. He was willing, gladly to give himself in tireless service and sacrifice for their souls that is their spiritual warfare. Yet - he was loved less by them. But that did not make a difference. Even if he had no hope of a return of love from them, he would keep on loving them."

Paul had very few who came to him but Onesiphorus came often to refresh him in his chains. Onesiphorus was a sacrificial giver and encourager. His visits were a breath of fresh air to Paul and helped him to keep ministering to others from his dungeon.

As Onesiphorus ministered to him, it gave Paul more power to minister to others. I am sure his times with Onesiphorus left him feeling more loved and more uplifted.

The world needs more Onesiphorus's, men and women who despite their own busy lives will take time to go to those in chains and refresh their spirit's. People who are sick, depressed, hopeless, rejected etc. Are you truly doing all in your power to make others' lives better? Be a refresher and start today. Many ministers and missionaries who may be feeling discouraged just need an email, a private mail, or letter to help them persevere.

Many people in chains feel forgotten. Reach out with the loving arms of our Saviour and be that one person who cares. Scripture says, *"In the last days people will be lovers of their own selves."* In other words, they are too self-focused to care about others. Don't let that be true of you - be an Onesiphorus not just to other Christians but to the unsaved too for you might just find that through your ministrations to them, the unsaved will see the love of Jesus in you and come to know Him.

128

The God Of Tender Mercies And Compassion

Isaiah 66:13 *"As one whom his mother comforteth, I will comfort you."*

Psalm 40:11 *"Withhold not thy tender mercies from me O Lord; Let thy lovingkindness and thy truth continually preserve me."*

The Lord has so much kindness and compassion upon you. Think of the love, tenderness, and compassion that you have had from the people in your life. Your mother holding you close and taking care of you when you were a child. The tenderness people show you when you are going through a difficult time. In times of bereavement, sorrow, and care there has been someone to hold you and cry with you. Someone who has shown you continually kindness. Think how amazing that tenderness felt and then imagine how all that is just a drop in the ocean beside the compassion and tenderness of the Lord's ministering love upon you.

Do you feel unloved today? Then the Lord is saying, *"I have loved thee with an everlasting love."* (Jeremiah 31:3)

Is what you are going through so thick and black that you cannot sense the Lord's presence with you? To that, He says, *"I will never leave thee nor forsake thee."* (Hebrews 13:5)

To someone who is so far through that you feel like giving up the Lord is saying,

"He giveth power to the faint; and to them that have no might he increaseth strength. Even the youths shall faint and be weary, and the young men shall utterly fall: But

*they that wait upon the LORD shall renew their strength;
they shall mount up with wings as eagles; they shall run,
and not be weary; and they shall walk, and not faint."*
(Isaiah 40:29-31)

Also, He is promising you, *"A crown of life in glory."* (James
1:12) if you will keep enduring. He loves and adores you more
than anyone else in this world does. Ask Him to let His tender
mercies and lovingkindness come to you today no matter how
painful your situation is and He will come and comfort you, ease
your burden, minister to your need and help you fight again. As
the hymn says:

Ask the Saviour to help you.
Comfort strengthen and keep you.
He is willing to aid you.
He will carry you through.

129

The Wedding

Anyone who knows me knows I love to watch the Walton's! I love anything to do with 'The Walton's'! But until recently I had never seen John Junior's wedding. (I've seen all the rest of their weddings and loved them all.)

Unlike all the other ones, John's was high drama from the start. An interfering Aunt on the bride's side did her best to make things a nightmare! This got too much for John and he went home to Walton's mountain. His bride arrived soon after but again there was high drama as they had a major fight which made John wonder if he was doing the right thing.

When the wedding day arrived the bride and John's sisters had just come down the aisle and were standing at the front of the church when high drama struck again. John's sister in law had just gone into labour in the church! His sister who had been a bridesmaid, his brother who had been playing the piano and the other bridesmaid sister dashed out to a side room! The bride and groom looked at one another. What do we do? Do we reschedule? They decided to continue but what a wedding! The screams and wails of a woman giving birth went on throughout all their vows. Then when the minister said, "You may kiss the bride", the wail of a baby went up from the side room and someone appeared to say the baby was a girl! Then John could finally kiss his bride.

In John's case, it seemed like every obstacle that could be thrown at him was to prevent him from marrying his beloved.

Maybe you are in a season of constant high drama. There is something you want to do - something you believe to be in the will of God for you and yet there is nothing but obstacles and everything that hell can throw at you to stop you from stepping into the purpose God has for you!

Satan from the beginning has caused high drama and tried to stop every purpose of God from coming to pass. He is the fallen angel who brings nothing but obstacles and discouragement. But he cannot win! The purpose will be fulfilled.

2 Corinthians 2:11 *"That we would not be outwitted by satan, for we are not ignorant of his designs."*

He's the adversary who prowls around like a roaring lion seeking to devour (1 Peter 5:8). He's also the deceiver and accuser of the whole world. (Revelation 12:9-10)

God sees beyond enemy lines and He is calling us not to be outwitted by satan's schemes - but to fight a good fight (1 Timothy 1:18). To take the sword of the Spirit, which is the Word of God, praying always. (Ephesians 6:17-18)

God is sovereign over satan. He is on a leash and can only do what God permits so no matter how many obstacles are in your life and no matter what high drama is happening to thwart God's purposes for your life - satan cannot win!

Your God is the one who turns what is meant for evil into good. He will give you the power to conquer satan and walk in every purpose that God predestined for you before the beginning of time.

130

Sweet Friendship That Refreshes The Soul

I have a friend that has journeyed most of my life with me since we started Bible College as teenagers. She is now married, is a pastor's wife, has two children, helps in the church charity shop and is hundreds of miles away in distance but she always makes time for me. I have part of a letter she wrote to me in 2007 inside my bible and on low days when the illness gets too much for me, I get that letter out and re-read it! Faithful friends are a treasure, they are precious and few, but I am truly thankful for the friends I have.

Proverbs 27:9 *"Ointment and perfume rejoice the heart so doth the sweetness of a man's friend by hearty counsel."*

Proverbs 13:20 *"He that walketh with wise men shall be wise: but a companion of fools shall be destroyed."*

Proverbs 27:17 *"Iron sharpeneth iron. So a man sharpeneth the countenance of his friend."*

Proverbs 17:17 *"A friend loveth at all times and a brother is born for adversity."*

A good number of years ago I went through something horrific that lasted for months on end and made my last year of my theology degree a nightmare. My smile hid the pain to everyone. But my dear close friend that I lived with did not even know either. I remember crying hard one day wishing I could tell this friend, but I am not good at opening up. I bottle things so my dear close friend only saw the smiling Joanne.

I will never forget the time I finally opened up. The dam broke and I just sobbed in her arms for what seemed like an eternity and then I poured months' worth of events to her. She was so shocked. Yet her tenderness, her compassion, her gentle encouraging words, her love, and wise counsel soothed an aching spirit like a balm. She decided to treat me to a day in Portrush.

In her presence, I laughed again. I felt like Joanne again. We ran in and out of the sea giggling like children. We went to the amusement park and went on the waltzer ride (my fav ride) three times. We went for fish and chips and just watched the ocean as we ate and talked about the amazingness and goodness of our God. We got ice cream and candy floss and went round all the gift shops picking up special treasures. We went into a photo booth that sketches your picture! We had great fun. But more than that I knew I had a sweet precious friend who had refreshed my soul and whom I knew I could fully trust never to repeat information. For she is wise and has no gossiping tongue. As iron sharpens iron, we can build each other up.

Choose close friends wisely. Sometimes people only want to get information out of you so they can repeat it. But a godly friend will conceal the matter and pray you through.

My Jesus is also my dearest closest friend. There is not a worry or fear I cannot give to my beloved. He is the friend who laid down His life for me, is always there in the best and worst of times. I can sob my heart out and I can lift my heart in praise to Him knowing nobody loves me more unconditionally than my beloved Jesus.

Are you struggling today? Turn to Jesus as you will find no truer friend than the one who died to save you and pluck you from a lost eternity.

If you are feeling friendless on earth and know Jesus as Saviour ask Him to send you a wise, godly, edifying, uplifting, caring, non-gossiping friend as He sent me. He will provide!

131

The Seventh Hour

I read a Grace Livingston Hill book called, 'The Seventh Hour'. In it, she quoted a scripture that I was drawn too.

John 4:52 *"Then he inquired of them of the hour when he began to amend. And they said unto him, Yesterday at the seventh hour the fever left him."*

The son of a certain Nobleman was sick, and he came straight to Jesus. He had faith in the ability of Jesus to heal because he came to Him and begged Him to come to the child's bedside to heal his son. But Jesus did not go. He sent him home with the promise of, your son lives. Without any visible proof the nobleman believed Jesus. At exactly the seventh hour while the boy's father had been talking to Jesus he had been healed. Seven was the number in the Bible for perfection and completeness.

In Grace's book a group of young people who were earnestly believing for one of their mothers to receive the miracle of Salvation. It looked hopeless as her heart was so hardened to God. But her 'Seventh Hour' appointed time came, and she yielded to her Saviour just before she died.

Are you believing for something and it looks impossible? You have prayed till you are blue in the face and you see no change. Discouragement reigns in your heart for you feel like things are never going to get better. Many a time I have felt that way with losing years of my life to an illness that is not shifting.

Let me encourage you today. Ecclesiastes 3 talks about there being an appointed time for everything under the sun and how God makes everything beautiful in His time.

Maybe you are wrestling with depression, maybe like me, you are physically sick, maybe your marriage is hanging by a thread, maybe your heart is broken by grief or over a wayward child. There are so many situations that people cry out to Jesus for help. Yet that help does not seem to be coming.

Remember this, your cries have already reached God's ears and your 'seventh hour' appointed time for release WILL come. God has never made a promise yet that He has not kept yet and He's not going to start with you!

I found this poem online on a site called 'Take off the Mask'. I pray that it is an encouragement to you all.

In God's perfect time,
Every pain shall be comforted,
Every year wiped away,
All our wounds shall be healed,
All our fears cast away,
In God's perfect time.

Take heart precious child of God, there is a 'seventh hour' of release for you too!

132

Death And Life In The Power Of The Tongue

I watched an episode of 'Little House on the Prairie' where Mary Ingalls had to start wearing glasses. Mary was bullied badly because of them so much so that she felt ashamed to wear them. The cruel words changed what was a blessing to Mary in helping her to see to being something that caused her shame and pain.

We all start in primary school learning the alphabet and putting words together. From then on, we can express ourselves freely. Without words, we would not have our precious Bible. Without words, the Gospel would not have been passed down from generation to generation for 2000 years.

The Bible has a lot to say about words.

Ephesians 4:29 *"Let no corrupt communication proceed out of your mouth, but that which is good to the use of edifying, that it may minister grace unto the hearers."*

Proverbs 10:19-20 *"In the multitude of words there wanteth not sin, but he that refraineth his tongue is wise. The tongue of the just is as choice silver."*

Proverbs 11:9 *"An hypocrite with his mouth destroyeth his neighbour."*

:13 *"A talebearer revealeth secrets."*

Proverbs 18:7 *"A fools mouth is his destruction and his lips are the snare of his soul."*

What way do you use words? Behind closed doors are you slandering and gossiping about another person? Are you with your tongue destroying them? Could your pastor read your texts and private emails without causing you shame? Do you use your lips for lies to destroy another's character? In public as a professing Christian do people hear corrupt communication coming out of your mouth? Complaining? Talking about the boss or other workmates? Running others into the ground to exalt yourself?

This is behaviour that brings dishonour to God. In James, it says you cannot with the same mouth bring forth clean and dirty waters at the same time. How can you with the same mouth try and sing worship songs in church? Is it real? Or is it a show to impress the pastor? In the sermon on the mount, Jesus said only the pure in heart shall see God. In other words, have a deep close relationship with Him. Pure in heart shows you have honoured God with your thoughts and words. The LORD has seen you have honoured Him. Your tongue is as silver. Your words are pure. Your worship is pure because you are not using the fountain of your mouth to pour forth dirty waters.

If everything you said was recorded and played in a church would you be ashamed? Would you be removed from any leadership role you hold as a result? Jesus is with you every second of the day. He hears all and it breaks His heart when His children use their tongues for destruction as it puts off the unsaved from coming to God.

Get before the Lord this day and ask Him to purify your heart and lips and use the words of your mouth from now on to build up and encourage others.

133

Bluebells

As a child I adored bluebells. They grew wild at the moss where I loved to play. I loved to pick the bluebells and bring them home. There were vases of them in every room.

Knowing most flowers are symbolic of something I wondered what the meaning of bluebells was. So I found this. The most popular meaning of bluebells is humility and gratitude.

It is associated with everlasting love and constancy. They are a symbol of undying love and unfailing devotion. I thought the meaning of this was beautiful. There are so many lessons that we as Christians can learn from the bluebell. The Bible is all for putting others needs before our own.

> Philippians 2:3-4 *"Let nothing be done through strife or vain glory but in lowliness of mind let each esteem others better than themselves. Look not every man at his own things but every man also on the things of others."*
>
> Romans 12:10 *"Be kindly, affectioned one to another with brotherly love preferring one another."*
>
> Mark 10:45 *"For even the Son of Man (Jesus) came not to be ministered unto, but to minister and give his life a ransom for many."*

We live in an 'I', 'me', and 'mine' generation. Prosperity churches teach it is all about you and your needs and what God can do for you like He's some kind of cosmic genie. Generally, people forget about others for they are so consumed with their own lives. But Jesus is calling us to be 'bluebells', to be devoted to one another, to replace the 'I' with the 'O' for others. In lowliness of mind esteem others better than yourself. Stop the prideful thinking that you are the best and the whole world revolves around you and your wants and that you are a godsend to the world. Get out there and lift others up. Even the King of kings came to serve others and not to be served and He is calling us to follow in His footsteps. He wants His 'bluebell' children to help the hurting, the sick, the needy. To show great brotherly love to everyone you meet. To be a rainbow in somebody else's cloud and stop letting your own cloud consume you so that you become selfish.

We are called to be selfless and to serve others. We are called to have an attitude of gratitude. You can put people off coming to Jesus by the words of your mouth by constantly gossiping and complaining both of which are sins. Let the words of your mouth bring the Lord great glory. Be daily grateful for your Salvation and every tiny thing that makes you smile. A grateful heart is a powerful magnet to the hurting.

1 Thessalonians 5:18 *"Give thanks in all circumstances."*

No matter what your circumstances are today reach out to someone else with love and compassion letting the love of our precious servant King radiate from you, so He can look down from Heaven upon you today and say, "I'm proud of my 'bluebell' child."

134

The Heirloom

An heirloom is described as something of special value handed down from one generation to another. I have a special heirloom. It has no worth in the eyes of the world or no material value but to me, it has great value.

I was given 'Lucy Doll' as my third birthday present. I have cherished her my whole life and even change her outfit from time to time. Lucy is an heirloom; she was my mother's doll before she was mine. It was loved and cherished by my mother. I hope someday the Lord will bless me with a little girl of my own to hand her down to or a niece if my brother marries! But I will make sure whatever way things work out I will keep 'Lucy Doll' in our family and hope she stays there for generations. But for now, I will keep her in perfect shape and she proudly sits on my chest of drawers.

You can be a spiritual heirloom by passing down the most precious gift, mankind has ever received. The Gospel of Jesus Christ. Material things fade away, but the Gospel will never fade away. The Lord wants you to carry the light of His word to a generation who largely wants nothing to do with Him.

Your life can and will make a huge difference if you pledge before God that no matter what you're going through, no matter what life throws at you, no matter how busy you are that you will obey the command of your Saviour.

Mark 16:15-16 *"Go ye therefore into all the world and preach the gospel to every creature. He that believeth and is baptized shall be saved, but he that believeth not shall be damned."*

We as God's children must obey the Lord's commands. This is not just for missionaries this is for every child of God.

2 Corinthians 3:2 *"Ye are our epistle* (letter) *written in our hearts. Known and read of all men."*

Ask the Lord to stir up in you a powerful passion to reach the lost. You may be the only Christian some people will ever meet whether in hospital, in a workplace or to a newcomer in your neighbourhood. Can they read you like a letter and see the Lord Jesus? Have you tried to talk to them about eternity and their need to accept Jesus as Saviour rather than let them go to a lost sinner's hell?

A woman from my church used to sing these words:

In this world of darkness.
We are given light.
Hope for all the dying.
How will they know that Jesus loves them,
and He died to save them?
Carry the light.
Go and tell the children,
they are precious in His sight.
Go and preach the Gospel
until there is no more night.
In the name of Jesus Christ, Carry the light.

135

I'll Say Yes Lord

Considering I am a wedding-aholic I like to watch *'Say Yes to the Dress'*. For those of you who do not know what it is, it is where brides-to-be go to a famous store in New York to buy the wedding dress of their dreams. Some days it is so funny because they bring the biggest crowds with them.

The opinions of all these people confuse the bride to be and distract her from what she wants. Some of the dresses are the ugliest dresses I have ever seen! Yet the bride stands clapping her hands jumping for joy saying I'm saying yes to the dress! Though I do realise that every bride has their idea of what they would like and should be free to choose what they like without others dictating to them.

It made me think, have you said 'Yes' to God's plans for your life? Has He laid it clearly on your heart what He wants you to do? But you are pausing, taking in the opinions of everyone else and delaying instead of obeying.

Psalm 16:11 *"Thou wilt shew me the path of life in thy presence is fullness of joy."*

Psalm 25:4 *"Shew me your ways oh Lord, teach me your paths."*

Proverbs 4:18 *"The path of the just is as a shining light, that shineth more unto the perfect day."*

This comes from the old hymn, *'Trust and Obey'*.

But we never can prove the delights of His love,
until all on the altar we lay.
For the favour He shows, for the joy He bestows.
Are for all who will trust and obey.

What has the Lord laid on your heart to do? Witness to someone, take a Sunday school class, help at a summer Bible camp - you alone know. But only in saying, 'Yes' are we on the path of life and that path will shine brighter the more you surrender to His will and keep obeying His Word. Like the hymn says, "We never can prove the delights of His love, Until ALL on the altar we lay."

The Lord wants you to walk in His perfect Will, obeying Him no matter what the cost. That thing He has laid on your heart to do just leave aside the opinions of others and your desire to go your own way and say YES Lord. YES to obedience, YES to your life being used more greatly for the Lord's glory, YES to bringing delight to His heart, YES to surrendering all not some, YES to making Jesus your Saviour and lover of your soul your top priority. Will you say YES to God's path and His leading? At the end of the day, He is all that truly matters.

136

You Have Great Worth In God's Eyes

I watched a true-life film called, *'A Narrow Escape'*. It was about American navy soldiers stationed in Korea during WW2. A baby was found abandoned on a dumping ground. They named the baby - Daniel. The navy doctor became very attached to the child. The child took to him like he was his father. But it was against protocol for a navy man to adopt a child found on duty. Plus the man believed his identity and career where who he was, and he could not be anything else.

The baby was brought on board the naval ship after the war to be adopted by an American family. But the doctor fell more and more in love with four-month-old Daniel. His wife and he could not have children and when the boat was stationed in port for a while his wife visited and instantly loved Daniel. She asked her husband to step down from his career so they could have the child. But he kept refusing. Kept saying my naval career is who I am. But eventually, when he thought the child was going to another family, he broke down and cried. He realised his work was not his identity and he loved baby Daniel and his wife more than his career.

It spoke to me. The LORD says you have worth for who you are, not what you do. Your worth does not depend upon your career, your ability to have children, your relationship status, or your financial gain. Your worth rests alone in your relationship with Jesus as Saviour. He who lives in you is your Heavenly lover who loves you for who you are! Even before a tiny baby can 'do' anything the mother loves him or her for who their child is not for their performance. The mothers love is unconditional and that is what God's love is like towards you.

Colossians 3:3 *"For you are dead and your life is hid with Christ in God."*

Colossians 2:10 *"And ye are complete in him."*

Other scriptures about your worth in God.

Matthew 10:31 - you have more value than the sparrows.

Zephaniah 3:17 - The Lord rejoices over you with gladness and singing.

Isaiah 43:4 - you are precious in His sight.

Psalm 139 - He formed you in the womb, He adores you, He says you are wonderfully made.

Deuteronomy 7:6 - He calls you His treasured possession.

Remember your worth is not found in what you do, it's about how the Lord sees you.

137

Miracles Happen When You Least Expect It

I watched a true film called, *'Half a Dozen Babies'*. It was about a young married couples' desperate plea to have a child. Naturally, it was impossible for both. The doctor suggested fertility tablets and to afford them they had to cash in their life insurance policy and use all their savings. But months went past, and it was not working. The husband said they needed to look into adoption as they had no more money.

Then at work one day (the wife was a nurse) her best friend told her about twins that had just been born and how the parents had been to a specialist and tried a new fertility drug and it worked! The lady persuaded her hubby to go to see this specialist. He told them one dose of it was over $1000. It looked impossible. They had spent everything they had. But then the next day the wife went to a pawn shop and sold her engagement and wedding rings. They now had enough money for just one more try but she promised that after that she would listen to her husband and go down the adoption line.

The miracle of life happened! The long-awaited, almost hopeless seeming miracle came to pass! The scan showed five babies! The doctor advised them to abort some as it was too risky to the mother's life. But she refused to kill any of her babies. When they were born, one had been hiding and six children all came into the world at once. They were America's first sextuplets. Four boys and two girls!

It was a massive miracle when all hope was lost the Lord blessed them with not one but six children to love and cherish!

Maybe today you are hanging by a thread. You have lost all sight of hope. There have been many tears, many times of getting your hopes up only for them to be crushed and now you just feel defeated and beat.

The Lord wants to remind you of these scriptures today.

Jeremiah 32:27 *"Behold, I am the Lord of all flesh: is anything too hard for me?"*

Isaiah 60:22 *"When the time is right, I the Lord will make it happen."*

Matthew 19:26 *"With God all things are possible."*

Hang in there! Do not give up in the waiting season for God's got this.

138

Staying Fresh In Your Walk With God

We all like to keep ourselves fresh. Clean body, clean face makes us feel fresher. Have you ever bought a punnet of strawberries and they looked fine when you bought them but once you took the top layer off, underneath they were not fresh at all? They were all blue and fluffy. Yukky!

Or have you ever bit into what you thought was a ripe banana to find it black and mushy inside? Eughh! Or you are about to enjoy a yogurt and after the first spoonful it is so sour you can barely swallow it. Foods that are not fresh certainly don't hit the mark.

The Lord gives us fresh grace and fresh strength to get through every day. We do not have to live off yesterday's grace for He has fresh grace for every day.

Lamentations 3:22-23 *"It is of the Lord's mercies that we are not consume, because his compassions fail not. They are new every morning. Great is thy faithfulness."*

2 Corinthians 12:9 *"My grace is sufficient for thee, for my power is made perfect in weakness."*

No matter what your struggle is today, remember the Lord has sent you fresh grace to endure today for He is faithful. The psalmist cried, *"Quicken me O Lord"*. A prayer he prayed many times in the psalms. He is saying Lord refresh, restore and renew my walk with you. In other words, freshen me up. Do not let me go stale. Do not let my heart go cold, I am calling out, light the fire again.

Stay fresh in Jesus. Do not let your walk go stale as old bread and remember you have fresh grace to see you through every day, even in your pain.

139

Dare To Speak Out God's Truth No Matter What

I read a book by Grace Livingston Hill. It featured two sisters. One who was evil and one who loved the Lord. The bad one was called Athaliah. She simply scoffed at anything to do with God. She was full of hate and anger and did the most awful things.

There was an Athaliah in scripture. The daughter of Jezebel. Athaliah was very evil (2 Chronicles 23). She stole the throne and murdered all her children and grandchildren, all the royal seed. She was ruthless and desperately wicked. The only child that was preserved was Joash, who was taken and hidden. She was given up to her evil ways. Eventually, she was killed when they brought forth the real royal heir. After her death, the kingdom was restored to God. They went to the places of Baal (idol, occultic worship) and tore down the false gods. The house of the Lord and worship of Him was reinstated in the land.

2 Chronicles 23:21 *"And all the people of the land rejoiced, and the city was quiet after they had slain Athaliah with the sword."*

The name Athaliah means, 'The time of the Lord' which is fitting for the biblical Athaliah only got away with turning the land to evil, the word of God ignored, occultic worship replaced the worship of the true and living God, for a time.

Sadly, the world we live in now has become the 'Athaliah' generation. The Word of God has been rejected by society. To many, it is just a stuffy outdated old book and anyone who stands up for truth is called narrow-minded. God's been left out of schools, nurses can no longer pray with patients, wicked abominable ways abound and are celebrated like the murdering of children in the womb, homosexuality, rape, children being captured and sold into the slavery for prostitution, fornication, adultery, domestic abuse, pornography, lust, theft, hatred, slander, lies and the rise of false prophets who preach false salvation.

Even Christians are going the same way as the church of Laodicea and compromise God's Word so they 'can do what's right in their own eyes'.

We as God's children need to turn to prayer. We need to pray hard that those who are rejecting the Saviour will get a chance to repent before death claims them or the Lord returns, and they must face judgement day without having Him as Saviour.

We need to 'Dare to be Daniels', to stand alone and to keep speaking out the truth, the whole truth, and nothing but the truth of God's Word even when we are mocked and scorned and called all sorts of things. Noah kept trying to reach the lost to the very end. They scorned and mocked him. They did not believe a flood was going to destroy the earth and refused to get into the ark. Jesus is our ark - the only door and only way to Salvation. Christian today we need to wake up from our sleep and carry the light of the Gospel to this dark world. Keep witnessing to others. Keep trying like Noah did till the very end. In Ezekiel, it says, if we fail to warn the lost, their blood will be on our heads.

Let us take our stand in an 'Athaliah' generation and see the world won for Christ before it's too late.

140

Johnny Jump Ups

I was reading a book and the girl stood and admired 'Johnny Jump Up' flowers before she went to her destination. I was like - what on this earth are they? So I investigated it. 'Johnny Jump Ups' are what the Americans call Viola flowers. They are wildflowers that need no tending too. They are bright-faced and extremely hardy. They can survive the worst winter frost and are the first flowers to blossom every spring. Because of their hardiness and far-reaching territory. They have been used for cooking and healing for centuries. Salves were made to treat wounds and sores and various infusions have been remedies for many internal problems. They can also be called 'Heart's Ease', 'tickle my fancy', 'jump up and kiss me' and called 'Stepmother' in France and Germany.

Two things about them spoke to me. Their endurance at surviving the worst winters and yet blooming first in spring. I think that is a lesson to all who are struggling to keep enduring. It is winter for you now and you think spring is never going to come. You feel defeated. Yet the Lord is saying,

Philippians 4:1 *"Stand fast in the Lord my dearly beloved."*

Joshua 1:6 *"Be strong and of a good courage."*

God is saying you are going to survive this harsh winter of seeming hopelessness that you find yourself in and bring you to a place where you will bloom in God with great beauty.

The fact that these flowers were used as a healing balm reminded me that Jesus is our precious Healer. Only He can bind up your wounds and make you whole again. That does not always happen in the way we want it too. But He cares for us deeply and wants us to bring our hearts greatest weights to Him so He can take them and fill you with His precious healing balm of divine love. As for one of the nicknames for the flowers, 'Heart's Ease' let Jesus be your heart's ease today.

141

Buckwheat Cakes

I was reading a novel by an Aunt of Grace Livingston Hill called *'Buckwheat Cakes'*. I'd never heard of them before. In the story, a recently married wife was struggling to make the Buckwheat cakes that her hubby loved. They were either sour, doughy, fat, or foul-tasting. The girl made it her ambition that when her hubby went away on business, she would make the train journey to his parents to learn how to make them.

On the way home her train got stuck in the snow. A girl beside her was reading her Bible and talking about her Saviour. The girl determined in her heart that her new ambition in life was to know the train girls Saviour.

Buckwheat cakes are the smell of autumn breakfast in West Virginia. Every year in Preston county they have a Buckwheat festival which marks the start of autumn. They are lighter than pancakes and usually served with either maple syrup or sausage.

This quote was taken from the very first American cookery and woman's history book. "The buckwheat cake was in her mouth. The tear was in her eye."

It was her joy to promote health and happiness in her home. The buckwheat cakes symbolised harmony in the home, of happiness in a southern marriage.

Buckwheat is a plant that has been grown in America since colonial days in the 1800s.

All of this spoke to me. They may be a symbol of joy in

marriage, but I think they have a wider meaning. For a start, they mark the start of autumn a beautiful season of bright colours and joy as children play through the fallen leaves. It is a symbol that no matter how bad your circumstances - joy will come again.

As for happiness in the home. We can learn from this and carry it through to all other relationships. The key to a happy marriage is selfless service one to the other. The Lord wants us to bring joy, kindness, and love to all those around us.

Romans 12:13 *"Share with the Lord's people who are in need. Practise hospitality."*

Romans 12:10 *"Be kindly affectioned one to another with brotherly love in honour preferring one another."*

Ephesians 4:32 *"Be ye kind to one another, tenderhearted...."*

Philippians 2:4 *"Look not every man on his own things but every man also of the needs of others."*

Remember the Buckwheat cake today and spread as much joy and love as you can to others for many are suffering and need your tender touch.

142

So Precious In His Eyes

Isaiah 43:4 *"Since thou wast precious in my sight, thou hast been honourable and I have loved thee."*

How often do we truly feel precious in the Lord's sight? We are often more aware of all our shortcomings than feeling precious. But God is saying you are His precious jewel. He loves you more than you will ever know, think or imagine.

Think of all the things in the world that are considered precious. Like gemstones or jewels. You are more precious than all the jewels in the world.

Think of the things in your life you consider precious. Not just things but people too. Your closest family, your dearest friends. God loves and adores you with even more affection than you love the most precious person in your life.

No matter how low you are feeling today let the fact that you are a precious jewel in God's eyes, comfort you and sustain you in your trial.

143

Jasper The Rescuer

I read a Grace Livingston Hill book called *'The Finding of Jasper Holt'*. This scripture came to mind as soon as I started reading it.

Psalm 69:1 *"Save me O God for the waters have come up to my neck."*

In the book a train crashed, throwing from it, its passengers. One very frail girl called Jean landed in deep waters. She thought she was going to die when she felt a strong hand grasp her and pull her to shore. This stranger had risked his own life to save another from drowning. It turned out the man was called Jasper. The name means 'treasurer' and it is believed it was one of the names of the Magi the Royals from afar who brought gifts to Jesus. The walls of Heaven are also made of the precious stone Jasper (Revelation 21:18). It is a very precious stone that is a symbol of courage and endurance.

Jasper in the story was a real treasure for Jean would have surely died if he had not saved her. Maybe today you are in a circumstance that makes you feel like you are drowning. The waters have come up to your neck and you feel you are going under. In our case, Jesus is our Jasper our Heavenly treasure who loves and adores us and will not see us going under.

Maybe so many of you feel like that today. Like you have been treading water too long and you are going under. But my dear friend Jesus will not let you go under. No matter how you feel He WILL rescue you, He WILL comfort you. He loved you enough to sacrifice His very life and die in your place, so He isn't about to let His precious child drown under the pressures of life for He has amazing plans for you. Never forget that! Your worth is more in His sight than rubies.

144

What The Enemy Means For Evil The Lord Can Turn To Good

I finished another book by Grace Livingston Hill called *'The Mystery of Mary'*. In it, the enemy meant great evil in her life to harm and destroy her. It was still in the day when people married their cousins. Everybody belonging to Mary had died and her wicked cousin had obtained a fake wedding certificate and intended to have her sent to a mental asylum so he could steal the fortune her parents had left her.

At the train station, she managed to escape and a kind man called Tryon took her under his wing. The plans of the enemy had been destroyed by her rescuer. After that life turned out to be more beautiful than ever. What the enemy meant for harm against God's child, He turned it into good.

Sometimes satan tries his very best to send blockages to stop God's children being all they can be in God and doing all they can in His service. He means to destroy God's purpose for you and leave you ineffective. But you must become wise to his plots and ask your Heavenly rescuer the Lord Jesus to help you and turn all that hell sends at you for good.

The devil sent a massive blockage of discouragement to my life. I had started writing a new book for His glory in 2013 but I got discouraged. The devil paralysed me with his lies that there was no way possible that I could write another book. I gave in to the enemies lies for a season BUT the Lord's purpose prevailed, and He gave me the divine anointing to finish it and now it is being published! I thought the enemy had totally blocked that, but the Lord's purposes will always prevail.

In the story of Joseph, his brothers had tried to wreck his life by throwing him in a pit and selling him as a slave. But no matter what they did to him the Lord's purpose still prevailed and he became second in command in Egypt.

Satan will try to block your service for God but do not let him. Ask the Lord who is your amazing Saviour to help you resist satan. If you have been almost destroyed by the enemy's plot know that what the enemy meant for your harm the Lord will turn into good for you and for His glory.

145

In My Distress

2 Samuel 22:7 *"In my distress, I called unto the Lord and he did hear my voice out of his temple and my cry did enter his ears."*

I finished reading *'Stranger within the Gates'* by Grace Livingston Hill. This quote touched me. "And to you who are troubled by things in your life that are bringing you disappointment and sorrow there comes this message of peace, that God has not let anything come to you that's not going to work out for some good for you to the end that His glory might shine through you and you may pass on the message of joy and Salvation to others."

Things might be distressing for you now and you desperately need your Saviour to come to your side and hold you for you feel like you are falling apart. But He has promised to bring good and great glory out of your situation no matter how bad it looks. You cannot see it now in your distress but one day God will use all you have been through to draw others to Himself.

My situation is too impossible for it to work out for God's glory, you say. He is still the miracle-working God no matter how you feel!

The words to an old song from years ago ties in. "Sometimes the night can be so long and it feels in the darkness, all hope is gone. Then a voice gently whispers my child it is I and Lo I am with you, you'll always be mine. He'll see you through. There's nothing Jesus can't do when you've done all you can and you've come to the end. He'll see you through."

Your God can turn your deepest distress and cause something glorious to come from it.

146

Expect Gladness

Proverbs 10:28 *"The Hope of the righteous shall be gladness."*

Or the Hope of the child of God shall be gladness. Ever remember the days when you were like the wee girl in the photo. As happy as the cat that got the cream. Carefree, wellies on, splashing through the puddles despite the rain still coming. I did it so often! There was nothing I loved more as a child than getting the wellies on and having a good splash in the puddles. It did not matter how muddy I got! I was in my element!

Life has a way of taking the moments of joy and replacing them with hard trials and sadness. Maybe you have endured much sadness for many years. You wonder if you will ever get through this struggle.

I am writing this today to say you will get through this struggle. You will enter a season of joy again. For the Lord has said the Hope of His child shall be gladness. Those puddle jumping joy-filled days of beauty will come again!

Hope is a rainbow. Things are about to change.

147

When It's All Too Much

Psalm 55:8 & 22 *"Hasten my escape from the windy storm and tempest... Cast thy burden upon the Lord and he shall sustain thee he shall never suffer the righteous to be moved."*

Sometimes things get so overwhelmingly bad that you just want to hasten your escape from the storm. Earlier in this passage, David said fearfulness and trembling came upon him. In other words, his circumstances were crippling his spirit to the point he just felt defeated.

Sometimes we get into the same place. We cry the load is too heavy Lord, I cannot bear it. Our spirits are downcast and wonder if we will ever be free of the nightmare circumstances we are going through.

The Lord understands. He sees you cannot carry this load by yourself. He sees the fearfulness and trembling. He sees the defeat in your spirit and how much you want to hasten from the windy storm. You have had promises of hope from the Lord but at the minute you are in the bleak season of waiting and it's crippling you.

We need to cast our burdens upon the Lord and let Him sustain us. He is not going to let you crumble even if you feel like it right now. To cast means to throw away from you as far as possible. Throw the mountainous struggle into the arms of Jesus. To try and carry it yourself is like going around with a heavy rock tied to you all day. Give that rock to Jesus, tell Him you cannot cope anymore and let Him sustain you. He loves you so much and does not want you to close Him out of the struggle and if the only prayer you can pray when you're at your worst is 'Lord help me', He sees and understands. He is with you right now. Holding you up. He will not see His child destroyed by his/her circumstances. This windy storm and tempest will not destroy you. Take heart, you are in His hands.

148

Floramel

John 10:10 *"The thief cometh not but to steal and to kill and to destroy. I am come that they might have life and that they might have it more abundantly."*

I started reading a book last night called *'Stranger within the Gates'*. In it, a deceptive, manipulative woman who wanted to get in with a wealthy family, told many lies to a young man. She told him so many lies and turned on the tears. She told him an awful man had been harassing her and she would never feel safe until she was under the protection of marriage. The young man protested at first, but she deceived him so much that he agreed. His beautiful looking Floramel was a thief, come to kill, steal, and destroy his family and get her hands on the family fortune.

Satan does the same. He can disguise himself as an angel of light and use certain people as wolves in sheep's clothing to come along and play on your naive side. But through them he is trying to destroy your walk with God, he is using them to stop you moving forward into all you could be in God. They will manipulate you; you will feel afraid of them but at the same time be too terrified to break off the friendship. All that will come from that relationship on their side will be gossip, slander, constant complaining and negativity. It will wear you down so much. The more slander you listen to about other people, the more your walk with God suffers. The thief is using them to kill, steal and destroy and keep you from service for God.

Satan also fires at us constant lies. He will tell us anything that is against his word. He will tell you anything to kill your walk with God. He will tell you are useless, worthless, that you will fail if you dare try anything for God. The only way to fight him and stop him from killing your walk with God is to quote the Word of God at him. If he says you are useless you say I am made in the image of God and have great worth in Him. If he says you are a failure you say I was born for a purpose and in God's eyes you are a pearl of great price. Jesus wants your walk with Him to be abundant and so close to Him. He wants to use you powerfully for His glory. Beware of his lies. Beware Floramels who have two different faces. One that is all smiling and the other that is cruel and destructive.

Do not let satan kill your walk with God. Do not let him steal from you. Do not let him destroy all the Lord is calling you to do.

Fight hard with the sword of His Word today and be on your guard lest any apparent friend is doing you more harm than good.

149

Funeral Potatoes

Mum was watching 'The Pioneer Woman' cookery programme. She had to listen twice for she thought she had heard wrong. The lady had made funeral potatoes! When she told me I got a mental image of a potato wearing a black coat! Curiosity was going to kill the cat, so I researched to find out about them.

In the South of America, they serve hot comforting foods after a funeral. Over here it is just tea with sandwiches and buns. I thought but why are they called funeral potatoes.

Well, they are stodgy and full of cheese and bacon and tinned soups. They are called that as they are comfort food. Ever turn to food during tragedy and despair?

Three years before I took sick, I had a trial far more devastating and heart-breaking than all the years I have suffered physically. My immediate reaction to the agony was to cry non-stop and eat packets of buns and large amounts of chocolate. I ran to friends for them to hold me and continued to eat rubbish. I still felt empty and full of despair. Comfort was not coming from food or constant running to friends.

One night I finally stopped running and trying to comfort myself. I fell to my knees in the bedroom and sobbed and sobbed and sobbed calling upon the Lord to comfort me and hold me close. Something awesome happened. The room was suddenly filled with the most amazing sense of the Lord's presence I have ever felt. It was like He was in the room with me. I dared not open my eyes for the whole place felt like Holy ground. I poured out my agonised heart to the Lord and He filled me with such supernatural comfort that I can hardly describe it with words.

After that night I continued to fall to my knees every time the pain got too much instead of eating non-stop and running to friends and I sensed His voice telling me He would carry me through the pain and agony.

Are you in pain and agony today? The bible describes the Lord as the God of all comfort. He has sent us His Holy Spirit to be our constant comforter.

2 Corinthians 1:3 *"The God of all comfort... who comforteth us in our tribulations that we may be able to comfort them wherewith we ourselves are comforted of God."*

Psalm 119:76 *"Let, I pray thee, thy merciful kindness be my comfort according to thy word unto thy servant."*

Turn to the Lord of all comfort to heal your broken heart today. He wants to pour in His comfort into your heart in a beautiful way. He cares about all you are going through and wants to hold you close through the agony. Run to the Lord of all comfort today to meet your need. He is longing to fill your heart with His healing balm and be there for you in your desperate time of need.

150

More Than Conquerors

Romans 8:37 *"We are more than conquerors through him that loved us."*

The dictionary describes 'Conqueror' as one who overcomes, one who wins the war for his country or overcomes an adversary. Other names for it are victor, champion, hero, winner, warrior, or fighter.

To think God calls us conquerors, even when we feel like we are drowning, is amazing. I marvel at it! Most days I do not feel like a warrior. I feel I am being overcome by a nightmare illness that will not go away. I would not describe myself as a victor or hero, yet God says I am. If I stay in the fight and do not let the illness overcome me and stop me serving the Lord that I love with all my heart He says I am a conqueror! I marvel at that! Feelings tell me I am worthless and useless but that is not what God says.

Looking at all the people who have been champions of their circumstances. I marvel! My friend was told her child was so badly brain damaged that she would never speak or walk. The little girl has proved them all wrong and is walking and talking and is an extremely sweet caring child.

A girl who attempted suicide by lying on the train tracks survived by the grace of God. She lost both legs but found the Saviour thereafter. She now runs 'Kristen Jane Anderson reaching you' ministries and has led many suicidal young people to the Saviour. She also married and has two children.

I read recently about a girl who survived an abortion. They took the life out of the child to kill her yet against the odds she survived and campaigns today for the rights of the unborn children. The famous man Nick who was born without arms and legs has a successful worldwide ministry taking the Gospel to millions. He did not let his extreme disabilities cause him to give up, instead, he asked the Lord to use his weaknesses for the glory of God and extension of His Kingdom.

I could go on with story after story, but the point is you are an overcomer. Your circumstances might be utterly dire. You might feel sunk, totally unusable to the Lord. You might feel beat but God says you are His warrior and as long as you stay near to Him and continue to ask Him to use you despite your weaknesses He will use your life in incredible ways. Ways you never thought possible if you leave your limits in the Lord's hands.

He says you are more than a conqueror so no matter how low you feel believe it because God cannot lie!

151

The God of the Weary

Psalm 60:5,11-12 *"That thy beloved might be delivered. Save with thy right hand and hear me... Give us help from trouble for vain is the help of man... Through God we shall do valiantly for he it is that shall tread down our enemies."*

In a picture I had seen, a girl looked like she had laid down in defeat. In utter weariness. She must feel so defeated and numb. I have been in that place. Coping with illness leaves you feeling like how on this earth am I going get through this. I remember a worship song from years ago.

> Hungry I come to you for I know you satisfy.
> I am weary but I know your love does not run dry.
> So I wait for you.
> Jesus, you're all this heart is living for.

If you are so weary from constantly coping from the circumstances of your life. Your marriage is in dire straits. Your adult children refuse to speak to you. You are in a bullying situation where you are hanging by a thread. You feel you cannot hold on during illness. You are suffering from depression and cannot see a way out.

The Lord says you are His BELOVED. No matter what is going on He adores you and He has said that His beloved will be delivered. He will save with His right hand and help you. He knows that in certain circumstances vain is the help of man. Many people do not want to listen to you when you are in dire straits. They only want to listen when the garden is rosy. Fair-weather friends!

Some medical conditions cannot be treated so again vain is the help of man. But despite there being little help from man God our Lord is the greatest helper and support we could ever ask for. He says that through Him we shall do valiantly - in other words triumphantly! He shall tread down our enemies. Everything the enemy is throwing against you He can deliver you from. Maybe in the likes of sickness, the wait will be long, but the enemy of illness is not too big for God. Nothing is! Weary soul, run to your Saviour today and cry out to Him to deliver you for He loves you deeply and can make a way where there seems to be no way.

152

From Trouble To Comfort

Psalm 77:2 *"In the day of my troubles, I sought the Lord. My sore ran in the night and ceased not. My Soul refused to be comforted."*

:14 *"Thou art the God that doest wonders. Thou hast declared thy strength among the people."*

In this psalm, David was in deep agonising despair. His soul refused to be comforted. He was falling apart, and he was in a hopeless state. Have you ever been there?

I watched a true-life film about a teenage girl who was in so much despair and inner turmoil that she was starving herself to death. She saw nothing to live for. Maybe you are in a place of such despair and despondency that you feel utterly empty inside. There is numbness there that ceases not and no matter what people say, the heaviness does not lift. You cry to God but inside you feel helpless. God cares for you and loves you as much in your heartbreak times as He does in your sunshine times in your life. How did David turn things around in this psalm? How did the girl in the film go from wanting to die to being determined to get well and live again? Both encouraged themselves. They changed their thoughts of utter despair to ones of 'No, I believe there is Hope, No, I'm not staying in this state.'

David loved the Lord and even though he felt despondent, he started to encourage himself in the Lord. It says many times throughout Scripture 'and David encouraged himself in the Lord.' He started by reminding himself that his God never changed and if God were able to do wonders in the past, He could still work a wonder in his life now. The God he served was and is the one who parted seas for His people to cross, who fed His children with manna from Heaven. His Lord was and is the one who made the heavens and the earth. He let his thoughts turn to the power of his God and lifted them off his own powerlessness.

Later in the passage, he said Lord I know that you with your own arm redeem or in other words rescue your people. If you are despondent today try doing what David did - encourage yourself in the Lord. Make a list of Scriptures that talk about His faithfulness, goodness and miracle-working power and hold tight to them. Your God with His strong arms will rescue you!

153

God Our Protector

For years and years right up to before I took sick, I was a sleepwalker! My mum often found me at 3 a.m. fully dressed in my school uniform, putting chocolate pop tarts into the toaster. I did that so many times and have no recollection of doing it for apparently, I always answered, 'I'm just getting ready for school'.

It happened once at CEF camp when I was twelve. There was a set of drawers at the bottom of the room that stored some of the other girls' belongings. I was in the top bunk at the opposite side of the room but in my sleep, I climbed down the ladder and went over to the set of drawers and took all the clothes out and chucked them all over the floor. Apparently, the other girls asked what I was doing, and I said, 'I just can't find the bug spray.' They laughed about it all week, but I could not believe the messy bombshell in the dorm was caused by me.

The Lord had protected me. I could have done myself damage by falling out that top bunk, but God kept me safe. I remember another incident when I was twenty and at Bible College living with four other girls. Again, apparently, they found me in the middle of the night laying out towels, getting the shower gel, shampoo, and hairdryer out. When they asked what I was doing I apparently said, 'I had to get a shower because I couldn't be late.' They steered me back to bed and I did not remember a thing when they told me in the morning. Again God protected me as the room I shared with my roommate was directly at the top of the stairs. I could have done myself great harm.

One more incident when I was twenty-two (I took M.E. at twenty-four). I was living with my CEF friend Naomi for a while,

while I was doing my PGCE to save me getting the train to and from Ballymoney to Belfast every day. One night she found me unlocking the front door and I was about to walk into the streets of Belfast in my pyjamas and bare feet. I thank the Lord that He woke Naomi, otherwise I was in great danger. We did not live in a safe part of Belfast. God protected me from harm by waking Naomi up just before I stepped out onto the street.

Our God is the God who protects His children. I have proved that in my life. He has kept me from danger many times. He is my strength, shield, and divine protector. If there is something you are worried about today, if you feel you are in danger or full of fear then remember God might let you bend but He will not let you break.

Look at these scriptures and take comfort from them.

Psalm 20:1 *"May the Lord answer you in distress, may the name of the God of Jacob protect you."*

Psalm 121 *"The Lord watched over you - the Lord is your shade at your right hand... the Lord will keep you from all harm..."*

2 Thessalonians 3:3 "But the Lord is faithful and he will strengthen and protect you from the evil one."

154

Always Darkest Before The Dawn

I started to read *'Dawning of the Morning'* by Grace Livingston Hill. The girl in the story was called Jemina which means 'dawning of the morning'. I was reminded of a Scripture.

Psalm 119:147 (KJV) *"I prevented the dawning of my morning and cried."*

According to the KJV dictionary, the word prevented in this context means 'anticipating'. So it could also be read: *"I anticipated the dawning of my morning."* Oh, what a beautiful verse. After years of suffering, I have been anticipating the dawning of my morning - the birth of a new day, full of healing and hope. There is nothing more beautiful than seeing the sun coming up first thing. Every Easter as a child and teenager my father and I went to the 'dawn service' in Ballintoy. I loved it! Standing there at dawn on Easter Sunday worshipping my Saviour for conquering death while watching the sun come up. It was glorious.

Maybe your circumstance has been awful for ages. My word for you today is to keep on anticipating the dawning of your new day. When a new day will be birthed, and you will leave behind the darkness. 'It is always darkest before the dawn' was a quote I heard at the start of my illness! It has been a long night-time season! But the Dawn is coming! I have expressed it as best I can in this poem.

Anticipating the Dawn

It's been a nightmare for years and years.
Because of Illness, there have been many tears.
But amidst the suffering and all my fears.
A light of hope has shone because I know 'My God hears.'
So, in all the thinking time amidst lying in bed.
I've had time to dream of healing. Of marriage. Of having a child.
Hopeful dreams go through my head.
I'm anticipating the dawning of my morning and know someday
I'll celebrate when the shadows have fled.
Onward I go. Not giving up. Believing beauty will be restored in
sufferings stead.

No matter how low you feel today ask the Lord to help you
keenly anticipate the dawning of your new day.

155

Marigold. Worldly Or Consecrated Wholly To Jesus?

I read a book called *'Marigold'* by Grace Livingston Hill. Marigold had once loved her Saviour with all her heart. He had all of her. She was dead to self and alive to Christ. However in trying to get the attention of a young man who was not a believer she started to walk away from God. She started to run with this man to worldly places that she could not take her Saviour too or feel that if He returned to earth, she would be ashamed to be found in such places. Her love for the Lord waxed cold. Her thoughts, attitudes and words became worldly and selfish. You cannot be married to one man and have flings with as many other men as you like. You are either fully surrendered to and have offered your life in wholehearted devotion to your Heavenly Bridegroom or you are playing the spiritual whore on the one you claim to love.

The girl in the book finally realised her life was meant to be dead to the world so she could be a living witness to the purity and love of her Saviour. You cannot serve two masters. If you love the things of the world, the love of the Father is not in you and you are in direct rebellion to Him. When you pray take my life and let it be consecrated Lord to thee, it should mean you are laying your life down as a living sacrifice, your body as the temple of God and desire that your life will draw many others who will see the Saviour in you.

Galatians 2:20 *"I am crucified with Christ, nevertheless I live, but Christ liveth in me and the life which I now live in the flesh I live by the faith of the Son of God who loved me and gave himself up for me."*

1 John 2:13 *"Love not the world, neither the things of the world. If any man love the world the love of the Father is not in him."*

James 4:4 *"Friendship with the world is emnity with God. Whosoever therefore will be a friend off the world is an enemy of God."*

Matthew 6v24 *"No man can serve two masters."*

After reading the book I investigated what Marigold means.

- The Marigold plant represents sacrifice. The sacred offering of oneself to God.

- Named after Mary the mother of Jesus who surrendered her everything to God even though she could have been stoned to death for expecting a baby outside marriage. Mary's goal was the total surrender of her will to God even though it could have cost her everything.

- It thrives during the autumn season and survives the driest weather.

The Lord is looking for 'marigold' servants who will obey Him no matter what the cost and who will not be a bride with the dirty stains of the world soiling her dress for that brings great heartbreak to our Heavenly Bridegroom.

If you feel like Marigold you have wandered away from the Lord and compromised yourself with the world then repent of your sins and rededicate your life to the Heavenly Bridegroom wholeheartedly and from this day forward vow to honour Him in everything. Give your all to the Saviour today He loves you and longs that you will fully surrender and be His Marigold.

156

The Jewellery Box

Matthew 6:19-21 *"Lay not up for yourselves treasures upon earth... But lay up for yourselves treasure in heaven. For where your treasure is, there will your heart be also."*

When I was younger, I used to own a beautiful jewellery box. It was the prettiest box I had ever seen. Inside a little ballerina popped up and it played music each time I opened it. I loved it and it was a treasure to me. The treasures it contained were just inexpensive jewellery that I had bought at the market in Portrush during Sunday school trips. None of it had any worth but the box itself had great worth to me.

When I was fifteen, I got home one night from a friend's house to find out that my precious dog Tessa had been killed. I cried sore and ran to the room where I opened the jewellery box for it is comforting music. But that was the day the music stopped, and the box no longer played music. I felt deeply sad. But there is a lesson to be learned from my little treasured box. The Lord does not want us gathering and accumulating and constantly storing up treasures on earth. For we cannot take any of it with us when we pass away.

How can we gather up treasure in Heaven? Well if you are a child of God the most important thing is serving the Lord with your whole heart and giving Him your all, not holding anything back. In Isaiah 61 we find a list of callings we are to fulfil that is treasure in God's eyes.

- Anointed to preach good tidings. Meaning to spread the Gospel wherever you go. To make it your priority to see other souls snatched from the fire.

- Sent to bind up the broken-hearted

- Sent to proclaim liberty to the captives.

- The opening of the prison to them that are bound.

- To comfort all that mourn.

Throughout Scripture, we find even more things that to God is storing up treasure in Heaven. Unselfish giving to others in kindness to make their lives brighter. Unselfish giving to missions to further the carrying on of the Gospel in places all over the world. Comforting widows and orphans. Prayer - we may not think this one as important but every prayer we pray in intercession for others goes up to Heaven before the throne room of God as a sweet fragrance.

Aiming to become more Christlike with every passing day. We are here for the Lord's purposes and how we obey Him and serve others, stores up great treasure in Heaven for you. If you are only focused on this life and getting more and more, you are laying up treasures on earth where the Word says the moth and rust do corrupt. Be more Heavenly minded than earthly focused for life here is brief but eternity is forever. Aim to give your Saviour your all today and in total surrender choose this day to start laying up treasures in Heaven instead of accumulating more on earth.

157

The Time Of The Singing Of The Birds Will Come

Song of Solomon 2:12 *"The flowers appear on the earth, the time of the singing of the birds is come, and the voice of the turtle dove is heard in our land."*

This was the verse in a book I was reading. It was called 'The Time of the Singing of the Birds' by Grace Livingston Hill. It was about two men who had endured great hardships and great trials during their service in WW2. Life was bleak for both as one was in a prisoner of war camp and the other so critically injured that the doctors were sure he would die. But he proved them wrong and lived only to get the news that his beloved mother had died while he had been unconscious. The other man eventually escaped from the POW camp and began a long arduous journey trying to get to safety.

The trials of life were great for these men but one of them held tight to the promise that the time of the singing of birds would come. A season of great unspeakable joy that would follow sorrow. Both men saw that promise come to pass after the war when they had a double wedding with the girls that they loved more than life.

It was a sweet Christian fiction story, but it encouraged me to believe that verse for my own life. Yes, things are bleak. Yes, they are hard with the trials of severe illness, but that verse reminded me that the place of sorrow and hardship will not be permanent. The time of the singing of the birds, the time for great rejoicing and joy will come. The time to see the goodness of the Lord yet again in the land of the living will come. I lay here listening to the most beautiful sounding bird singing outside my window. It was so sweet. So uplifting. I guess that is the double-knock for the Lord telling me for sure 'The time of the singing of the birds' will come and it will come in your life too. I love Scriptures that begin with 'And it came to pass.' Let us believe God for it.

158

Lightning Flashes And The Power Of Our God

I do not know what you think about lightning storms. Maybe you love them and like to watch the flashes out the window! But me? I have the quilt right over my head and with every roll of thunder and every time the room lights up, I jump! It scares the life out of me! I knew someone who got into a cupboard every time there was a thunder and lightning storm for she was so scared too!!

Some interesting facts about Lightning. It looks beautiful but there are dangers behind its beauty. It is unpredictable. It strikes earth more than 100 times per second. The Empire state building is struck 100 times a year. At its peak power, a single lightning strike is a staggering 1,000,000,000 watts. A large thunderstorm is believed to contain enough energy to power the whole of the U.S.A. for twenty minutes. A single lightning strike is more than five times hotter than the surface of the sun. Each year in Britain thirty people are hit by lightning.

Exodus 20:18 *"All people perceived the thunder and the lightning flashes and a thick cloud upon the mountain and a very loud trumpet sound, so that all the people who were in the camp trembled."*

Lightning is just a visual demonstration of God's power in the Sky. He is mighty and very powerful. But we lose sight of that. We see only our problems and only the mountains we face. The Lord wants to remind you today that no matter how impossible your circumstances are God is powerful. He can do what we cannot do! The same God that created this earth, who made us from the dust of the earth, who threw the stars into the sky, who causes the sun to rise every day is the same God who will demonstrate His power in your circumstances in His time.

> Jeremiah 10:12 *"It is he who made the earth by his power, who established the world by his wisdom and by his understanding stretched out the heavens."*

> Genesis 18:14 *"Is anything too hard for the Lord?"*

> Job 42:2 *"I know that you can do all things, and that no purpose of yours can be thwarted."*

He has got it all in control. Our all-powerful God holds us in His hand and is mighty and strong and much more than able to intervene in your circumstance with His mighty power. So next time lightning strikes remember the power of your almighty God and that He can do all things.

159

Tied To The Lord's Heart Strings By Love

Romans 8:38-39 *"For I am persuaded that neither death, nor life, nor angels, nor principalities, nor powers, things present, nor things to come. Nor height nor depth nor any other creature shall be able to separate us from the love of God which is in Christ Jesus our Lord."*

What a comforting verses. No matter what life throws at us nothing can separate us from the Lord's love. We are tied to His heartstrings by love. No matter how dire things are for you, no matter how many things are coming against you, no matter how bleak and black life looks, no matter how heartbroken you are, no matter how desperate you feel - you are safe in the loving arms of your Saviour.

He is your shelter through the enemy's attacks. He is our protection through life's worst storm. No matter what comes, nothing can separate you from your Saviour's love. That is all that truly matters in life, belonging to our beloved and being safe for time and eternity in His hands. Feeling low today? Know that you are being held so tight. Like the old worship song said. 'So close I believe You're holding me now in your arms I belong. You'll never let me go.'

160

Feeling Helpless?

Psalm 35:1-2 *"Plead my cause O Lord... Fight against them that fight against me. Take hold on spear and buckler and stand up for mine help."*

Have you ever felt like everything is coming against you all at the one time? You feel helpless. You feel so knocked down by the enemy that you can no longer stand the pressure. Like someone drowning in a river who cannot help themselves unless someone jumps in and pulls them out, you are in that same place today. You look around and wonder if you will ever get pulled out. At times like that, we need to ask the Lord to plead our cause and fight against them that fight against us. That could be the enemy's attacks of illness, circumstances, problems in marriage and the list could go on.

Once we cry 'Jesus fight for me', He will come to your side with His sword and shield. You might not see your circumstance change immediately but calm will be restored to your spirit and you'll know that your precious Lord is pulling you out of that river you are drowning in and fighting for you. He has got you. You are not going to crumble. With Him on your side, you are not going to lose this battle. He loves you and adores you. Trust Him to plead your cause.

161

The Significance Of Cherry Blossom Tree

Isaiah 51:3 *"For the Lord shall comfort Zion. He shall comfort all her waste places and he will make her wilderness like Eden and her desert like the garden of the Lord. Joy and gladness shall be found therein, thanksgiving and the voice of melody."*

I have always loved cherry blossom trees. They are so exquisite and gorgeous. The significance of the cherry blossom in Japanese culture goes back hundreds of years. In their country, the cherry blossom represents the fragility and beauty of life. It is a reminder that life is almost overwhelmingly beautiful but that it is also tragically short. When the cherry blossom blooms for a short time each year in brilliant force they serve as a visual reminder of how precious and precarious life is. It is a symbolic flower of spring showing a time of renewal and the fleeting nature of life.

It made me think. Life is so beautiful but sometimes we are like horses with blinkers on. We get so focused on what we do not have and cannot see the beauty right in front of us - the precious relationships in our lives. Appreciate the beauty of these relationships for no one lives forever. Do not neglect what is in front of you. A girl I went to school with got married and there was a beautiful picture of her kissing her mum. Her mum is now passed away from cancer. It broke my heart to read it. Love those who the Lord has blessed you with. Value the beauty of the simple things in life even if your circumstances are hard. The smell of flowers, the aroma of perfume, cups of comforting tea, precious talks with your family and closest friends, knowing you are precious enough to be in someone's prayers. Do not live your life with blinkers on. See the beauty now and appreciate all you have. Thank God every single day for your blessings.

Maybe your life is so hard right now but another lesson learned from the cherry blossom and the Scripture in Isaiah 51:3 is that God can bring springtime back to your life. He can cause you to blossom. He can cause your life to become like the garden of Eden. But in the waiting, He does not want us complaining and spending every day with a bad attitude moaning about how hard our lives are. Because of complaining many of the Israelites never got to live in the promised land.

Do not complain as you wait. Appreciate what is beautiful while it is still right there in front of you. Job said, *"Naked came I out of my mother's womb and naked shall I return. The Lord gave and the Lord hath taken away. Blessed be the name of the Lord."*

Praise Him while it hurts. Live to let His beauty shine through you. Make the lives of others all around you more beautiful and as you wait for springtime to come in your life keep thankful and deeply grateful for the beauty that remains for the Lord blesses those abundantly who have grateful hearts.

162

The God of All Comfort

Isaiah 51:12 *"I, even, I, am he that comforteth you."*

Remember what it was like before all the child protection laws came in. You fell and hurt your knee at school and the teacher cleaned it up, then took you up on her knee and held you when you cried. Then gave you sweeties because sweeties solve everything! I remember being on children's camps and if I were having a homesick day the leader would hold you close bringing comfort. I remember snuggling up on Grandpa's knee and feeling so safe, loved, and secure.

Just before my body collapsed with M.E. I was one of the leaders on a youth weekend to Bushmills. I had struggled hard against my body all that year, but a diagnosis had not been reached so I kept pushing on. That weekend me and my friend Diane was in a little leader's room with bunk beds. I felt so sick but for the children's sake tried to maintain a bright appearance. But I knew there was something badly wrong with my body.

One afternoon we all gathered to play rounders. We were not outside five minutes until I collapsed on the ground. I was carried to the room and lay curled in a ball so weak and so exhausted. I started to cry. What is wrong with me? Why can't I make my body function? I was crying my heart out when my friend Diane came in. She held me tight and just let me cry. I was so cold. It was August but my body would not thaw. Diane produced a pair of thermal pyjamas out of her suitcase. She had no idea why she packed them but now she knew! She put the pyjamas on me and then went to get me some tea, scones, and biscuits. Her comfort and love eased my tears. I did not know what was wrong, but I knew God would not fail me. I felt His presence so strong through Diane's embrace.

What about you today? Are you in a season where you feel everything is spinning out of control and you feel no comfort, no rest, no peace? Your mind is in overdrive trying to work out what is going on in your life. Please be encouraged that the God of all comfort is right there in your midst. He will not fail you no matter how you feel.

Lord, I pray your comfort on all those who are so broken today. Oh Lord fill them to overflowing with a beautiful sense of your self. May they know your tangible presence standing in their midst and please comfort them, even send friends to comfort them. Oh my Lord help them to feel your comfort and a beautiful sense of your love. Work everything out for your glory and their good in their lives precious Lord. In Jesus name. Amen

163

Perfect Peace

John 14:27 *"Peace I leave with You, my peace I leave unto you: not as the world giveth, give I unto you. Let not your heart be troubled neither let it be afraid."*

> When peace like a river attendeth my soul.
> When sorrows like sea billows roll.
> Whatever my lot, thou hast taught me to say,
> blessed hope it is well with my soul.

Life can get so stressful at times that peace goes out the window and instead of life being like a calm river it becomes a stormy sea.

I read a book called 'Out of the Storm'. It was a Christian fiction book. In it, the sea was so tumultuous that the ship the people where on was battered to pieces and it sunk. All the lifeboats had gone and yet two passengers remained. They made a makeshift raft but while the man was jumping off the sinking ship, he banged his head and went unconscious. The girl on the raft with him was terrified for the seas where so rough and she had a sick man on her raft. Somehow, they survived and got to land. The seas were so stormy it was a miracle they made it through.

How do you feel today? Do you feel like the storms of life are battering so hard at your life that you feel you are sinking? You feel you are going under. I'm talking to myself as much as anybody else for I'm clinging to a makeshift raft crying out to my Saviour to bring me to smooth seas to a place of peace.

The Lord wants you to know today that no matter how bad you feel. No matter how stormy the seas of your life are, that you are going to make it to dry land. He is saying be at peace amid troubled waters today, don't let yourself be terrified for your Lord is the one who can come to you in your storm and lift you out of troubled waters and draw you near to Himself.

Know no matter what you are going through today It is well with your soul and nobody can take that away from you. You still have not lost your most treasured Lord. Run to Him and let Him lift you out of troubled waters.

164

Be The Star That You Are

Daniel 12:3 *"And they that be wise shall shine as the brightness of the heavens and they that turn many to righteousness as the stars for ever and ever."*

There is a lot on the media about what it is to be a 'star' today. There are loads of programmes like 'Britain's got talent' where people long to have their five minutes in the spotlight. Some think being a star is to be like a model. Others think it is to be like a certain actor/actress. The only way to shine like a star and get attention from others is to throw themselves into the spotlight of life and enjoy the temporary glory.

In this verse, God tells us what it truly means to shine like a star. These people will shine as the brightness of the heavens. You ever see the sky at night when it is lit up with stars? It is glorious. I used to see it many years ago when I went to bottle feed my pet lambs at night.

God says that is you if you care for the souls of others. It is you if it is your only burning desire to see others snatched from the fire and won for Him. This is the only stardom that matters. This is the only stardom that counts. For how awesome it would be when your life is over to be met in Heaven with a host of people that are there because you led them to the Saviour. There is nothing sweeter in this earth than taking the hands of a lost soul and leading them in the sinner's prayer. I have had that honour many times and it brings me to tears that Jesus can use even me - simple flawed me. He can use you too and in His eyes, you will shine like a star if you ask the Lord to give you a heart for the lost. You do not have to have your health to lead others to Calvary. You do not have to be a great orator. All you must be is fully surrendered, and ready to let God use you. Go shine like a star!

165

The Compassionate Lord
Of The Afflicted

Isaiah 63:14 *"In all their affliction he was afflicted and the angel of his presence saved them and in his pity he redeemed them and he bare them and carried them."*

I looked at a picture and seen how afflicted a girl was. During a storm, she looked so desolate. You may feel like every fiery dart from hell is coming against you today. You may feel like the storm in your life is raging, the thunder and lightning surround you. There seems to be no end to your affliction.

But the Lord is saying He sees your affliction. He sees the pain. He sees every demon in hell that is coming against you. He sees your despair. And yet He is saying, "My precious child. Every affliction you face afflicts me too for I hate to see my beloved in pain. I weep when you weep. But I am working on your behalf though you may not see. I am fighting the enemy on your behalf. I will send the angel of my presence to rescue you. I am holding you up and carrying you. I know you are so scared. I know you feel that life has reached a dead end, but I am still a redeeming God and I will intervene. Let me hold you close today and watch and wait for your deliverance draws near."

166

The God Of 'I Can't Cope Anymore' Moments

Psalm 62:1-3 *"Save me, O God for the waters are come unto my soul. I sink in deep mire. I come into deep waters where the floods overflow me. I am weary with my crying: my throat is dried: Mine eyes fail while I wait for my God."*

Do you ever feel like you are sinking? You love the Lord, but you are weary with the stress and the crying. You feel like you are sinking in deep waters. People tell you to trust God, it will all work out, but you are so overwhelmed that everything feels like it is spinning out of control. David felt this way in this Psalm.

God is still your God in your I can't cope moments. He sees when you are overwhelmed, and your tears are your only prayers. Do not feel like a failure. God understands. He sees when you have reached your tipping point and He is holding you close. Just let Him hold you. Just cry in His arms. Just know many others feel this way too, even the man in the Bible described as a man after God's own heart. Do not be sore on yourself precious child of God. He is holding you tight. He will keep you from falling.

167

An Unquenchable Thirst For God

Psalm 42:1-2 *"As the Hart* (deer) *panteth after the water brooks, so panteth my soul after thee O God. My soul thirsteth for God, for the living God."*

Has there ever been a time in your life when you were so thirsty that the tongue was stuck to the roof of your mouth? I can only remember one occasion where this happened to me. I was studying for my finals in my degree. I had two completed but one left to go which was spaced out weeks after the first two. I had memorized for the final exam until I was driving myself mad so on a sunny day, I took a few hours off. I was soul thirsty for my Lord. Desperate to hear His voice.

I was going through something awful at the time and did not feel like I could talk to anyone. I knew if I went down on my knees in the student house, I would only be down ten minutes until I got distracted and felt I should go back to more study. So I left the house and walked. As I walked, I poured out my bottled-up soul to my Saviour. I talked and talked, and I walked sensing the Lord walking beside me. I had been communing with the Lord so long I realised I had walked for miles. I felt so thirsty and I kept hoping I would pass a shop soon. Eventually, I did and bought two bottles of water, pure orange, and some sandwiches. The water was like the best thing ever at that moment for I was so parched.

I sat down on a grassy area and ate my lunch and read the Bible I had with me. I was desperately seeking God for answers over a seemingly impossible matter. I was soul thirsty and longed for my God and experienced great physical thirst that day too. I had sought the Lord every day on my knees in prayer and studied

His Word in my room, but I needed that day of totally abandoning all to be with my Saviour and pour out my heart.

What about you today? Are you desperately soul thirsty? Your life is in ruins and you cannot find answers. You have strayed from the Lord in your spirit and went straight to friends and leaders for advice instead of going straight to the one who made you and holds your life in His hands.

My soul is still daily thirsty for my Lord. Unless I have been with Him and communed with Him as a friend to friend and read His Word, I would be like someone trying to live in a desert without water. My spiritual walk would soon die, and I would become a backslidden form of my former self - a form unusable to my Saviour for He cannot use lukewarm Christians.

Get your thirst for the Lord back. Pour out your bottled-up soul to Him and commune with Him as a friend to friend. He longs for you to thirst for Him for only He satisfies. Nothing and nobody can take the place of sitting at the Master's feet. Letting Him daily fill you with living water that He will pour into your soul which will make you a powerful stream to impact a thirsty land that needs God so much.

168

Seek To Help Others Not Drown In Self-pity

Galatians 6:2 *"Bear ye one another's burdens and so fulfil the law of Christ."*

I read a quote that said: "We rise by lifting others."

We are most free in God when we choose to help others no matter what our circumstances are and refuse to drown in self-pity that renders us ineffective to God. Going into a shell and saying my pain is too great to come out of this shell is worldly and carnal and not Christlike. You set yourself and others free when you choose self-sacrifice over self-pity. The people who inspire me the most are people whose lives are horrific, yet they rise above by remaining sweet-spirited and doing all in their power for others.

Sarah suffered from severe depression. Sarah wanted to die. Her depression was so bad she had to go to her doctor every week as he wanted to keep a close eye on her. But Sarah even though she was in mental agony still visited the sick and encouraged others. She was involved in every outreach possible. Helped her friends with everything. She cried the whole way in the car to places and the whole way back, but she did not let her pain stop her from bearing others burdens and being a living witness to the Lord she loved.

It wasn't until one night she was with a friend and had listened to all her friend's problems and prayed them through with her, that suddenly her friend said oh Sarah I never ask you how you are. I am so sorry. Sarah broke down and told her close friend the truth. Well, I have severe depression and want to die. I am heavily medicated. Her friend burst into tears saying I cannot believe you have been doing all these things for God and others and myself and I did not see you were suffering.

But Sarah continued to reach out with the Gospel and lift others even though she was in a place of utter mental darkness. She kept going until finally, the black fog lifted. (Sarah is a made-up name but the lady permitted me to share.)

Since I became physically sick I have met people who even though they suffer so much choose to let their lives be a living sacrifice laying themselves down for others. People with cancer, severe M.E., and M.S. They refuse to curl up and die and use their sicknesses as an excuse to go into self-pity mode.

When Jesus was on the cross He was in utter agony yet He took time to forgive the dying thief beside Him and also make sure His mother would be cared for when He was gone. He was still bearing other's burdens in His suffering.

We rise and are truly free when we choose to lift others and choose selflessness over self-pity. By making that choice you are saying Lord no matter how much I suffer it will not stop me living for You, serving You and lifting the weak. I choose You over selfishness because I know You can work through my weakness when I am wholly surrendered to You. Let my life bring You praise despite the agony.

169

Wish or Pray?

Daniel 6:3&10 *"An excellent spirit was in him... He kneeled upon his knees three times a day and prayed and gave thanks before his God."*

As a child, I loved making wishes on those dandelion heads that you could blow, and all the little parts went flying everywhere. I wished I would marry a man with a heart of gold. I wished I would have a beautiful baby girl. I wished the time would go quickly so it would be time for the Sunday school trip! (We only went to Portrush once a year and I loved going to Barry's amusements). I wished the summer Bible camp would hurry up and come as it was the highlight of my year. I wished everybody that was sick would get better. I wished I would grow up to make everyone else's lives better. I wished...

But since I've become older I've realised this quote to be so true, "Why wish upon a star when you can pray to the one who made it."

My almighty God and beautiful Saviour has sent some amazing answers to prayer when I've least expected them. I am still believing Him for healing in my body and I am not giving up on that!

In 2008 I was admitted to hospital for a fortnight. I was told my body was in such a bad state I would never be better. I remember my late Granny Peden coming that day and I just broke down in her arms. Then Pastor Taylor came, and I broke down with him too. I was at my absolute weakest emotionally. I had lost all my fight. I am not telling this story to bring any glory to Joanne because it was nothing to do with me and all about God's power working through His weakest child. But the girl in the bed beside me was screaming in pain. The morphine had not worked, and she was crippled with pain. She was crying and said 'You're a Christian, aren't you? Please pray for me.' I did not feel like praying. I felt defeated. But at that point, if I pushed hard, I could still get out of bed briefly. She was right beside me so I got out of bed pushing my weak body as hard as it would go. I sat on her bed and held her tight and asked the Lord to take her pain away. I then got back into bed where I continued to feel defeated. But then an hour later she said Joanne the pain is gone. As you prayed, I felt a heat going into my tummy and now I feel no pain at all. I was in utter awe of God. It was not me. It was the power of prayer. And I could not believe He had heard me on a day I did not want to be on earth anymore!

Prayer is our most powerful weapon. This year I have already seen amazing answers to prayer. A friend who had five miscarriages now has a baby. My uncle gave his life to Jesus before he died. A friend with depression was healed. A publisher accepted my second book. God made a way where there seemed to be no way! And the list could go on!

Do not wish - pray! Every prayer is a powerful weapon that causes strongholds to come tumbling down. If you are believing God for something today, please do not give up! Every prayer goes straight to the throne room of God like a sweet fragrance.

Oh, we may not know why He does not answer immediately at times, but He will hear and answer in the way He sees best for us for He is the one who holds the bigger picture. We only see little snapshots, so we do not properly understand. Pray and believe. God hears.

170

Are You Feeling Trapped And Depressed?

Psalm 24:15 *"Mine eyes are ever toward the Lord, for he shall pluck my feet out of the net."*

In one of the episodes of 'Little House on the Prairie', Carrie fell into a mine. Everyone was trying their best to get her out, but they were making it worse. The more they dug the more mud fell into the mine, trapping her further. It all looked hopeless. It looked like she was going to die down there until a neighbour's child remembered there was another entrance to the mine and they rescued Carrie just before the whole mine collapsed.

I was once locked in a wardrobe by a friend! We were young, and she thought it was funny. It was in their attic. I felt suffocated and so afraid. The door would not budge, and no one heard me screaming. I was terrified and the more I panicked the less I could breathe. Finally, after an hour she let me out laughing and skipping with joy at her 'joke' It left me a little afraid of tight spaces after it! I remember at Queens University the Theology Department was on the eleventh floor and I always took the stairs as I feared tight spaces!

Are you feeling trapped and depressed today? Do you feel you are in such a tight place that you feel suffocated and like you cannot go on anymore? Are you afraid and so overwhelmed by life's circumstances you feel like giving up? Then remember today's Scripture, *"Mine eyes are ever toward the Lord for he will pluck me out of the net."* He WILL pluck you out of the thick dark pit you are in.

171

Beautiful In Your Saviour's Eyes

Psalm 139:14&17 *"I will praise thee; for I am fearfully and wonderfully made: Marvellous are thy works, and that my soul knoweth right well. How precious also are thy thoughts unto me O God."*

Jeremiah 1:5 *"Before I formed thee in the belly I knew thee; and before thou camest forth out of the womb, I sanctified thee and ordained thee a prophet unto the nations."*

Permission to share this story from a support group member as long as I use a different name. So let us call her Amanda as I like that name as it means worthy of love.

Amanda loved Jesus from a young age but was horrendously bullied at school for five years. She was called ugly, trash, a disease so no one came near her. The bullies had warned that anyone who spoke to her would also be bullied.

Years passed and she saw herself as ugly, avoided mirrors, had no confidence, felt unworthy of love. Then a man noticed her, but he was abusive. He called her for all the names under the sun. He also claimed to be a Christian and used the Bible to manipulate her. The abuse became horrific, but she did not leave for she believed he loved her. They got engaged. His words to her were, you are mine now and the second we are married I will start battering you into submission. She was terrified, alone, isolated from all friends. The life draining out of her. This was love, she kept telling herself, it is all I am worth. Eventually, Amanda with a lot of help from her pastor had the courage to walk away.

However, the next two years were still horrific. In both workplaces, she was targeted and abused by both bosses. She believed it was all she was worth. After some time passed Amanda stopped believing satan's lies. She started believing she was fearfully and wonderfully made by God. That she had worth and she was beautiful in His eyes. She believed God formed her in her mother's womb and she was born for a great purpose. She believed that God thought precious thoughts about her, and she was greatly beloved by God.

How about you? What circumstance are you in today? Are you trapped in an abusive relationship? Is your marriage causing you great pain? Are you being bullied? Are you in a circumstance that makes you feel worthless, useless, ugly, and purposeless? Then let me encourage you today. You are not what your accusers and abusers say you are. You are fearfully and wonderfully made by the Lord God Almighty; He declares you as His beloved, of great worth and on this earth for a great purpose that only you can fulfil. He is telling you today to cast away the enemies lies and believe all the beautiful things His Word says about you. Believe them not just in your head but let them absorb deeply into your heart too. You were formed in your mother's womb by a God who has great tasks for you that only you can do. There is no other you! You are a unique and beautiful creation. No one else has your fingerprints and every hair on your head is counted by our God.

He is declaring, "You are beautiful my sweet one! Please believe my voice over the enemy's voice for I do not want my precious one trapped in fear for one more day. You will accomplish great things for my glory my beloved, unique creation. Your very name is engraved in my nail-scarred hands. Absorb my love today and believe all I say about you my darling pearl of great price."

172

Our Heavenly Bridegroom

Revelation 21:2 *"And I saw the Holy city, new Jerusalem coming down out of heaven from God made ready as a bride adorned for her husband."*

I have had the wedding bug since I was asked to be a flower girl at my uncle's wedding! I adored the whole day! Getting my hair in a French plait, my beautiful white dress, and pink flowers. Seeing the bride in all her glory coming down the aisle. Hearing the vows of two people vowing to love each other in sickness and in health till death do they part! I loved it all! It was one of the best days of my life! Only seven years old but on top of the moon happiness wise.

Through Scripture Jesus is described as the Heavenly Bridegroom and we as His church His bride. It made me think. Do we love and cherish our beloved in the best of times and the worst of times? Do we always aim to keep ourselves pure and holy for our beloved? I remember the words of the hymn, "When the bridegroom cometh, will your robes be white? Are your garments spotless are they white as snow. Are you washed in the Blood of the Lamb?"

Child of God, your Heavenly Bridegroom loves you dearly but like a bride getting ready for her wedding day, we should spend our lives getting ready to meet our Heavenly lover. Do not let your robes of white become impure and black, so spotted with the things of the world that your Lord can barely recognise you. His word clearly says, *"No man can serve two masters."* You are either living for and loving God or serving satan and letting your robes become spotted and impure. The Lord wants His children to be pure in heart. His word says that the pure in heart will see Him. Keeping ourselves pure by not feeding our minds on junk and not running to worldly impure places, aiming to be holy and set apart from Him, letting our thoughts and speech reflect His glory are some ways we can reflect our beloved. I sang a duet in church with a friend once and meant every word: "O that I would be made pure. That I would strive to love Him more. That every work of my hands would accomplish all His plans so that He be glorified. O for a heart. To serve my God. A heart that is ever broken to His will. O for a heart to serve my God my king, a heart that's ever delighting Him."

I know I want a pure heart. I have vowed to forsake all worldly pleasures. I want to be pure in heart and in His eyes so that when the day comes that I see Him face to face I will be able to fall into His arms, with a peace in my spirit that I kept myself unspotted and in love with my Heavenly Bridegroom all the days of my life.

I do not want to be the bride with the soiled dress when I meet my beloved, what about you?

173

Stay In The Fight

Psalm 144:1 *"Blessed be the Lord my strength which teacheth my hands to war and my fingers to fight."*

Fighting! Most siblings grow up fighting. My brother and I must be the exception to the rule as we never fought once! We were always friends and still are.

But when I think about today's verse, I think of a song that comes on the radio. "You're an overcomer stay in the fight till the final round. You are not going under cos God is holding you right now. You might be down for a second feeling like it's over, that's when He reminds you: you're an overcomer."

Sometimes we lose all sense of fight, that's when we need to ask the Lord our strength, to teach our hands to fight and our fingers to war.

Satan doesn't want us to make it. He will constantly send fiery darts when we are down. We are told to resist the enemy of our soul. We are in a war. The enemy wants to keep us from fulfilling our purpose in God and his best weapon is discouragement. That is why we need to ask God to help us fight him off. He will fill our minds with lies - that is his favourite tactic. He will say you have no worth; you are not worthy to be loved, you are useless, and the list will go on. The only way to fight back is with the truth of God's words. Make a list of what he says about you and write them all down. Every time the enemy says you are worthless you can come back at him with, I am a jewel in God's crown, I am a pearl of great price. Fight him with the sword of God's Word when discouragement starts.

How else can we fight? I learned last year that during WW2 the soldiers in the trenches used to sing 'Abide with Me' when they were afraid when enemy planes were flying overhead. They united in song remembering God was their strength. We can fight the enemy by keeping on singing praises to God in the trenches of life. When everything feels bleak and scary God will honour you with His peace. We can fight the enemy by staying close to our Saviours side in prayer and Bible reading.

If you feel you are losing the fight, God will not let you be overcome. You are His and if you are far through, He will fight for you. You might be down for a second, feeling like it is over, but God says, I will not let the enemy defeat you, my darling child. My purposes for your life will come to pass. Remember satan is already a defeated foe. He is only roaring like a lion trying to destroy you but all he can do is roar! Your Lord defeated him on the cross so do not let a defeated foe defeat you when you have Almighty God on your side!

174

Fear Not

Hosea 13:9 *"But in me is thine help."*

As a child, even though I had given my heart to Jesus when I was six, I suffered from a lot of nightmares. If I did something wrong at all I was sure I was going to hell or if Jesus were to return to earth that he would say depart from me I never knew you. Bedtime for a few years was full of nightmares. I could see the devil coming to take me and I woke screaming for my father. He told me the same thing every time, as I had given Jesus my heart that nothing could separate me from Him.

As the years went on, I grew more and more afraid of the end of the world. I was sixteen when an elderly friend came to see me. He said I do not normally do this but this morning the Lord laid a message so clear on my heart for you saying, "Fear not you are my child." At those words, all fear lifted, all fear was gone. The nightmares stopped. I knew I was secure in my salvation. God had me in the palms of His hands.

What about you? Are you trembling in fear today over something that is happening in your life? The Lord is saying give the fear to Me for in Me is thine help. No matter what terrifies you today, big, or small the Lord is saying to you what He said to me all those years ago. "Fear not you are my child." Those things that terrify you He will lift. His perfect love for you will cast out fear. Give Him your fear today and He will give you His peace. He is standing ready to help.

175

Looking Unto Jesus, The Author And Finisher Of Our Faith

The Lord laid this on my heart recently. You see, I am as guilty as anybody else of getting my eyes off Jesus. When I get my eyes off Jesus and unto my illness and circumstances I start to drown. Weariness sets in and the battle feels too big. I am not the only one! In Scripture when Peter took his eyes off Jesus while walking on water he started to drown. Jesus lifted him, but he had to get his eyes back on Jesus again. He is the author of our lives! He is not going to leave us stuck in the same chapter forever. If we dwell on our circumstances we start to drown however if we get our eyes back on our all-powerful Lord, knowing He holds our lives in His hands who sees the end from the beginning, then seeing his lovely face and worshipping him will refocus our eyes. Get them back on the King of Glory! I am speaking to myself here more than anyone else. I am saying come on Joanne stop focusing on all the people who have had M.E. for what seems like a zillion years and get your eyes back on your amazing, good, and caring Lord who has spoken so many promises over your life.

Lord Jesus, I refocus my eyes on You right now. Come heal my weary soul. Sharpen my spiritual vision to lift my eyes to You my wonderful Redeemer and please do not let me drown. You know the end from the beginning, and I know You have a fresh start for Joanne Peden in your time. Oh Lord the wee girl in the picture is gazing upwards and in doing so she is seen as a butterfly. A butterfly is a symbol of the newness of life and leaving the cocoon of pain behind. Keep my eyes gazing at You and your lovely face and get my eyes off circumstances oh dearest Lord I pray. In Jesus name. Amen

176

Turning Hearts towards the King

We've all saw that pretty girl that walks into a room and turns heads with her physical beauty. We may feel like plain Jane's in comparison, but the most important thing is not the beauty on the outside it is being beautiful in the eyes of the Lord. Having a pure heart full of love for the Lord, tenderness, gentleness, a loving heart, a spirit of generosity a peaceful serene spirit, a non-complaining/non-gossiping tongue. It is to imitate the Lord Jesus in His likeness in compassion, in humility of spirit, in unselfishness.

Study the Gospels and absorb how the Lord Jesus walked and talked and ask the Father to change you into the image of Jesus, for in doing so people will start to notice you, not your outward appearance but the inner beauty of the heart. Many will come to know the Lord as Saviour because of you turning hearts to the king. This does not just apply to women but men also!

Psalm 45:13 *"The Kings daughter* (or son) *is all glorious within..."*

Could it be said of you that you are all glorious within?

Proverbs 31:30 *"Charm is deceitful and beauty is vain, but a woman* (or man) *who fears* (or honours) *the Lord she shall be praised."*

The people who have made the most powerful impressions on my life were not outwardly attractive. I am thinking of one man who used to be my CEF leader. The love he had for everyone around him was out of this world. Many people came to know the Lord as Saviour because of George's constant witness in love for others, sending little gifts, looking after every child in his neighbourhood. He was all glorious within. He had a pure heart like a child and prayed and was kind to every single person around him. I gave the memorial speech at his funeral before I took sick and I still have it in my drawer. I read it from time to time because I saw in George the likeness and glory of my King and others saw it too and were attracted to him like magnets.

Let us ask the Lord to make us living witnesses who are all glorious within. Pray that we will become King magnets.

177

When Embarrassing Moments Become Divine Encounters

2 Timothy 4:2 *"Preach the word, be instant in and out of season..."*

1 Petet 3:15 *"Always be ready to give an answer to every man that asketh you the reason of the hope that is within you with meekness and fear."*

My dream was and is still to go into CEF, but I was advised by my Godly elderly pastor to do an R.E. teacher training year as a backup after my Theology degree. Though during that year I realised I could not have gone into R.E. teaching. I know some Christians can and do a brilliant job of it but I just personally couldn't tell children there where different options on ways to God through different religions when it burns in my spirit to tell the way through Jesus. But anyway, I had already enrolled for the year before I discovered I could never teach other religions.

It was the first week. We had not been to our separate classes yet and we were all meeting for group lectures. I did not know another person. I remember clearly that one day I was wearing a pink blouse and long black skirt. I had just gone into a lecture that was to last two and a half hours. It had just started and suddenly, I felt unwell. The next thing I remember was waking up on top of one of the lecture benches, with my blouse wide open and ambulance men getting me connected to oxygen. I was mortified to be lying half-naked in full view of everyone and I pointed to my blouse. A kind girl buttoned up my blouse and came in the ambulance with me to the city hospital.

The girl turned out to be a maths student from Armagh. She drove two hours every day to get to Queens University. She was so kind and caring. She refused to leave my side even though I was a stranger. She stayed in A&E for four hours with me. We chatted about general things then she said there is something about you - a hope in your eyes. What do you believe? So I gave her my testimony about how Jesus saved me as a child and how I believed He was the only way to Heaven, and I loved Jesus with all my heart. She was not a Christian but was interested. She said she had a Bible somewhere and asked me for passages she could look up when she got home. She took out her notebook and I gave her a list. Then my parents arrived, and the girl hugged me and drove her long journey home.

It was not an ideal place! I was on oxygen and hooked to a drip and doctors were in and out sticking needles in me. But it was a divine appointment. God wanted me to share the Gospel with that girl that day and even though it was not my ideal circumstances God still used me. I looked her up the next week. Went to the Maths department, with a gift of a necklace, a box of chocolates and a card. I never saw her again for the rest of the course as we were always in our subject groups. So I don't know if she gave her heart to Jesus but Jesus wanted me to sow the Gospel seed and I pray He watered it and she came to Him.

No matter what your circumstances, always be ready to give an answer for the hope that is within you. Be ready to share in and out of season. God has a way of divinely arranging circumstances so we can reach someone who needs Him. Even from my bed, I have met people online who wanted to know about Jesus. Where are you? Sick? In the workplace? On holidays? Your car has broken down and you are at the mechanic? You find yourself in a place you would not normally be in if circumstances had not put you in that place? Make the most of every opportunity to talk about Jesus. He wants to use you as His living light to carry the Gospel light, are you willing to let Him no matter how bleak your circumstances look right now? Dare to be a light.

178

Daisy Chains

Isaiah 55:6-7 *"Seek, the Lord while he can be found. Call on him while he is near. Let the wicked forsake his ways and the wicked man his thoughts and turn to the Lord and he will freely pardon."*

I remember as a child making daisy chains with a cousin on warm summer days. We made necklaces out of them, bracelets, and decorations for our hair! We felt adorned in our creations. However, the next morning our creations had withered up and died. Why did they die? Because they were no longer connected to their source. They could no longer flourish because they were not rooted in the ground anymore.

It is the same with us in our walks with God if we stop praying and stop reading His Word. If we stop praising Him and make everything else a priority over Him, it will not be long until be become like those daisy chains. Our spirits will wither up, our love for worldly things will increase. We will soon become more like satan than our Saviour.

If you have walked away from the Lord and your heart has become cold, cry out to Him to create in you a clean heart and renew a right spirit with you. Ask Him to renew the joy of your salvation (Psalm 51) and refuse to become cold in your spiritual walk again by staying near to your Saviours side, by being connected to your source of life and power again.

God cannot use carnal Christians, but He can use those who choose to love Him with their all and keep their hearts pure before Him.

179

Ellen, A Selfless, Loving Heart

2 Corinthians 2:15 *"For we are unto God a sweet savour, in them that are saved and in them that perish."*

Philippians 2:3 *"In lowliness of mind let each esteem others better than themselves."* (Regard one another as more important than yourself."*

Recently earth lost a true angel. Her name was Ellen. She was not to be found in the spotlight or at the front of any church, but she faithfully loved and served others with such a selfless heart. She was a dear family friend and was so good to me throughout my years of illness - always visiting - always bringing me Christian books. She adored children and they adored her! She taught Sunday school for years and made such a huge difference in children's lives. Her life was a sweet savour both to the saved and the unsaved for her happy, gentle, caring, selfless spirit meant she went out of her way to do anything for anybody. She loved Jesus so much and her life brought Him so much glory. I wrote this poem about her:

You were as warm and welcoming as a sunny day.
You loved with all your heart and made the sky for others
turn bright instead of grey.
You adored children and they adored you,
they flocked to you without delay.
You made life better for everyone else.
Your sweetness, gentleness and caring heart
are only some on a long list I could say.

You had such a love for Jesus.
A wise and Godly heart.
Many children will be in Heaven because you cared for their
souls, you sowed the Gospel seed.
You did your part.
The children in your classes saw Jesus in you,
they loved your warmth and inner beauty.
From you, they were never apart.
In prayer you lifted them,
in care you taught them the way,
you gave their lives the best start.

You will be dearly missed by many
for you touched so many lives for God.
Your compassion, goodness and love for all will mean the
Gospel will still be carried to many others,
at home and abroad.
You're safely home on Heaven's shores
with your precious Saviour,
receiving your well done faithful servant
and Heaven's applaud.
We'll miss you so much but
it comforts our minds to know
that you Ellen are safe in glory and will no longer
through life's harsh battles have to plod.

Are you an Ellen? Do you care more for others than you do
yourself? Do you do all in your power to forward the Gospel? Are
you a sweet-smelling savour to all those that know you?

Would your life be so successful that someone could pen
these words about you when death claims you? Be an Ellen. Be a
compassionate heart in a selfish world and watch what awesome
things the Lord does through you.

180

Too Many Easter Eggs!

Hebrews 12:1 *"Let us lay aside every weight, and the sin which doth do easily beset us and let us run with patience the race that is set before us."*

I was always a keen runner before my illness. I especially loved cross country at school. I loved the feeling when you got to the end knowing you endured miles in all weathers. I was usually one of the first to finish. I loved running. It just brought me so much joy.

One Easter I received six large Easter eggs. I devoured them in very little time! I have always been a slim build. Mum says I am a thoroughbred because I eat what I want but always remain the same. I did not realise the effect on my physical fitness until I got back to school. Cross country was first on the agenda. I was so unfit and overloaded with sugar that I puffed, and I panted round a trail I usually flew through. I came last! Last! Even the slowest girl in the class beat me! I was mortified! I felt so ashamed!

Hebrews 12:3 *"For consider him that endured.. lest ye become wearied and faint in your minds."*

What weights and sins are you holding onto that are hindering your walk with God? Have you something you call your pet sin? You know it is wrong, but you stubbornly hold unto it and refuse to repent of it. Maybe it is a burden you are carrying that you cannot hand over to the Saviour. He wants to carry your burdens. He wants to lift the weight off your shoulders. Give it to Him. Do not run the race of life with rocks in your backpack that hinder your spiritual progress. Jesus loves you and wants you to hand them over. The weight that so easily beset me all those years ago in my cross-country race was that I had overindulged on junk and that was the weight that hindered my amazing progress.

Maybe you are in agony today. You are so depressed, life is in a hard place, you feel faint in your mind. Life's got too much for you. Consider all Jesus endured. His cruel sufferings, His beatings, His bruises, His cruel painful death. Think, if Jesus could endure, so can I! I'm not going to let anything hinder my spiritual progress, no sickness, no trial, no grief I'm going to press on, loving God with all my heart, getting rid of sins that interfere with my walk with God, I'm going to give Him every burden and be the best I can be for Him so He can use me despite bad circumstances! I am going to run and hear the words, 'Well done good and faithful servant, come in and receive your reward.'

Let go of ALL weights. Be the best you can be in God.

181

Your Name Written in Special Places

Isaiah 49:16 *"Behold I have graven thee upon the palms of my hands...."*

Revelation 20:15 talks about those whose names are written in the Lamb's book of life not having to endure a lost eternity. Revelation 20:12 talks about other books being opened along with the Book of Life.

I have always been addicted to books. Even from I was six years old I was reading full novels! I prefer books to films. There is nothing I love more than getting lost in a good book. All the books I read now are either Christian teaching books, Christian biographies, or Christian fiction. It is the standard birthday and Christmas gift from family and friends to ask what books I do not have and buy them or give me a voucher for me to get the books I want. My family have long since given up asking me if I am sure I do not want something different for a change, but the answer is always the same... books, please. To me, books are the greatest gift of all!

If you know the Lord as Saviour your name is written on the palms of His hands. Your name is also written in the Book of Life. Every believer's name is written in that book as soon as they become saved. No one can enter Heaven without having their name in the Book of Life.

Then other books will be opened. These books will record all the Christians self-sacrificing service for the Saviour and kind good deeds and the names of souls they have led to the Lord. These things are recorded so that when the rewards are being given out in Heaven you will be bestowed honour according to your love and obedience to the Saviour. The Gospel itself is not by works, it's fully dependent on accepting Jesus as Saviour for the price was already paid on the cross so all that is left to be done is for you to accept the gift of Salvation.

It rejoices my heart to know my name is written in Heaven! When the great Heavenly roll call is taken my name - Joanne Peden, will be read out and I will be welcomed into Heaven. It also brings me great joy to know I am so precious to my Saviour that my name is written on His hands! As for the other books and Heavenly rewards, there will be no reward so sweet to me apart from the gift of seeing my blessed Saviour's face. Of taking His hand and holding it tight, of falling to my knees and worshipping Him.

I like books with a happy ending and for those with their names written in the Lambs book of life, there will be a joyously happy ending. But maybe you have never accepted Jesus as Saviour and know your name is not written on the Heavenly roll call book. You can fix that today by coming to the Lord, falling to your knees, repenting of your sins, and asking the Lord Jesus to be your personal Saviour and making yourself wholly His. Then you too will have your name written in Heaven.

182

The Day I Bolted

2 Timothy 1:7 *"For God hath not given us a spirit of fear but of power and of love and of a sound mind."*

I received beautiful earrings in the post from a friend. She made me a pink bracelet a few weeks ago and wanted me to have matching earrings to wear with my new pink dress when I can finally get out of the house again. I was so touched.

It brought back to my remembrance the day I went to get my ears pierced. I got the money for it as a twelfth birthday gift. My cousin and I set out to find somewhere in town that would pierce ears. We trekked through jewellers and were refused as I had no adult with me. We trekked through endless hairdressers and were told they did not pierce ears. We were about to give up when finally one hairdresser said they did pierce ears. This scary-looking man came out and said he was going to get the gun. I suddenly felt really scared of him and went running out the door shouting, "I don't want my ears pierced anymore!" My cousin was standing outside laughing her head off! You are such an idiot Joanne were her words. But she was not letting me give up. I am not letting you chicken out she said. So we found another hairdresser called 'Amanda's' and yes, they pierced ears and it was a lovely lady that put me at ease. The fear left me, and I let her pierce them. I did not even feel it. My cousin and I laughed all the way home at how I took off like rocket terrified in the first place.

God has not placed within us a spirit of fear. He wants us to lean on Him and wholly trust Him. When fear enters our mind, He wants us to talk through the fear with Him and let Him bring calm amid our panic.

Philippians 4:1 *"So stand fast in the Lord my dearly beloved."*

Are you full of fear today? You are still dearly beloved to your Saviour no matter how you feel. He wants you to talk through the fear with Him and let Him replace it with His love and peace. He is saying stand fast. You can do this because His Spirit is in you and with His Spirit of power in you, you will never be defeated. Cast your cares on your Lord. He wants to hear all about it, for everything that burdens your heart, the Lord wants to know about. You are His and nothing will ever separate you from His love. Come into His arms.

183

Passion Or Performance?

I was listening to a 'Brooklyn Tabernacle' webcast and it triggered this little thought. He said for some people being a Christian is all about performance - acting a certain way in front of the pastor and being a different person when they are not about. They pretend to be sweet and Godly and do things to be noticed but their heart is afar off from God. They are not living for the audience of one - the living God - they are living for an audience of what mere mortal man thinks about them. The pastor went on to say that for some people even getting up to the platform to sing is just about performance. He said he would rather have a sweet Godly singer who is just up there that others might see Jesus and be drawn closer to Him than an expert singer who is just up there to 'look at how awesome I am.'

A few years ago I was in the hospital and someone who never acknowledges me in life came to visit me. It was a strange visit the person barely spoke and left very quickly. The next day my pastor came and said it was nice of 'so and so' to come to visit you! This person only came to see me so they could report back to the pastors about their good deed.

1 Peter 1:24 *"For all flesh is as grass and all glory of man as the flower of the grass. The grass thereof withereth and the flower of the field falleth away."*

In other words, the men and women that you are trying to impress and living to bask in their glory are just mere mortals like the rest of us, who will one day be lowered into the ground in a casket like the rest of us. Stop living for the glory and praise of people and start living for the glory and honour of the One who sees you when you are no longer performing and trying to win people's approval. The One who sees the real you and yearns that you would fully surrender your life to Him and live it wholly for His glory alone. Forget about all those around you, it is the King of king's and Lord of lord's you will spend eternity with. It is Him alone that you will stand before and give an account of your life.

1 Corinthians 1:31 *"Whatsoever ye do, do all for the glory of God."*

He alone is all that matters. He alone is the One who is with us every second of the day. He alone sees us at our best and our worst so stop the performing and start getting passionate about the One who died to save you and rose that you will also live eternally. Make it your vow before God today that you are wholly available ready to do His will whatever it costs and though you may not be recognised for it this side of eternity develop a passion for the souls of those who are drifting into a lost eternity instead of trying to make yourself look good to men.

Only one life.
Twill soon be past.
Only what's done for Christ will last.

184

Do not Blame God

Job 10:7-8 *"Thine hands have made me and fashioned me together round about me, yet thou dost destroy me."*

In other words, if you had not let me be born, I would have been spared this miserable existence. At this point in Job's journey, he was blaming God for what happened to him.

We should never blame God for what happens to us. We live in a fallen world, and sickness, tragedy, and pain are caused because man has chosen to push God away from the very start. I, Joanne, do not blame God for my illness. Blaming God makes one bitter and I never want to end up that way. Satan and man's rebellion against God is the reason why there is so much pain in the world. I may have suffered for years but I love my beloved Saviour so much. I do not blame Him at all. I don't want to develop the victim mentality but I want to have a victor mentality and not let life's circumstances destroy me for I know my Lord can bring so much good and glory out of everything the enemy means for evil.

"Sometimes we are to blame for our circumstances if they have come as a direct result of disobedience to God."

"Life's course is not determined by the dreams we dream but by the choices we make."

"For example, Lot chose all the plains of Jordan (Genesis 13). Lot chose selfishly and only left Abraham the bare plains of Bethel. He pitched his tent towards Sodom. He became caught up in the affairs of sinful men. He destroyed his wife, home, and family by the power of choice. Don't choose worldly pleasures over the Lord God for it will only end up in your destruction."

"I would rather eat dry bread than walk away from God." Pastor Taylor.

Other people chose to follow God. In Hebrews 11:25, Moses chose to suffer affliction with the people of God rather than have all the pleasures of Egypt. Joshua's choice, *"As for me and my house we will serve the Lord."* Ruth's choice, *"Thy people shall be my people and thy God my God."* Christ's choice, *"Not my will but thine be done."*

Choose to follow Jesus no matter what. Through pain, through sorrow, through suffering, through tragedy, through grief. Choose to say I am thine Lord completely devoted to you, no matter what. Because walking away from God is NOT an option. You might feel pleasure for a while, but your life will end up bleak, dry empty. Satan will reign in your life and not your beloved Saviour and like Lot, you will end up in destruction. Choose life today. Choose to praise your Saviour through the storm and never walk away. Do not blame God. Make the most of your poor circumstances and let the Lord use them for His glory.

185

A Happy Holiday

Job 13:15 *"Though he slay me, yet will I trust in him."*

It was just a few months before my body utterly gave way to M.E. We had an Easter break from work. My body felt exhausted, weak, faint but my friend so badly wanted to go to the Faith Mission Bangor Easter Convention that I just could not let her down. So she booked the B&B and we set off for four days. The times in those meetings were so aflame for God that my spirit felt challenged to be a light in this dark world no matter what my body was doing. I fainted in a couple of meetings and had to miss a few afternoon sessions but while my friend was out, the little room I was in became Holy ground. It was like God was preparing me for what was to come. I heard God voice so clear, "Will you still love and serve me if life takes a turn for the worse?" To which I replied. I am thine Lord. Come what may I will always love you.

The sense of His presence in that little B&B room was out of this world. My friend came in from a walk and went – wow, what happened to you? Your face is glowing! To which I replied I have just awesomely met God, let us get some tea, scones and chocolate and I will tell you all about it.

It's almost like that Bangor holiday was my divine preparation for what was to come for four short months later I collapsed at work and my body never worked properly again since and years later it's still not working. But do I still love and serve my Saviour? – Yes, He is my everything. If you heard Him telling you that things were going to go black, would you still love Him as much in darkness as in the time of blessing?

186

I Serve A Risen Saviour

The difference between all world religions and Christianity is that Jesus is NOT in a grave! He has conquered death and is alive! Buddha is in a grave, Joseph Smith is in a grave, the founders of Hinduism and Islam are in graves. But Jesus is alive!

He conquered death! Death is not something that has to be feared anymore. For if we place our trust in Jesus and accept Him as Saviour, we can be sure that death will not be the end for us too! Our bodies may go into a grave, but our souls will go straight to Heaven to live eternally with the One who suffered for us in our place! Then when He returns to earth the second time - because He has promised to come again.

Our bodies in the grave will rise to meet Him in the air and our soul and body will be reunited and then we will have our glorified, immortal body - just like the body Jesus had when He came back from the dead! He showed Himself alive to over 500 people! The women who went to the tomb that first Easter Sunday found it empty and ran to tell the despondent disciples that Jesus had indeed kept His promise and conquered death! He loves you with an everlasting love and longs for you to come to Him to share in eternal life in Heaven which He paid for on the cross if only we will trust Him.

I Joanne Peden do not fear death! I know the minute I close my eyes in death I will awake in my Saviours arms! What joy! What happiness! No more sickness, sorrow, or pain! In all my years of suffering, I have said every day, because my Saviour lives, I can face tomorrow. Come what may, my risen Saviour is alive in my heart! He is also alive in Heaven seated at the right hand of the

Father, interceding for His own beloved and interceding for those who have not yet accepted Him. Beautiful Jesus. Awesome Lord.

Maybe you are in a tomb of despair, a tomb of fear of death, a tomb of utter defeat. Jesus, risen Saviour, and conquering King is reaching into your darkness right now and saying "Darling just come to me. Come into my arms. Let me make things well with your soul. Let me carry you through the harsh trials of life. I am reaching in right now because I love you. Will you come into my arms?"

187

Black Saturday

I am borrowing the term 'Black Saturday' from the yearly band parade because I can think of nothing better to call today. Black Saturday - the bleakest day on earth. Jesus had died. Oh, He had promised to rebuild the temple within three days - to come back to life again. But it seemed only the heathen Roman centurions believed that for who posts Roman guards outside a tomb?

I can imagine the sadness of His followers. I can hear them saying, "That's it, it is over now." We thought He was our Messiah; we gave up years following Him but He's dead. He promised so much but this is the end of the line, none of what He said is going to happen. I can imagine the despondency, the heartbreak, the disillusionment. Black Saturday! The day of God's total silence. The day where it looked like all hope was gone and no promises were coming to pass.

1 Thessalonians 5:24 *"Faithful is he that calleth* (or promised you) *you who will also do it."*

Psalm 42:5 *"Why art thou cast down O my soul and why art thou disquieted within me?"*

In the despair of the darkness, the followers of Jesus lost sight of His promises. What about you? Are you in a 'Black Saturday' of the soul? God has promised to do something in your life through His Word, but you have become despondent. God's abandoned me you cry. He has forgotten that which He promised, and you have gone into soul downcast mode. He said He would heal my marriage, He promised we would have a child, He promised He would heal my body, He promised He would save my family, and the list could go on. But now all you see is blackness. Utter silence from Heaven. Years have passed you are getting more and more detached from the promise. Dear friend, please let a spark of hope ignite in your spirit today. In the silence and the darkness, in the black night of your soul, God is moving behind the scenes bringing His promise to pass.

What He says He will do! The despondent disciples didn't believe He would rise from the dead as He said but we all know He is very much alive today and seated at the right hand of the Father in Heaven.

He will bring to pass ALL He has spoken unto you. Do not lose heart. Light will soon shine in your darkness O weary soul.

188

The Lamb of God

As a child and as a teenager, I kept little lambs. They had to be bottle-fed four times a day! The midnight feed wasn't much fun though, but I loved my wee lambs. I loved their sweetness, and gentleness and how they cuddled up to you. To this day I will not eat lamb at all because I was so attached to my pet lambs that the thought of eating lamb puts me off.

John 1:29 *"Behold the lamb of God, which taketh away the sin of the world."*

Isaiah 53:5-7 *"He was wounded for our transgressions. He was bruised for our iniquities: the chastisement of our peace was upon him and with his stripes we are healed... He was oppressed and he was afflicted, yet he opened not his mouth, he is brought like a lamb to the slaughter and as a sheep before her shearers is dumb so he openeth not his mouth."*

Jesus is the Lamb of God. He came to be the once for all sacrifice, to die in our place, to take the punishment for our sins all upon Himself so if we place our trust in Him can go to Heaven when we die. Like a lamb going to the slaughter, He opened not His mouth. He could have called ten thousand angels to rescue Him, to save Him from the wounding and bruising and death on a cruel cross but He chose not to. He chose to die in our place.

"With His stripes, we are healed." is a verse that is largely taken out of context by prosperity preachers. With Jesus' sacrifice, we can be healed from sin. Every single one of us if we call upon Jesus, repent of our sins and make Him the Saviour of our life. By choosing to reject Him, you choose to go to a lost sinner's hell,

but He suffered so you would not have to go there. He wants you to be healed of sin and He made a way to make it possible. Some use this verse as a 'name it, claim it, put it on the wall and frame it' to claim for every physical illness. But that is not the context that this verse is in. It is about Salvation. It is about being made right with God for all eternity. If you thought of that verse as a 'claim it' for all illnesses, you are very wrong. If it were true that we could claim it for all sicknesses, then nobody would ever die. I know some of the Godliest people who died of cancer who looked to Jesus for their healing, but it did not come in the form they wanted - Jesus took them home to Heaven to heal them.

Thank the Lord for dying in your place and rejoice that you are going to Heaven when you die because of our suffering Saviour. If you have never placed your trust in Him consider making this the day when you make things well with your soul and accept Jesus' gift of Salvation. He died in our place for our eternal freedom. Ask Him into your heart, repent of sins and make Him King of your heart.

189

The Gift

A friend sent me a beautiful pink bracelet in the post with a heart attached. I was overwhelmed and touched! I love pink and I love hearts! It made me think. In Ephesians 4 we are told to be kind and tender-hearted one to another. Recently, I have experienced so many people being kind and tender-hearted towards me.

Why does the Lord ask us to be kind and tender-hearted one to another? Because it makes a massive impact on others' lives. We live in a world full of harsh, judgemental hearts who love to tear down, gossip, cause others pain. We live in a world where people are so caught up in their own world's that it is all about, I, me, and mine with no thought for others. Even the Bible says, *"in the last days men* (and women) *will be lovers of their own selves."*

Throughout my years of illness, I have been subject to harsh judgement. Some say it is all in my head and I am making it up. I have been accused of not looking sick. People have started rumours to say I do not have M.E. but Anorexia. Again not true. Of course, I eat. I want to be well and live. If I did not eat, I would be dead. M.E. affects every system of the body including the bowel which is why at times I have appeared too thin. In spells when I could get out of the house for an hour, I was bombarded with people saying you look fine so why aren't you working? Little did they know the number of days in bed it would take to recover from going out for a short time. I have received some of the cruellest private mails from professing 'Christians'.

I did not choose to be sick, but I have had little sympathy because I have M.E. and not another Illness. M.E. is still viewed ignorantly even though there is medical proof to show it is in the blood, brain, and immune system.

At the same time, I have experienced the tender touch from some of the most selfless hearts in the world. Choosing to be kind and tender-hearted despite your circumstances. Choosing to be kind and tender-hearted when you are well and able shows you make time for people, no matter how busy you are. It shows you are an imitator of Jesus. It helps the unsaved see the kindness of the Saviour and many have come to faith because tender-hearted Christians have reached out beyond themselves. I heard of a man who reached out to so many people through buying their groceries, buying them furniture, helping with everything all those around those needed. The result? After he had shown all that kindness, he asked the recipients of his kindness to go to Gospel meetings. The number of people that got saved because of the kind, tender-heartedness and love for their souls was phenomenal!

Be kind and tender-hearted in a harsh world and just watch how our Lord and Saviour moves through you to bring others to a saving knowledge of Himself.

190

A Selfless Heart = A Jesus Heart

I received this beautiful 'Love You to the Moon and Back' picture from the lady I call my beloved second mother. It is always what we say to each other every day and it meant so much to me. What can I say about Patricia? She has been sick and bedbound as far as I can remember. Yet, despite the agony she is in daily, she makes the world better for everyone in it by her selfless love, gifts in the post, always checking on her friends to make sure they are okay. Just constantly loving and constantly giving. As a child when we went to visit her, I would curl up on the bed beside her and gain so much from her words of encouragement and comfort. She has always made me feel like I can reach for the stars and achieve anything in God.

The strongest people are those who continue to care for and love others despite their problems. Patricia is a perfect example of that and throughout my years of sickness, I've looked to her as my inspiration and have done all in my power like her not to get into an attitude of self-pity where I forget everyone else and wallow in my pain.

Does Patricia receive as much love as she gives in return? No! The verse I have written on the flyleaf of my Bible which I've made my life's motto says: *"I will very gladly spend and be spent for you, though the more abundantly I love you, the less I be loved."* 2 Corinthians 12:15

This was true of the man writing these words - Paul in his prison cell. He could have said I've enough problems of my own, so yours are not my concern. But he did not. He continued to reach out in love from his prison cell by his letters which we still have today as a big part of our Bible. Though Paul in his prison cell was largely forgotten and unloved and uncared for he spoke about it at times. He had one-man called Onesiphorous who did not forget him in his chains. This man loved and cared for Paul tenderly and selflessness, when everyone else was too busy, caught up in their own world.

Jesus loves selflessly too. How it must break His heart that after Him going to a cross to suffer and die for everyone - people still reject Him. People push Him away and say I am a good person, I do not need Jesus, I do not need salvation. He suffered that if all men would repent of sins and turn their lives over to Him that they would be guaranteed to go to Heaven and not hell when they die. How does Jesus respond to those who keep pushing him away? He keeps loving them. He keeps praying to the Father that they will surrender their lives to Him. Our selfless Saviour is not giving up on you - He loves you to the moon and back! For those who know Him be imitators of our selfless Saviour today. Develop an attitude of love towards others and dare to reach out even if you receive little love back. Your reward will be great in Heaven!

191

Life's Defining Moments

Prayer is a powerful weapon. Two of my life's most defining moments were answers to prayer.

Firstly, I was eleven years old. I was standing by the bedside of my beloved grandfather. He had major bowel surgery and we were gathered as a family as we were told he was not going to make it. I looked at my precious beloved encourager in that bed and prayed in my mind 'Jesus help him please'. Doctors had no hope for him. Then suddenly, I fainted. I came round in my uncle's strong arms and was being placed in a hospital bed for nurses to revive me when suddenly, I witnessed a miracle. My beloved Granda who had beforehand been so still in the bed and not speaking was now sitting up in the bed in a real panic, help my Joanne, he was shouting. Upright in the bed my selfless dying Granda was more worried about me than he was himself! After that day Granda got fully better and lived twenty more years until he went to glory.

Secondly, I was at Bible college. We had been assigned to a group of unreached, unchurched young people from the Somerton Road, Belfast. Every week we prepared our epilogues and tried to make the Gospel as clear as possible and prayed hard that God would save those young people. But we seemed to have hit a brick wall. One weekend I came home from University and my family had been to see a Christian play at the town hall called 'Heavens Gates and Hells flames'. My brother had bought the video, so I watched it while being at home. While I was watching it, the Lord spoke clear - this is your answer to the souls of the young people. So back up at University, I talked to the group leader and asked if we could act out a few scenes from the play instead of epilogue the next week. He agreed. What we witnessed was a miracle! It was like the Gospel just clicked in all their minds that night. They understood and we led fourteen young people all individually in the sinner's prayer. I got back to college and worshipped God the whole night. Did not sleep a wink. I was so excited at how God had answered prayer.

Many times since God has intervened in my life. Some things to personal to write on here. But those two major answers to prayer were my life's defining moments.

His word tells us to ask and we will receive, knock and the door will be opened. We are told to be constant in prayer and pray continually. Oh, sometimes the answers do not look like the ones we want! I did not think I would be still sick after all these years. But we have an amazing God who does answer prayers. He manifests His power! He heard an eleven-year-olds cry for her Granda and a nineteen-year-olds cry for the precious souls of the youth. God came in His power and answered.

James 5:17-18 *"Elijah was a man subject to like passions as we are, and he prayed earnestly that it might rain: and it rained not on the earth by the space of three years and six months. And he prayed again, and the heaven gave rain and the earth brought forth her fruit."*

And he prayed again! He did not stop when he saw no results the first time. Pray dear friend as you have never prayed before. Our precious Saviour hears and answers prayer!

192

George - The Bird With
The Broken Wing

When we were children an injured pigeon turned up outside our house. Thankfully, we got to him before all our cats did! We named him George. He had a broken wing, so we put him in our garden shed and fed and watered him every day until his wing started to heal. We grew very attached to George. He became our pet and we loved going to hold him and pet him every day. However, the day came when George's wing healed. We took him out to the yard and he just walked about. I kept saying fly! You were made to fly, you dumb bird! If you do not fly the cats will eat you! He just kept walking around for about an hour. But then eventually George took off and flew! He was doing what he was created to do! Oh, we missed him. But we could not keep him in captivity when he was made to soar through the air.

It made me think. So many of us are like birds with broken wings. We make excuses to not fulfil all our purposes in God. We do not soar because we walk around with a broken wing making excuses why we cannot do this and cannot do that.

In Jeremiah 1 We are told that before God even formed us in the womb, He had purposes for us to fulfil that only we could fulfil. In Ephesians 2:10 we are told we are His workmanship (masterpieces) created in Christ Jesus for good works that God prepared beforehand.

What is the Lord asking you to do that you keep making excuses about? Do you have a lovely voice but will not sing in church because of fear? Do you think the Lord wants you to teach a Sunday school class, lead the Youth, serve in G.B. or B.B., do some form of outreach like reaching out to the lost through a team that gives out coffee/tea and tracts to those coming out of pubs? Does He want you to be an encourager, yet you keep saying no Lord I cannot even encourage myself never mind anyone else! Does He want you to share your testimony, yet you keep saying I cannot, I am too shy, I cannot get up and speak? Is he calling you to go to Bible College and devote your life to His service? Does He want you to reach out with the Gospel to your workmates? Does He want you to go and care for the broken, the sick, the elderly, to share His love with the needy? Is he asking you to give of your money to fund a specific mission? You might be disabled like me but that is still no excuse for being a bird with a broken wing.

Put your mind to it and seek God for ways to reach out from bed, He will give them to you. He created you do soar, to be all you could be in Him. Don't you long for the words *"well done good and faithful servant"* when you meet our Lord in paradise? Then make this day the day you refuse to be the bird with the broken wing and soar high in the sky and be all you were created to be. No more excuses. No more I cannot! But I pray that God will give you the courage to fulfil your purposes that you were placed on this earth for.

Soar precious friend. Soar! Fly high!

193

The Ice Cream Van

I used to stay with my Granda a lot as a child. Every Thursday after playing dolls with me for hours and letting me 'do his hair' we would go and feed the swans. After swan time it was time for the ice cream van to come round. Every week Granda asked me the same question! I always asked for a 99 with lots of chocolate sprinkles. Granda used to say, "Why is a 99 called a 99 and not a 98 or a 100?" I used to giggle because it was so predictable that he was going to say that! To this day I do not know why a 99 is called a 99!

But thinking of my late Granda's words made me think of the question why? Why do people get struck down with an illness when they have so many dreams? Why do some mothers have to lose a child whether through miscarriage or the death of an older child? Why are some children born with great mental and physical difficulties? Why do some lovely people end up in abusive marriages? Why is there so much suffering? The list goes on.

In the book of Job, while he was suffering so intensely, he asked a lot of why questions. He even asked God why he had to be born, why had he not died at birth. Job was in great distress. But by the end of the book of Job, the Lord revealed Himself unto Job and made all things well.

Sometimes we must trust Him even when we do not understand. Isaiah 26 says, *"Trust ye in the Lord Jehovah, for in the Lord Jehovah is everlasting strength."* In Proverbs 3 we are told not to lean on our own understanding but in all our ways to acknowledge the Lord and He will make our paths straight. The thing is we will never know the answers to the why's this side of Heaven. We need to trust that the Lord loves us deeply and when we do not see His hand in our circumstances, we need to trust that His heart towards us is one of pure gold. He is to wise to be mistaken and He is too good to be unkind. Yes, there is evil in this world because man chose satan's ways over God's ways. It was never what God intended for planet earth, but He gave man freewill. He wanted people to love Him of their own freewill and not be forced into it like programmed robots.

If your heart is breaking with a 'Why?' Go to the heart of the One who loved you enough to go to a cross to die for your eternal Salvation. Pour out your heart to Him. Let Him comfort you in your distress. Leave what you do not understand in His hands and know that behind the scenes, despite what satan tries to do, He is fighting off the enemy and working for your good. You are adored and loved by the King of kings and Lord of lords. Leave your 'why' in His hands and let Him love you through your storm.

194

The Mystery

As some of you know I suffer from an eye disease called Keratoconus that can only be corrected by special lenses. Glasses do not work. I am part of a K.C. support group and the other day a lady posted a funny story.

She had taken her lenses out the night before and went to put them in again the next morning. But she discovered one was missing. She got her hubby to search the house as everything was too blurry for her to search too. The full-day went past, and the lost lens did not show up. Then that night they were putting their five-year-old daughter to bed when she said, "It hurts now mummy." Her husband looked in their five-year-olds eye and found the lost lens! She had gone into her mother's room, took the lens out of its case and put it in her eye. When asked why she did it, the little girl replied, "I just wanted to be like mummy."

It made me think. Who are you imitating? Is the greatest role model in your life to be like Jesus? In Philippians 2 it talks about how selfless and loving our Saviour is. He wants us to be imitators of Him.

In Corinthians, it is written, "Ye are our epistle written in our hearts." Your life is a living letter to all those around you. Do people see Jesus in you? Do they see selflessness, gentleness, kindness, care for the lost, love for the broken, a beautiful spirit that never complains or puts others down? A spirit that wants to see others built up and is so self-sacrificing that there is nothing you would not do for others.

Are you like Him in your love for spending time in prayer with the Father? Are you like Him in speaking the truth of His Word like

He did even when it is not popular? Are you like Him in His purity? You do not want any unclean thing to come out of your mouth or go into your mind. Do you want your life to be a living letter that screams Jesus lives here? Then ask Him to make you more like Him and study His word to see how He walked and talked and let His Word transform your mind and let it transform you into the likeness of Christ. I once said of my late Granda, I want to be like Granda because Granda is like Jesus. Could people look at us and say that. Make that your highest goal and desire. I know it is my highest goal and desire.

195

In The Middle Of It All

I was listening to a service. The soloist sang the words, "In the middle of it all, he was always there beside me." She went on to give her testimony and tell how she has suffered from manic depression since she was nineteen. Even though she's a gifted singer and pushes herself to the front of the church often, she's consumed with a dark cloud, a dark cloud that leaves her so despondent that sometimes she can't drag herself out of bed for weeks. She was feeling upset one night at church because she could no longer pray, but another sister in the Lord comforted her with the words, "The Lord knows your heart, He knows you want to pray and just can't, He sees your desire to honour Him and your frustration that you can't. Just sing choruses and hymns when you do not have your own words, God will accept those as your sacrifice of praise."

I thought the lady was so brave that despite her manic depression she still got up to a platform to minister in song to others. That is real faith, honouring God even when you do not feel like it.

In the middle of it all, He was always there beside me reminding me of Scriptures. He will never leave me nor forsake me, He shall not fail nor forsake, when you pass through the waters I will be with you and the rivers they shall not overflow, when you walk through the fire you shall not be burned, neither shall the flame kindle upon you. Your Saviour is never going to abandon you whether you suffer from mental illness or physical illness or you are in a place of extreme pain due to life's circumstances. He adores you. You are still His darling child. His strong hands are on your life for good.

196

Childhood Memories

I was thinking about all the wonderful memories childhood brought. The hours out playing with a skipping rope and hula hoop. The hours spent playing tennis against the wall. The joy of playing Barbie's with my cousin. Then the joy of playing Supergirl and Superman with another cousin, running through the town pretending to rescue people from danger even climbing trees to save those 'on top of buildings as we imagined'!

Running through the fields playing on my own creating a whole magical world I called myself Lucinda. Every time through the fields in my imagination I went on a magical adventure to Unicorn land. Oh, I had some amazing times in those fields. Sometimes I was a doctor performing surgery, sometimes I was a nurse caring for the sick but most of all I was a mother! Oh, I cared for my dolls like they were real! I bathed them, changed them, cuddled them, took them out in the pram, fed them. I still have my most precious doll - Lucy who I plan to pass down to a daughter of mine someday.

Then there was the joy of going to CEF camps every summer. Going on the Sunday school trip to Portrush once a year! Having sleepovers with friends where we ate far too many sweets and chocolate and laughed the whole night! Oh, and cartoon time for that hour every day! There was no 24/7 kids TV then. But how we loved that hour when we got lost in the care bears, the raggy dolls, She-Ra Princess of power, Fragile rock and others that I have forgotten.

Riding bicycles, playing with my brother, making mud cakes, and pretending we owned a cafe. Oh, and coming home from school every Friday to the Bunty and Mandy and Judy magazines with a yummy Mississippi mud pie chocolate yogurt! Oh, such memories!

But as I thought about the joyous times, I thanked the Lord for happy memories because in seasons of pain and suffering we can recall God's goodness in the past and believe that good times will come again.

In Nehemiah, the verse goes, *"The joy of the Lord is my strength."* Many days we do not feel joy for the suffering is so bad. Many a day we wonder if we will always be in a season of pain and despair but in Ecclesiastes, the verse says the time to laugh and the time to dance will return no matter how bleak it looks now.

In the meantime, the joy of the Lord will be our strength. You don't have to feel joy for it to be there, it creeps up through happy memories, through holding onto Scriptures of promises of hope, continuing to live to give and bless others even when your heart feels heavy and being thankful for your Salvation daily for it is the greatest miracle of all.

Hold on, dear child. Joy comes in the morning. The time to laugh and the time to dance and rejoice will return no matter how impossible it looks right now. Our God specialises in things thought impossible. He can do just what no other can do.

197

Trapped

I had a dream. It might not be someone else's idea of a nightmare, but it certainly was mine. Due to my personal beliefs, I do not go to pubs/nightclubs or drink alcohol. But in this dream, I was in a nightclub. There was loud worldly music playing with lyrics full of swearing, filth, and other things I would not mention. Everyone was dancing and drinking. The dancing was suggestive and sensual, and I have never seen so much alcohol flowing. The girls were all half-naked while I was dressed in what you would wear to a funeral.

Meanwhile, in the dream, I was going around the place frantic. Asking how did I end up here? Was I kidnapped? Did someone drug me and bring me here. I got more and more frantic all I could think was if my dear Lord and Saviour was to return this night, I don't want Him to find me in this den of iniquity. I frantically found a payphone and phoned every taxi firm I could find but they were all booked up. I went round a few sober-looking people and asked for a lift home but they just laughed and said relax little lady, have a few and let your hair down. Then I noticed the bars on the doors and windows. I could not get out I was well and truly trapped. At that point, I woke up screaming please let me out and was so relieved it had only been a dream.

But it made me think. So many people today are trapped in circumstances, not of their choosing. Life for them has become a prison cell. Trapped in abusive marriages, trapped by Illnesses, trapped by their own minds as they suffer from thick depression that they cannot get free of. Trapped in jobs where they have abusive bosses, trapped in some other circumstance that looks like the prison bars in my dream.

The word trapped means ensnared. No way out. But the Bible tells us, *"He who the son sets free is free indeed."* For those who know Jesus as Saviour, you can be in the most horrific circumstances and still be free in your spirit. Free to choose right attitudes, free to keep loving your Saviour and shining for Him in your prison cell, free to choose to keep praising Him like the saints in Scripture did when they were trapped in their prison cell. Free to trust Him that He knows what He is doing, and in His time, He will open a door of hope to replace the valley of suffering as it says in Hosea 2.

Hang in there dear suffering, trapped friend. Do not give up for the Lord will come through for you. And as you wait, choose to praise Him in your prison cell for He is still God and He is still good even when we do not understand why or what He is up to. When you cannot see His hand, trust His heart. My prayer for you is that the Lord will rescue you very soon from your prison cell.

198

Continue To Touch The Lives Of Others When You Are Suffering Yourself

A scripture one of my closest friends sent me about a year after I took sick has always stuck with me.

2 Corinthians 6:10 *"As sorrowful yet always rejoicing, as poor yet making many rich as having nothing and yet possessing all things."*

The part of the Scripture that touched me most was, *"as poor yet making many rich."*

Even in our sorrowful situations in life that feel depressing and a struggle, we can still make many rich in the Lord. It is still possible to be used of God in your most sorrowful state if you determine in your heart to rise above it and not be absorbed by self-pity. You can encourage new believers in their faith through letters and maybe buying them a good devotional that will help build them up. You can encourage missionaries through letters, cards, and emails. You can share the greatest news of all, the Gospel through social media and perhaps putting a Gospel tract in with an encouragement package you have sent to an unbeliever. You can still contribute to the life of your church through prayer and by having great compassion on others that are sick and depressed.

The key is to let compassion reign in your heart stronger than feelings. Feelings will pull you down and cause you to press the stop button on all you might accomplish for the Kingdom of Heaven. It takes effort, it takes determination but never let your circumstances get in the way of you being there with love and compassion for others.

In a book by Grace Livingston Hill called *'The Honour Girl,'* the following scripture was quoted.

Romans 14:7-8 *"For none of us liveth to himself and no man dieth to himself. For whether we live, we live unto the Lord and whether we die, we die unto the Lord: Whether we live therefore or die, we are the Lord's."*

The girl in the book had been living an extremely selfish, self-centred, 'It's all about me and my wants life.' Then she read that Scripture and changed her ways and made her life a sacrifice of compassion and selfless service for others for the rest of her days.

To quote Mary Ingalls from *'Little House on the Prairie'*, "It's the folks that have the least that give the most as they know what it is to be in sorrow and pain."

No matter what your circumstances are today - stop living to self. You may be sorrowful, but you can still rejoice in your great Salvation. You might be poor in the eyes of the world, but you can make others rich through encouragement, kindness, compassion, prayer, continuing to shine the Gospel light and refusing to drown in self-pity. In the eyes of the world, you might have nothing, yet you still possess everything in your Saviour's eyes. All may change but Jesus never! Glory to his name!

Determine this day to make others rich in God.

199

The Lord My Hiding Place

Psalm 32:7 *"Thou art my hiding place; thou shalt preserve me from trouble; thou shalt compass me about with songs of deliverance."*

My favourite game when I was a child was hide and seek. I liked to find the strangest places to hide. I did not just go behind the curtains. I would have found some cupboard and squeezed myself into it somehow. It was always more fun in friends' houses as there were more places to hide.

Though the best place to hide when you are afraid or distressed or in despair is to run to the Lord and hide in Him. The song says, "You are my Hiding Place. You always fill my heart with songs of deliverance whenever I am afraid. I will trust in you."

When we run into His arms His comforting presence saves us from distress. He will fill our hearts with comfort when we are weak. He will whisper words of hope into our weary spirits. He will refresh us and renew us and give us the strength to keep going. He will also fill us with songs of deliverance! We can sing our way through the storm with the songs that the Lord fills us with when we hide in Him. Go to Him today weary heart and let Him ease your distress and fill you with songs of deliverance.

200

The Miracle

1 Samuel 11:18 *"So Samuel called unto the Lord and the Lord sent thunder and lightning and rain that day, and all the people feared the Lord."*

Sometimes God works behind the scenes quietly and we do not get the answers to prayer that we would like but we still accept that Jesus loves us, and His goodness surrounds us always. Though other times He demonstrates His power in a visible way like how He sent the thunder and lightning so that people would know Him.

Not long ago a girl that I used to go to school with had a baby. You might say well that is nothing out of the ordinary, people have babies every day. But this friend had desperately wanted a baby for seven years and it looked like it would never happen. She messaged me and told me about her battle and desire for a baby, so I prayed every day. I kept praying even when I felt like stopping to pray because it looked impossible.

BUT God sent the long-awaited miracle child and she now proudly holds her son in her arms.

Another miracle I read about was about a girl like myself with severe M.E. Doctors, (just like they told me) told her she would never have any quality of life again and must accept she would never be well.

One night she and her sister were praying and worshipping the Lord together when the room was filled with an incredible sense of God's glory. She felt His healing power going all through her body. The pain was gone, the limp muscles felt strong and she felt energy like she had never known before.

The next day she went out running! She had not run in fourteen years! It was a thunder and lightning miracle. She since dedicated her life to the Lord's service bringing the Gospel to young people. She has now married and had children! It was a 'can't be done with the doctors' but it was an 'I will do it' with God.

We do not always see or hear of these thunder and lightning miracles, so I felt it was important to share them. Don't give up on praying for things on your heart and people you love who need healing, for you just don't know God might send a thunder and lightning miracle and many will come to know Jesus as Saviour as a result.

Though sometimes the miracle He sends is endurance to face every day and to be used amid weakness. That does not have the thunder and lightning shine to it but it is still a miracle.

To those who are waiting, myself included, do not stop believing. Do not faint in your Spirit and say, 'I can't' because God is saying 'oh, but I can.'

201

Created In God's Image To Be Who He Made You To Be

I read an article about a woman who had gone on a T.V. reality show a few years ago. When she went on T.V. she was happy with the way she looked with her long blonde hair and dark tan. But when the series aired things changed. Internet trolls where leaving horrific comments about her being brutally ugly. These comments continued for as long as the show was aired. At that point, something snapped in the girls' mind and she developed 'Body Disphormic Disorder' - a mental illness that means what they see in the mirror isn't reality. They see a distorted image of themselves. Some people with the illness hide in baggy clothes and avoid mirrors at all costs. But others go to the extreme of spending thousands on themselves and still see distortion.

This girl went the second way. She went utterly crazy and spent £60,000 having plastic surgery done to every part of her body. And to this day she continues having surgeries because she still cannot get the cruel comments of the internet trolls out of her head. She says going on reality T.V. destroyed her life. Once confident and bubbly she is now a depressed shell of her former self who is addicted to surgery. It made me sad. She was a beautiful girl but the bully's comments sank deep into her heart.

Genesis 1:27 *"God created man in his own image. Male and female created he them."*

We were all created individually to shine forth and bear the image of God in our unique way to have a mighty impact upon the Kingdom of God on earth!

There are no clones of you! Ecclesiastes 3:11 says, *"He hath made everything beautiful."* Beautiful includes you! No matter what rubbish bullies have spoken over your life it is lies from the pit of hell to keep you from being all the Lord purposed to be!

The word of God is a living book, and the Lord used this scripture to remind me that I have great worth in God's eyes.

Haggai 2:23 *"In that day will I take thee... my servant, said I the Lord and will make thee as a signet: for I have chosen thee."*

The signet ring was used by Kings. It was engraved with a design to identify his authority. It was used for Royal messages and to mark precious articles. It was an inseparable and valuable possession and in this verse that is what God was declaring Zerubbabel to be.

The signet ring is also used in Scripture as an engagement ring which in Bible days made a man and woman betrothed together in love forever.

Hosea 2:19 *"And I will betroth thee unto me forever."*

You have been knit together in your mother's womb for a purpose that only you can fulfil. Not only does Psalm 139 declare that you are fearfully and wonderfully made, but here the King of all kings and Lord of all lords is reminding you that you have His royal seal of approval upon you. You are His valuable jewelled possession. You are His beloved and you are betrothed to one another in a bond of deep love from the day of your Salvation for now and for all eternity. Moreover, He says, *"I have chosen thee to bear fruit that will last."* (John 15:16) So if the King of kings is calling you beautiful and valuable, loved and needed in building His Kingdom, then stamp out the enemy's lies in your head today by fighting satan head-on with Scripture. You have more value than you ever dreamt possible child of God. You have great worth, born for a purpose and are a precious jewel and you know what? Nothing anyone says against you can change that!

Conclusion

Maybe you have read through this whole book and are hurting. You would love to give your life to the Saviour that you have read about through these pages. Jesus went to the cross to die in your place once and for all to pay sin's price so that no one would have to go to a lost sinner's Hell after death. But he would never force Himself upon you. He's just longing for you to accept His gift of Salvation.

Acts 4:12 says: *"Neither is there Salvation in any other, for there is none other name under heaven given among men whereby we must be saved."*

John 14:6: *"I am the way, the truth and the life, no man cometh unto the Father but by me."*

John 3:36: *"He that believeth on the Son hath everlasting life, and he that believeth not on the Son shall not see life; but the wrath of God abideth on him.*

If you would like to accept Him as Saviour, here are the words that many have prayed to make things well with their souls. If you pray this prayer you will be made a Child of God. Find a good Bible believing church and if you don't own a Bible, please feel free to contact me and I'll make sure you get one.

"Dear Heavenly Father, I know that I'm a sinner and I ask for your forgiveness. I believe you died for my sins and rose from the dead. I turn from my sin, I repent of my sins, I invite you to come into my heart and life. I want to trust and follow you as my Lord and Saviour. Thank you for making me yours."

If you would like to contact Joanne, feel free to do so at: amyrtletree@hotmail.com